Gotta Find a Home 2:

More Conversations
with Street People

Book 2

The beggar, engraving by Alphonse Legros (1837-1911)

Gotta Find a Home 2:

More Conversations with Street People

Book 2

Dennis Cardiff

Gotta Find a Home: More Conversations with Street People, Book 2
by Dennis Cardiff
© *2016 Dennis Cardiff All rights reserved. Ontario, Canada*

Published by Dennis Cardiff

The author has tried to recreate events, locales and conversations from his memories of them. In order to maintain anonymity names of individuals and places have been changed.

Cover Illustration Copyright © 2014 by Dennis Cardiff

Cover Font is called DJ Gross and the *license can be found at: http://www.fontsquirrel.com/license/DJ-Gross*

Book design and production by Karen Silvestri, Karenzo Media

ISBN-10: 0-9939799-2-0
ISBN-13: 978-0-9939799-2-7

To my wife Daisy, for her love, patience and understanding; allowing me to spend hours at my computer, when she would have preferred that I spend them with her. To my sons Rik and Roger, from whom I continue to learn. To my street friends, aliases: Joy, Shakes, Alphonse, Baby Alphonse Jr., Serge, Rocky, Silver, Weasel and his dog Bear, who have passed away much too early. Still active on the streets are Wolf and his dog Shaggy, Little Jake, Mariah, Bearded Bruce, Jacques, Magdalene, Mary, Trudy, Chili, Loretta, Craig, Timmy, both Chesters and both Chucks.

How It Began

From Book 1

My lungs ached as frost hung in the bitterly cold December morning air, making breathing difficult. I trudged in the falling snow toward the building where I work, in one of the city's grey, concrete, office tower canyons. I dodged other pedestrians, also trying to get to work on time, I noticed a woman seated cross-legged on the sidewalk with her back against a building wall. A snow-covered Buddha, wrapped in a sleeping bag, shivering in the below freezing temperature. I guessed her to be in her forties. Everything about her seemed round. She had the most angelic face, sparkling blue eyes and a beautiful smile. A cap was upturned in front of her. I thought, There but for the grace of God go I. Her smile and blue eyes haunted me all day.

In the past I've been unemployed, my wife and I were unable to pay our mortgage and other bills, we went through bankruptcy, lost our house, my truck. Being in my fifties, my prospects looked dim. It could have been me, on the sidewalk, in her place.

I was told not to give money to panhandlers because they'll just spend it on booze. I thought to myself, What should I do, if anything? What would you do? I asked for advice from a friend who has worked with homeless people. She said, 'The woman is probably hungry. Why don't you ask her if she'd like a breakfast sandwich and maybe a coffee?'

That sounded reasonable, so the next day I asked, "Are you hungry? Would you like some breakfast, perhaps a coffee?"

"That would be nice," she replied.

When I brought her a sandwich and coffee she said to me, "Thank you so much, sir. You're so kind. Bless you." I truly felt blessed.

This has become a morning routine for the past four years. The woman (I'll call Joy) and I have become friends. Often I'll sit with her on the sidewalk. We sometimes meet her companions in the park. They have become my closest friends. I think of them as angels. My life has become much richer for the experience.

Contents

The Usual Suspects

(Alphabetical listing of Dennis' street friends)

People come and go on a daily basis on the street, so this list only includes 'the regulars' – the ones that Dennis refers to as 'the usual suspects'. This list will refresh your memory on their approximate ages and who their 'partners' are.

Alphonse – age 40, with Magdalene (Maggie)

Anastasia – age 60ish

Andre

Angela – Joy's probation officer

Anne – with Chester and Nick

Bear – Weasel's dog

Bearded Bruce

Bettie – daughter of Shakes

Big Jake – Joy's boyfriend

Bowser – Shakes' stuffed dog

Buck

Chantal – the 'religious lady' to stops by to chat

Chester – with Anne. Joy's 3rd roommate.

Chili – age 21

Chuck (Toothless) – Joy's 2nd roommate

Daimon – with Lucy in the Sky

Deaf Donald – age 35

Dillinger – Buck's dog

1

Debbie- with Outcast

Fran – daughter of Shakes

Gaston

Hippo

Ian – with Marlena

Irene – with Shark

Jacques

Little Jake – age 41

Joy

Luther

Lucy in the Sky – with Damon

Maggie (Magdalene) – age 22, with Alphonse

Marlena – with Ian

Metro – sells newspapers

Nick – with Anne. Pans to make money to help out his street friends by making them sandwiches.

Outcast - with Debbie

Raven

Roy – Joy's first roommate

Rocky

Trudy

Introduction

Throughout the past four years I have met many people, now friends, who for various reasons are, or were, homeless.

- Antonio slept on a park bench and was beaten; he had his teeth kicked out for no other reason than his choice to sleep outdoors. He is a small, gentle man who has a phobia about enclosed spaces.

- Craig slept on the sidewalk in the freezing cold. I saw him every morning and was never sure if, when I lifted the corner of his sleeping bag, I would find him dead or alive. Sometimes, he confided, he would have preferred never to awake.

- Joy fell on hard times. She slept behind a dumpster in back of the coffee shop. I saw her with blackened eyes, bruised legs, cracked ribs, cut and swollen lips. I usually see her sitting on the sidewalk panning for change.

I can't do much for these people except to show them love, compassion, an ear to listen, perhaps a breakfast sandwich and a coffee. I want to do more. To know them is to love them. What is seen cannot be unseen.

When I'm with the homeless, I don't judge. I ask a minimum of questions, only enough to keep the conversation moving. I don't interrogate or ask about their past. Mostly, I listen and try to understand. I am often asked why I am there. Although the reasons are deeper, I usually answer by saying,

"The conversations here are more interesting than where I work." I visit these people on the streets, on the way to my place of employment, and at noon hours.

What I have learned over the past four years has changed my life. These people, who I consider to be my friends, are alcoholics, drug and other substance users. Some work as prostitutes, some have AIDS, most or all have served time in prison for various offenses. All of them I would trust with my life. They have welcomed me into their street family. I am honored to be considered a member.

I have heard sickening stories of abuse as children and babies born with drug dependencies. Most have mental and physical illnesses, suffer beatings, broken bones, stabbings, and have a fear of abusive partners and the police.

Authority in any form is seen negatively, as a means to control their lives. The homeless shelters are noisy, infested with bedbugs, the scene of fights and a place where personal items are stolen. Many homeless people prefer to sleep inside common areas such as bank foyers, outside under bridges, or behind dumpsters.

I have recalled conversations from memory and recorded them on these pages. I've attempted to be as accurate and truthful as possible. I haven't used any recording devices, so recollections may be faulty. I leave out details that I think may incriminate, but I don't interpret, explain or edit.

What they say is what you read. I have changed names and locations for purposes of privacy. My friends don't choose to be addicts. It's a disease and should be treated as such. They need help. They can't do it on their own, but they want it on their own terms.

August 2012

He Died Two Days Ago

7 August 2012

Monday mornings have always been considered unproductive days for panning. The reasons given are that office workers, returning after the weekend, tend to be tired, grumpy and not particularly generous to those in need. Therefore, I wasn't surprised to see that the spots usually occupied by Joy and Silver were vacant. I looked farther up the street and saw Magdalene.

"Hi, Magdalene, do you mind if I sit down?"

"Hi, sure, sit."

"How is your baby?" I asked.

"He died two days ago."

Baby Alphonse Jr. would have been eight weeks old. I had talked with Magdalene last week. Social Services had found a nice place for her and her husband Alphonse to live, near the hospital. The last time I saw them as a couple was before the birth. They were both excited about their expected son. I was shocked to hear that their baby died. I never know what to say at times like this.

"I'm terribly sorry to hear that. You must feel devastated." I put my hand gently on Magdalene's shoulder, knowing that she doesn't like to be hugged.

"I'm okay."

"How is Alphonse taking it?"

"I don't know," she replied.

"I'm asking too many questions. You have my deepest sympathy."

"Do you have a cigarette? No, I remember, you don't smoke. I'll see if I can find one." She stood up and walked to an outdoor ashtray, near the door to the coffee shop. She picked out a couple of butts and returned to her spot.

"Perhaps, I'll see you at noon, Magdalene. Once again, I'm so sorry. Remember, you are loved by many friends."

At noon I walked to the park. Sitting on the curb, hiding under a baseball cap and behind a bushy gray beard, was Serge.

"Hi Serge. I haven't seen you for the past week. Have I missed anything while I was away?"

"No, every day the same thing." I noticed that he had a black eye.

"Did you fall again?"

"Yes, I fell. I was walking between two cars to have a pee, and I fell." This is Serge's standard excuse for black eyes. A few weeks ago he had two, probably from beatings. He doesn't want to cause any trouble for anybody. Also, he's afraid of repercussions.

Walking further up the sidewalk I met Trudy. "Hi, I was so sorry to hear that Magdalene's baby died."

"I didn't know that. When did it happen?"

"She said it was two days ago."

"I saw Alphonse this morning, but he wasn't talking to anyone."

"That's the reason. I'm sure he's very upset. He wanted so much to be a father."

"Dennis, do you have any more of those grocery store cards? I was just talking to Nick. He said he was hungry."

"Sure, I'd be pleased if you gave one to Nick. I really admire what he does to help people. If you see Larry, tell him

6

that I've finished the first three volumes of *Conversations with God*. He recommended them to me. I really enjoyed them, so if he has any more suggestions, I'd be interested in hearing them."

I next went to what Shakes calls his office, a curb beside an underground parking garage. "Hi, Shakes, I have a pair of track pants for you (*$8.00 at Goodwill*). Do you want to try them on?"

"Thanks, Dennis, I'll try them on later, after I've had a shower."

He continued, "You know, Dennis, I've been in this spot for seventeen years. At first it was just a dirt parking lot. The owner asked me if I'd pick up any trash. I said, 'Sure!' He gave me five bucks a day. Now it's become a condo city.

"Yesterday, I went to visit my daughter, Bettie and my grandson. It was Bettie's birthday. She was in bad shape. Her boyfriend had beaten her up."

"I'm so sorry, Shakes. I also heard that your daughter, Fran was beaten, and her boyfriend, Gene is now in prison. I heard that she has hairline fractures in her spine from when he jumped her."

"Yes, Fran was there too. They're both in rough shape. I can't understand these guys.

"Dennis, would you mind doing me a favor? Would you buy me a salad from the restaurant behind us? Maybe, coleslaw, or potato salad, whatever they have… and pepper… and don't forget a fork."

"Sure, Shakes." I came back with his salad and said, "Perhaps, I'll see you tomorrow."

"Sure, I'll be with the rest of the congregation."

It Seemed Like a Good Idea at the Time

8 August 2012

Joy approached me at the park. I hardly recognized her. Gone was her do-rag, and her hair color had changed from black to blond and looked professionally cut and styled. She was wearing a loose cotton, black on white print blouse with gray stretch pants.

"Joy," I said, "you look beautiful!"

"Thanks, I thought I needed to pamper myself for a change.

Outcast said, "It was brutal here, 104 degrees. The rain we had just increased the humidity, but didn't lower the temperature. I used up one of my inhalers. I have to go to the pharmacy today to get a new one."

Joy said, "I still don't have my health card, so I borrowed Chester's inhaler. That probably wasn't a good idea, but it's all I could do. I was hardly here at all last week. It was just too hot."

I said, "I was so sorry to hear that Magdalene's baby died."

"I didn't know that. What happened?"

"I don't know any details. I spoke to her yesterday morning. I asked, 'How is your baby?' She said, 'He died two days ago.' I asked how Alphonse was taking it. She said, 'I don't know.' Perhaps they aren't together any more.

"I mentioned it to Trudy. She had seen Alphonse earlier that day, but he wasn't talking to anyone."

Joy said, "Trudy was by earlier, but she didn't stay. She was acting funny. She probably knows something that she doesn't want to talk about."

Outcast said, "It sounds like Sudden Infant Death Syndrome. A baby can turn over in bed and suffocate. It happens a lot."

I said, "If anyone hears about funeral arrangements, please let me know. I'd like to attend. I was talking to Shakes yesterday. He was at Bettie's, for her birthday party on Sunday. She had been beaten by her boyfriend."

Joy said, "That Kit, what a scumbag, beating a woman six months pregnant with his twins, their son looking on. Someone is going to take care of this. I see him every day crossing in front of our apartment."

Shakes came over. I asked, "What kind of injuries does Bettie have?"

"Her face and ribs are badly bruised; beyond that, I don't know."

I asked, "Has her boyfriend been charged?"

Joy said, "We don't do that. We wait until someone is nearly beaten to death, and left in a pool of blood to die, as I was; or like Fran, with her back permanently fucked. That's the reason that Big Jake and Gene are in jail."

Outcast waved at a woman passing by on the sidewalk. "Did you see that woman I waved to? She's my boss. Two days a week I volunteer at the Salvation Army. She posted bail for me one time. I'll always be thankful to her for the help she gave me. She's not surprised to see me here. She knows that I'm an alcoholic and a drug addict… and always will be. I was sentenced to ten years. Of course, I didn't have to serve the full term."

I sat down on the grass with Little Jake. "How have you been this past week?"

"I'm not allowed to pan because I'm on probation. That sucks!"

"Have you had your court appearance yet?"

"That's on August 30th. I'll know what's going to happen then. I fell off my bike a few days ago."

"Where were you injured?"

"My knees and my elbows were scraped. I have bruises on my right leg. I was wasted. I don't know what happened. They found my bike in the hedge. It was in pieces, so I threw it away."

"You probably hit the curb. I've done that before and have the scars to prove it."

"Yeah, that's probably what happened."

"Riding drunk probably seemed like a good idea at the time."

Joy said, "Everything seems like a good idea at the time."

Willie said, "There is such a thing as common sense, and everybody has it to some degree. Even people with Down Syndrome, or any of the syndromes, have it. I've had some experience with that, mind you; I have a mental disability and I'm getting a pension for it, but my mind has two settings; either I'm polite, or I'm all out crazy. There's no in between."

He took off his shoe and said, "See how the middle three toes come up and down as one? I got three pins in them attached to another piece of metal in my instep. They're from jumping out of a three-story window. It seemed like a good idea at the time, but I wish I had just put my hands up and gone with the cops.

"What happened was that me and another guy were in a hotel room making a drug deal. He left to get some more, and the cops followed him back. We were both standing there, at the table, the scales at one end, the drugs at the other, when the cops broke the door down. I backed towards the balcony, said, 'I'm out of here!' and over I went. I landed in the alley, which was concrete. It would have been nice if I had landed in soft earth or even some bushes. I was lucky to have gotten off so easy, but I still went to prison. I could have saved myself a lot of pain.

"Now when I go through a metal detector at the airport, all the alarms go off. They ask me to take my shoes off. 'No problem,' I say. It happens all the time.

"On another occasion, I was at home listening to music. It was ten thirty. I had the volume up. Then I heard this pounding and kicking at my door. When I heard that, I figured somebody had come for a fight. I opened the door and this guy was screaming at me to turn the music down. I said, 'No!' I saw his fist coming up. I just reached over it and connected with his jaw. He took off, like a scared rabbit, down the street. I thought he lived next door. If he lived down the street. Why would he be complaining about the music? It wasn't that loud. I yelled after him, 'You can stop running now. I'm not going to hit you again.' I did turn the music down. Some people — go figure!"

Gingerbread Man

9 August 2012

The first person I saw at noon today was Bright Sky. I asked him, "How long have you lived on the streets?"

"Oh gosh, my parents died in 1999. I wasn't in very good shape, so that's when I decided to travel around the world in 800 days. I still haven't made it. I was down in Mexico for a while. I liked it there, but there is a lot of violent crime.

"I've lived in Montreal and Vancouver before coming here. In Trois Riviere, Quebec, I was arrested for hitchhiking and threatened with rape. Last year I appeared on a talk radio show. I announced my intention of running for Prime Minister of Canada, since our current Prime Minister Harper is doing such a poor job. Later, I was beaten by the Royal Canadian Mounted Police, who also confiscated my photography equipment, laptops and files. I still haven't been able to get them back.

"On July 14, 2001, I spoke at a City Council Meeting about the proposed Light Rail Transit Project and my Solar Monorail vision.

"In Europe, monorail systems are used almost exclusively for mass transit. With monorails there is not the problem of traffic congestion or snow removal. It's far more cost-effective to build up for monorails, as opposed to digging down to build subways."

I asked, "Do you know the people who congregate in the park? The group varies from day-to-day."

"I know of them, but I don't associate with them. I met some of them at the tent city. Shakes just lay on the edge of the fountain. I can't figure him out."

I said, "He's a very nice person. He's been panhandling down the street, beside the underground parking, for the past seventeen years. He comes from Montreal. While he was there, he was a boxer. He sparred with George Chuvallo and Shawn O'Sullivan. He must have been good. It's possible that he sustained some brain injury while boxing."

Sky said, "Getting a few knocks to the head can cause a lot of damage. I'm concerned about the baby carts that some people pull behind bicycles. I saw one involved in an accident right on this corner last winter. I took some pictures and asked the woman riding the bicycle if her child was wearing a helmet and mittens. She was an army girl. A couple of army fellows were there as well. They said, 'That's no way to speak to a woman.' The police arrived and asked what the problem

12

was. I tried to explain, but they wouldn't listen. They just told me to move along.

"Another time, I was attacked by a woman. I was taking pictures from across the street. She came up to me and said, 'Hey! I don't want my picture taken!' I said, 'I'm not photographing you, just the street scene.' She didn't believe me and grabbed my camera."

The next person I saw was Serge. His left eye was still black. He told me that yesterday he overslept until ten o'clock at the shelter. He said he almost never does that. This morning he was up at 7:30, thinking that it was Friday, PNA (*Personal Needs Allowance*) day, when he receives a check in the amount of $27. He had fallen again and showed me where he scraped his arm.

On the grass at the park were Hippo, André (*who had shaved off his beard and left only a moustache*), Silver, Daimon (*on crutches with his right leg in a cast*) and his girlfriend Lucy in the Sky.

I hadn't seen Daimon or Lucy since they were beaten up while trying to mug a black dude named Lucky. Lucy was knocked out and Daimon was left with a broken ankle. Whenever I'm near them, I feel like the gingerbread man faced by a pair of foxes. My thought was not if I will get mugged, but when and how bad. Hippo and André would have my back, so I'm safe for another day.

Garbage Day

10 August 2012

Today is garbage day. As I was waiting for my bus, it started to rain. A cyclist with a makeshift wagon rode past me carrying a clear plastic bag full of crushed cans. He stopped at a recycling bin on the curb, beside a driveway not far from the bus stop. He rooted through and found more cans he could get a cash refund for, from ten to twenty cents a can, depending on size.

Because of the rain, I wasn't expecting to see any panhandlers. As I looked towards Joy's usual spot, I recognized Shakes. He was standing, talking to a man seated on the sidewalk.

"Hi, Shakes! How are you doing?"

"Fine, Dennis, I was just checking to see who was sitting here."

"Is this Walter?" I asked. Walter had been panning across the street from Shakes last week.

"No, This is Al."

"Hi, Al, I'm Dennis." I reached into my pocket for a grocery store card and handed it to him. "There's enough credit on here to buy yourself breakfast."

"Thanks, Dennis."

"What about me, Dennis? Do you have one for me?" asked Shakes.

"I didn't think you ate at this time of day, Shakes. Of course, I have one for you."

Shakes said, "I slept at my daughter Fran's last night. She woke me up at 7:00 and said, 'Dad, I made some scrambled eggs and bacon for you. You have to eat something.' "

"How is Fran doing? Does she know if there is any permanent damage to her back?"

"She doesn't know. She's waiting to hear from her doctor."

"How is Bettie?"

"She doesn't know. Again, she's waiting to hear from her doctor."

"Her boyfriend should be charged," I said.

Shakes said, "I can't wait to see him myself."

"A lot of people can't wait to see him. I'm sure that Joy will lay a beating on him if he crosses her path."

"Yes, I know."

I said, "Yesterday, I saw Daimon and Lucy for the first time since his ankle was broken."

"Yeah, I saw them too. I found André asleep, so he didn't get to where he was going."

"Where are you going now, Shakes?"

"To my office."

Home Brew

14 August 2012

This morning I met André in front of the coffee shop. "Hi André," I said,"How was your weekend?"

"It was rough, man. I woke up Sunday morning and I had the shakes so bad I couldn't do anything. I just lay there in the hut all day. I drank plenty of water, but couldn't eat a thing.

"Monday morning, Shakes came over with a bottle. That made me feel better, helped with the shakes a bit. I couldn't even work. If you're panning and someone sees you shaking, like I was, they know any money they give isn't going for food.

"One good thing happened though. The Salvation Army came by and gave both Hippo and me sleeping bags. It's been three months that I've been sleeping in this thin jacket. They also signed us up for housing and ODSP (*Ontario Disability Support Program*). They're going to line up some places for us to see. From the ODSP, they'll put $450 towards the rent each month. I asked, 'So, where do I go to meet you guys?' They said, 'You don't have to go anywhere. We'll come to the park tomorrow and should be able to arrange something.' Imagine that, *they're* coming to see *me!*"

I said, "I see Alphonse across the street. I guess you heard that he and Maggie lost their baby."

"Yeah, he's trying to show a brave face. Imagine, trying to smile when you've lost a kid. He's really broken up."

I said goodbye to André and crossed the street to talk to Alphonse. "Hi Alphonse, I spoke with Maggie last week. She told me that you and her lost your baby. I'm so sorry to hear that. You must be heartbroken. I wish there were words to express to you how sad I feel. You both looked so happy the last time I saw you together."

"Yes, it's very sad, but what can I do? It's out of our hands. The baby was induced early because Maggie was using crack. We stayed at Ronald McDonald House while the baby was in the incubator on life support. After a week, they told us that he had a hole in his heart and his lungs weren't developed enough to supply his organs with oxygen."

Cocaine use during pregnancy can affect a pregnant woman and her unborn baby in many ways. During the early months of pregnancy, it may increase the risk of miscarriage. Later in pregnancy, it can trigger preterm labor (labor that occurs before 37 weeks of pregnancy) or cause the baby to grow poorly. As a result, cocaine-exposed babies are more likely than unexposed babies to be born with low birthweight (less than 5.5 lb/2.5 kg). Low-birthweight babies are 20 times more likely to die in their first month of life than normal-weight babies, and face an increased risk of lifelong disabilities such as mental retardation and cerebral palsy. Cocaine-exposed babies also tend to have smaller heads, which generally reflect smaller brains. Some studies suggest that cocaine-exposed babies are at increased risk of birth defects, including urinary-tract defects and, possibly, heart defects. Cocaine also may cause an unborn baby to have a stroke, irreversible brain damage, or a heart attack. (Wikipedia)

"There was no hope for him, so we consented to have them pull out the tubes. I was holding him when they took him off the ventilator. His breathing became very shallow. He died in my arms 45 minutes later. At the very end, as the doctor said would happen, he made little sounds like he was drowning. Then he was silent.

"Maggie asks me why I haven't been sleeping with her. Since she's been on crack, she sells herself on the street. I try to watch out for her. I want her to be safe. I see her go away with men and come back about an hour later with a fistful of cash. She spends it all on crack. I've contracted syphilis and other sexual diseases from her. Luckily, they were treatable with antibiotics, but some diseases aren't. I can't risk my life to make love with her. I don't know who she's been with.

"My brother and sister came down to be with us after the baby died. Maggie was jealous. She thought they had come only to comfort me. I told her, 'No, Maggie they came for both of us.'

"I still love Maggie. I don't know what to do." Tears were falling from his eyes. I put my arm around his shoulder and said, "I love you, man. Let it all out. I know you still love Maggie, and so you should. She's young, only 24 years old. She needs to mature. If she decides to get help, perhaps you can be together again like you once were. Perhaps it can be a new start for you. No one knows the future. All we know is this moment."

"I know I can't control what she does. I just wish she'd get off the crack before it kills her."

I said, "I have to go to work now, Alphonse. Will I see you at the park this afternoon? You take care. I love you, man."

At the park, Shakes was asleep on the grass. Wolf asked, "Dennis, do you have a cigarette?"

"No, Wolf, I don't smoke."

"Outcast, do you have a cigarette?"

"No, but Debbie has some at her place. She'll sell you some. Go ask her."

"I'd prefer if you could phone ahead, let her know I'm coming."

"Phone with what?"

"Phone with, I don't know, fifty cents."

"You expect me to spend fifty cents so you can get a smoke? I don't think so."

Wolf said, "It's just like when you told me that Debbie would lend me her library card. She said to me, 'Wolf, pay your thirty dollars in fines, and get your own card.' "

I asked André, "How has your day been since I saw you this morning?"

"It's been good. A lady at the coffee shop bought me a muffin and a large coffee with some kind of syrup in it. I couldn't taste the syrup until I got to the very bottom, then I could taste it. I was shaky after I finished. I really didn't need that. Someone else gave me an apple. I gave that to Al. I can't eat apples. I don't have enough teeth to chew them.

"See this space where my bottom tooth was? I pulled that myself while I was in jail. The tooth was loose and wobbly. It hurt when I bit into anything, so I got a piece of string, tied one end to the tooth, the other end to my bunk, then pulled. I had a package of salt — that's when they still let you have salt — put it in a glass of water and gargled. That's supposed to help it heal and prevent infection. It healed fine.

"For the past twenty-five years I've been in and out of prison: Alberta, Saskatchewan, Ontario, Quebec and the Maritimes."

I asked, "Which are the worst? Which are the best?"

"There isn't anything good about prison, but I'd say, of all them, the best were in Quebec. The very worst was the Don Jail. They didn't ask you to do things; they made you. I remember when I first arrived, a guard asked me to put my feet on these yellow footprints on the floor, and my hands on these hand prints on the wall. I guess my hand wasn't quite in the right position. He took it and smashed it against the wall. If you mouthed off, the guards would take you to a locked room and beat the shit out of you.

"Millhaven is bad too. It's a super maximum security prison. I'd done some bad stuff to get sent there. I'd been high on coke, acid, 'shrooms and my nerve pills. I got into a fight with this guy over something, I can't remember what. I slammed his face into a painted concrete wall, again and again and again. It left red face prints all over this yellow wall. When he came to court, his entire head was bandaged, except for his left eye. He had one of those casts on his right arm that held it

perpendicular to his body. His left wrist and right ankle were also in casts.

"When I was in Maplehurst, I worked in the kitchen and on maintenance. I walked into a storeroom and found two empty five gallon plastic pails. I thought to my self, *home-brew*. As I was walking down the corridor, back to my cell, I threw kites (*messages*) as I went along. I tried to get them under the cell doors, but some fell just outside. That wasn't a problem; with the flick of a towel the inmatess could pull them in. Everybody was pretty excited about this brew. I had access to everything in the kitchen including a couple of fingers of yeast.

"The brew was coming along really well, it was aging nicely when the head cook found it. He poured in some dish detergent, then dumped it down the drain. He said to me, 'What do you think of your brew now?' That got us really mad. I took some salami from the kitchen — some was whole, some was sliced. I stuffed it into one of the toilets as far as it would go. I stomped it with my foot. Some of the round part was still sticking out, but the toilet was really blocked. We had all agreed to flush our toilets at a specific time. When we did, water shot out everywhere. It was four inches deep in the kitchen, they couldn't use it because of the electrical appliances. The guards changing room was flooded as well.

"I asked the head cook, 'Does it still seem funny that you spoiled our brew?' Mind you, I was also on maintenance. It took me until one o'clock in the morning to mop up that mess, but we showed them."

Nick said, "I'm making up to eighty sandwiches a week that I hand out to homeless people. I start below the bridge. There's a group of homeless people who gather there, just like they do here.

"André," he said, "I walked past here his morning, but I didn't see you."

André and Silver were wondering what to do with Shakes, since it appeared that it was going to start to rain.

I walked with Nick towards the corner. I asked, "What kind of sandwiches do you make?"

"Egg salad, peanut butter and jam, meat with mustard and tuna. I'm up at about four in the morning. I use about two loaves of bread; pack them in my rucksack with my Bible, and distribute them until I run out. As people are eating, I read God's word to them. After that, I panhandle to get the cash to do the same thing next day.

"Yesterday, I was panning on one street where I've panned for fourteen years. I was sitting on the sidewalk with my hat out when a cop came along. He said, 'You've got your cap out. Are you panhandling? "

I said, "Yes officer, my cap is out. Do you see the cross on it, and my Bible? I give food to the homeless and spread the word of the Lord. I read from my Bible, and if somebody is hungry, I give them a sandwich. I don't sell it to them. Those don't come cheap. They cost me money. I'm just trying to get enough change to carry on my work."

"So, you're like Robin Hood, collect from the rich, give to the poor. That's a nice story, but you're going to have to move along."

"I'll move along, but I'll set up some other place." I went to the next block. He came again and motioned me to leave. I moved three times before I decided to call it a day."

We approached the next street when Nick said, "I left someone behind here." I walked to a bench where Bearded Bruce was sitting.

"Hi, Bruce," I said, "I haven't seen you for a long time."

"I just got out today. I didn't have to serve the full term of my three-month sentence, but I'm now free and clear. It's the first time in five years that I've been able to say that. I can make a new start."

I didn't ask, but I suspect the reason that Bruce didn't want to go to the park was because of the temptation of drugs and alcohol; the very things that got him in trouble in the first place (*twice he'd tried to sell crack to an undercover police officer*).

I said to him, "I'm on my way back to work, but you and Nick could probably use a sandwich. Am I right? Here are a couple of coffee shop cards. Maybe, you'd like to have lunch together."

"Thanks, Dennis," they both said as I walked away and waved.

Nick said, "I'll say a prayer for you."

"Thanks, Nick, I'd appreciate that."

Birthday

15 August 2012

Today is Shakes' 48th birthday, at least seventeen of those years have been on the street. The assembled group signed a card with a gram of weed in it.

Silver started early, at 5:00 in the morning. He pushed a grocery cart through an affluent neighborhood collecting empty beer cans and liquor bottles. He returned these to the beer store for a refund and had enough to buy Shakes two bottles of his favorite Imperial sherry.

Bearded Bruce said, "Inuk and I visited with a social worker to apply for housing, the Ontario Disability Support Program and for me to get copies of my health card, birth certificate and immigration papers. The immigration papers have to be notarized and cost $100.

'I'm expecting to get $450 from ODSP and another $300 from Welfare. Hopefully, I can find a clean, bug free apartment away from crackheads. That's my main complaint about the shelters. After rent, this should leave me about ninety-five bucks for all other living expenses. To supplement this I may still have to panhandle. Inuk and I have decided not to share an apartment, so that when we have a fight, each of us will have a place to come home to. Sometime in the future, I hope to find work as a camp cook for a construction or logging company. I have my chef credentials. What may stand in my way is the fact that, having served time in prison, I'm not bondable; however, I have never committed a violent crime and my social worker will help with references. I can even get a reference from the restaurant near where I panhandle. They occasionally bring me coffee and they'd say, 'Sure, Bruce's a good guy. He's never caused us any trouble.' If I wasn't there, it might be some drunken loudmouth."

Little Jake arrived and said, "I ditched Debbie somewhere downtown."

Bruce said, "You'll never learn. If you get kicked in the balls by a horse, you don't jump on the same horse again. If you do, expect another kick in the balls."

Jake agreed, "I know, I know." Shortly after, Debbie arrived.

Every time someone would pass on the sidewalk, Shakes would say, "Good afternoon ma'am, today's my birthday. Would you like to wish me a happy birthday?" Or André would say, "It's my friend's birthday today. How about wishing him a happy birthday?"

Bruce said, "That's the way to appear inconspicuous; sit in the middle of the sidewalk, shirtless, with a cowboy hat on and yell at everybody passing by."

Both Shakes and André had been drinking since early morning. Shakes was laying on the grass and André was constantly chatting or posing. Silver said, "Do you have a pause button somewhere, or do you go on like this from morning to night? I don't need TV; all I need is to come down here and watch you two clowning around. I've got my own movie channel right here."

Hippo was disappointed. He has a housing appointment with the shelter Thursday and all morning he thought this was Thursday.

I said to him, "Hippo, you need to get a calendar. You could scratch each day off, and you'd always know what day it is."

Bruce said, "Even if he had one, he'd need someone to remind him to look at it."

Butchering a Cow

20 August 2012

Sitting in the shade, on a park bench, I met William and Serge. Neither of them ever has much to say; they are both French-speaking, and their knowledge of English is as limited as is my knowledge of French. William is rather gaunt and pale, while Serge looks like a gnarled Santa Claus. We always exchange greetings and I look forward to seeing them. I can depend on Serge being there, being Serge.

"Hello, William, Serge," I said as I shook their hands. "It's a beautiful afternoon. Are you enjoying the cooler weather after the heat wave we had?"

Serge said, "Yes, it's very nice, especially sitting here in the shade. How have you been? I haven't seen you for a couple of days."

"I've been sick with a cold," I said. "That's why I wasn't here on Thursday or Friday. You haven't fallen again, have you?"

"No, I haven't fallen."

"Hi Hippo," I said, "how is it going with your application for housing?"

"It's going good. This afternoon I get to see a few places. If everything works out, I'll be able to move September 1st."

"That's great," I said. "Do you have any idea of which neighborhood you will be moving to?"

" I'm not sure, but they said it'll be nearby."

"That sounds good, it's just a forty minute walk to downtown. There are lots of stores, there's good bus transportation."

"Yeah, I'm looking forward to it. It'll be a bachelor, but that's big enough for me. It beats living behind a dumpster."

"How have you been feeling?"

"I'm starting to feel better now, but I was sick all weekend with a summer cold."

"André," I asked, "how have you been feeling?"

"I wasn't feeling so good this morning. The first sip I took, I started throwing up and coughing. When the Outreach Workers came around they asked, 'Are you okay?' I said, 'No, I'm not okay, I'm coughing up a lung here.' Getting all that phlegm out of my lungs felt good though. Back when I had my heart attack, I had double walking pneumonia. It was like I had a rock in my chest. I could only take shallow breaths, or it would burn my lungs.

"I've had my first bottle now and I'm feeling great. It's great being me."

"That's good," I said, "because everyone else is taken."

André said to a woman walking by, "Can I have a smile, please, just one? I'm sure you'd look even prettier if you smiled."

He said to me, "Some people walking around look so grouchy. Don't they know that if you want to be happy, you first have to act happy. Say, 'Good morning' to people, smile, say, 'Have a nice day.' I'm always happy. Even at the liquor store. Most of my friends get served once, then they're cut off for the rest of the day; not me. I go in with a smile on my face, say hello to the staff. When I'm at the check-out, I look the cashier in the eyes. And, I don't steal, except this morning. There was only one employee there and she was doing something on the computer. I stuck a bottle in the inside pocket of my jacket, picked up another and paid for that at the cash.

"One time, I had just come out of the liquor store and stopped to talk to some friends who were drinking. A cop came by and made everyone dump their bottles. I said to him, 'I just bought this. It isn't even cracked.' He said, 'Yeah, but can you prove you bought it, and didn't just steal it.' I said, 'I didn't keep the receipt; why would I? What am I going to do? Return a used bottle of sherry because I didn't like it? I bought it because I intended to drink it.' I walked back into the store and spoke to the manager, the guy that served me. I told him the situation. He came out and said to the cop, 'This gentleman bought and paid for a bottle of sherry. He refused the receipt because he was on his way out and had no need for it. He's a regular customer and he's never stolen from this store. I've watched him.' The cop let me keep the bottle.

"That's a nice electric bike going by," said André. "They cost over $800. My mother would never let me have a motor bike, not even an off-road one. My dad and brothers were race car drivers. If you want to know why I'm so crazy, you should see the rest of my family. All of us really like torque. Whatever we drive, we take it to the absolute limit. My dad rebuilt a Mustang and put a big Firebird engine in it. Everything had to be changed around to make the engine fit. When he first got it running, the hood wouldn't close. So he could go for a test run, he got me to stand on the front bumper. He chained my feet so they wouldn't slip, then he had me lie down on the hood. I grabbed onto the drip rails with my fingers. When he'd go a round a corner, he'd grab my wrist with one hand and shift with the other. This was on a gravel road. I'd be looking over the roof, feeling the car go one way, while the road behind was going another. I don't know what speed we were going, but it was fast. I saw my life pass before my eyes. I was only eight years old, so it didn't take very long. I hadn't had much of a life to that point. He was a great guy, my dad. God bless his soul." André made the sign of the cross on his chest and looked up.

"My old man was crazy. He had this pickup truck. He got some sheet steel and welded it to the undercarriage. We didn't know what he was up to, but it turned out that he was making a skid plate. He had the idea that he wanted to jump the neighbor's fence with the pickup. He built sort of a ramp leading up to the fence. Like I said, I didn't know what he was up to, so when he started the truck, I hopped in the back. There was no tailgate. I held onto the roll bar. All of a sudden, 'whoosh' we were airborne. He took out a whole section of the fence, but the skid plate kept any fence posts from coming through the floor into the cab. The truck wasn't damaged at all.

"Another time he had an old snowmobile that he rebuilt with a bigger engine. He had leather straps around the hood. I'd never seen anything like that before. The straps, it turned out, were to hold his shotgun. He'd go moose hunting with that. He'd be cruising at full speed with one hand on the throttle, reloading the shotgun with the other. I saw him get a moose. He had just crested the top of a hill and was coming down when he shot the moose in the back of the head. A perfect shot.

"We rented a house on eight acres of land. Back then, I think we were paying about $100 a month. My mother had a half-acre garden in the front of the house. Our neighbor's cows were always getting loose, trampling and eating the leaves of the vegetables.

"My dad said to the neighbor, 'My wife puts a lot of time and effort into planting and caring for that garden, she doesn't appreciate your cows coming over and ruining it. The next time I see your cows stray even one foot into our yard, I'm taking one.' Sure enough, it happened. Before we knew it, my dad had that cow slaughtered, hung by chains from a beam in the garage, and was butchering it — cutting it into pieces. He had to go out and buy a twenty-five cubic foot freezer to hold that cow. The neighbor came over and said, 'One of my cows is missing. You haven't seen it have you?' My dad said, 'No, I haven't, but you're welcome to take a look around the property. It might be out there somewhere.' "

Chester's cell phone rang. In his French accent he answered, "Hello? Yes, he's here." He handed the phone to Hippo. "Hello, oh, he never gave anything to me. Okay, thanks."

I asked, "Was that someone calling about your housing?"

"No, it was Loon. He said that he gave Weasel ten bucks to give to me. He was checking to see if I got it. I told him that I hadn't."

Joy said, "Yeah, if Loon gives money to someone to hold for someone else, he always follows up to see if they got it. I do the same. So when did he give Weasel the money?"

"Friday? This is Monday. Weasel is your friend, he lives with you guys. That's just wrong to hold out on a friend. This morning he was off to pan at the church. There are women there who bring him food and clothes. He sells the clothes to the crackheads and buys more crack. Hippo, you've got to do something about this."

André said, "Yeah, Hippo, stop being such a pussy. He's half your size, you can take him. I'm half his size and just last night I didn't like something he said, so I popped him one."

Joy said, "I've hit him when he's gotten out of line." He said, 'I can't hit you back because I'm not a woman beater.' I said, 'I dont fight like a woman, so you don't have to worry on that score."

"Yeah," said Hippo, "I'll do it soon. Right now I'm going to the hotel on a butt run."

"You're going on a butt run? Now?" asked André incredulously.

"Well, I also have to take a dump. I've been trying to hold it in, but now I have to go."

Hippo returned with his hand full of cigarette butts. He dumped them on the sidewalk in front of André. "Hippo, these are menthol. Haven't you got any class?"

"It's all they had," he said. Hotels often have sand ashtrays in their lobby. The cigarette butts are extinguished, but not crushed, like they would be in another type of ashtray or on the sidewalk.

29

Grumpy Juice

21 August 2012

Clouds were threatening rain. Joy asked, "Is that the girlfriend of Alphonse in the next block?"

"Yes, it's Magdalene. I spoke to her last week after she lost her baby. Later in the week I talked to Alphonse. He said it was a crack baby, a boy, induced prematurely. He had a hole in his heart and his lungs weren't able to supply oxygen to his other organs."

"I'm sorry," said Joy, "but she should be charged. Every kid I've brought into this world has been clean. I quit crack, cigarettes and alcohol while I was pregnant. That way, they at least had a fighting chance in the world. The night before my oldest was born, I smoked a joint. It showed up in the baby's blood tests. They were ready to take him away from me. I said, 'You're going to take my baby away because I smoked one joint? Over my dead body!'

"My sister had a crack baby. You couldn't even look at him or he would spaz out. Can you imagine what kind of life is in store for that kid?

"Alphonse is on the skids with a lot of people right now. He and Maggie have been sleeping in the hut with André, Hippo, Little Jake, Weasel and his dog, Bear. The dog sleeps by the door as a guard. Everyone knows that you have to be careful opening the door because Bear is behind it. Alphonse came by one night falling down drunk and just pushed in the door. It scraped Bear's paw and she had to get five stitches. Nobody's seen Alphonse since. Bear is still limping and has to have special ointment put on her paw twice a day.

"I just love Bear, she's really a sweet dog, but she has horrible breath. Weasel said to me, 'I feed her Dentabone.' I said, 'That's for removing plaque and tartar from her teeth. For her breath you have to give her Doggie Mints. If those don't work, she should be taken to a vet. That probably won't happen because all Weasel's money goes on crack. I gave Doggie Mints to my dog, Roxie; she was a boxer and had great breath. She used to sleep with me every night. I didn't even mind if she put her paw on my face when she slept. I couldn't tolerate that with any of the men I've lived with.

"Like me, she was epileptic. If I had a seizure, she'd pat my face until I came out of it. I'd do the same for her. One time she had a prolonged, grand mal seizure and died before I could get her to the vet."

I said, "I saw Bearded Bruce last Thursday. He and Inuk have applied for housing."

"Yeah, I met them at Chuck's new place. They were staying there. Maybe I should have held out at Chuck's a while longer. His new place is a huge two bedroom. I don't know about Inuk. She and Bruce have been together three years now, but while he was in prison, she was living with other guys. I met her one day with her oldest son. He isn't of legal drinking age, but he was staggering drunk."

I said, "Bruce and Inuk are each getting their own apartments. That way Bruce said, 'When we get into a fight, we'll each have our own place to go home to.' "

Joy said, "I don't know what's happening with Fran. They've called her into court about three times. She's so afraid of Gene, she doesn't even want him to see her. It was just in January that he got out of prison for beating her the last time. He was in a holding cell with my Jake before they moved him to Millhaven."

Chester stopped by to say hello. To Joy he said, "I didn't hear you leave this morning."

"If I'd stopped to make the bed, you probably would have heard me. Is there anything you want me to bring home?"

"I wouldn't mind some pot. Do you know where I could get some?"

"You could try the shelter. I could give you some phone numbers, but I don't know if anyone is coming downtown this afternoon. I saved some roaches. You might be able to get one joint with what's left in the can on the kitchen table.

"Chester, I want to use your phone later. I want to make an appointment.

To me she said, "I've been thinking of looking into some kind of employment. I couldn't do nine to five, but I'd like landscaping, maybe with flexible hours — of course, I'd want to be paid under the table. I'm good at growing flowers and plants. One time a neighbor had a couple of rose bushes that never bloomed. He was going to dig them up and toss them out. I said, 'Let me try to do something with them. I dug them up, replanted them somewhere else, and within a couple of months they had pink and white blooms on them."

Noon in the park was quiet. Weasel was asleep with Bear under a tree. André was drunk, professing his love for Joy. "We could make such a great team," he said to her.

"Yeah, sure we would," said Joy sarcastically.

Weasel awoke and asked, "What time is it?"

Bruce said, "It's only twelve ten. Go back to sleep for another hour." Later Weasel said, "I don't remember coming here."

Bruce said, "We started out up the hill. Then, we came down here."

"Weasel," said Joy, "you missed a great fight. That big native guy and André were scrapping. He pushed André down on his ass. André got into that karate stance he uses, but he was so drunk that he couldn't keep his balance. I kept egging him on saying, 'You shouldn't let him get away with that.' André took a swing, missed, and the big guy pushed him on his ass again. The cops were strolling through the park and didn't do a thing. I was sure someone would get a ticket."

Weasel walked over to Hippo. I overheard him say, "If you even try to get up, I'll knock you back down." He then walked down the line to Bruce who said, "Well, didn't we wake up with a gut full of grumpy juice?"

"What?" said Weasel, "Can I have a cigarette?"

"Of course you can," said Bruce.

I asked Bruce, "How are the arrangements coming for housing?"

"Monday, I got my first welfare check for $300. I'm waiting for my program to kick in. Nothing can happen until that's in place. Then we'll sign the papers for housing. Hopefully, we'll have a place in September."

William came by with a two-wheeled cart. "I got this from a bar that was being refitted. One wheel was off the cart, but I took it to the shelter and a guy helped me to get the wheel back on. We inflated the tires and it's good as new. The bar was throwing out a mini freezer, a fridge, all sorts of stuff. I saw some empty beer bottles in the garage and asked if I could have them. They gave me six cases of two fours, so I got $14.40 for those.

"Hippo, don't throw that wine bottle away. I'll take it."

"Come get it yourself," Hippo said.

William rooted through the garbage container for the wine bottle and also pulled out a large paper coffee cup with a plastic lid.

Joy said to me, "I hate it when he does that."

"William!" said Joy, "you're not going to drink out of that are you?"

"It'll be fine. I'll swish a little beer in it first, to clean it out. I forgot my cup at home." He pulled out a can of beer and filled the paper cup, so it looked like he was drinking coffee.

He said to me, "Would you like to know what I did with the coffee shop card you gave me? I didn't sell it to buy beer. I bought two coffee, a bagel with cream cheese — did you know that the coffee shop ran out of meat? I was in there at 10:00 two nights ago; they close at eleven. They didn't have any meat. I went in the next day, a bit earlier. I still had about a $1.50 on the card, and got some kind of meat wrap. I made good use of the card.

"I met a woman in the park once. I was sitting on a bench, shaved, dapper looking. We started talking. It turned out that we had both previously lived in Montreal. We talked about that for a while. She said, 'You're a very interesting man.'

"I was straight forward with her. I said, 'I left my wife because she had been cheating on me. I lost my job, my unemployment insurance ran out and now I'm homeless.' "

"She said, 'I left my husband because he had been cheating on me.' She was a beautiful woman, had lots of money, ran her own business. She said, 'I have some errands to run. Will you wait for me here for about twenty minutes?'

"I said, 'I won't wait right here. I was planning to go to the liquor store to buy a couple of bottles of beer, but that will only take about fifteen minutes, so I'll be here before you get back.'

"She said, 'Can I give you money to buy a six-pack? Then we can share a few beer.'

"I said, 'You don't have to give me any money. I've got a check on me for $547. I'll buy a six pack.'

"She said, 'You're so generous.'

"When I got back with the beer, she had two huge bags with her. She said, 'I've bought you a gift.' There were clothes in there, chips, chocolate bars. She even bought me a return ticket to Montreal and back. She said, 'If things don't work out for you here, come visit me in Montreal. The tickets are good for a year.' She gave me her address and phone number. I said I'd call her."

He continued, "My apartment was robbed. They took my backpack with her address and phone number in it. She'd told me where she lived, but I couldn't remember. I couldn't even remember her last name, so I couldn't look her up in the phone book. That's the way it goes. Perhaps, we'll run into each other some other time."

Phyllis Diller

22 August 2012

"Hi," said Bright Sky, "I'm glad to see you. Did you visit my website? What did you think?"

"It's great. I also listened to your proposal to City Council. It was very well presented."

"Thanks! Yesterday, I was on talk radio, but the host blew me off. I have a recording of the program if you'd like to hear it."

"Sure!"

"I'll rewind this. Anyway, what I was proposing was that the city investigate the building of a solar monorail, like they have in Bologna, Spain."

As the tape rewound, he went on. "Did you hear that we lost Phyllis Diller? She had a great laugh. I was talking to a friend about which celebrity we would most like to meet. My choice would be Doris Day. You're old enough to remember her. She's an animal activist (founder of *Actors and Others for Animals*, the Doris Day Animal League and the Doris Day Pet Foundation). I sent her an email saying that I'd like to meet her, but I didn't get an answer.

"See that guy, sitting on the sidewalk, with his hat out? I don't know what that's all about. I find it disgusting. Doesn't he have any sense of dignity?"

"There's something coming up on the radio that I want you to hear. Maybe, you've already heard it. President Obama's ratings have gone up four points because of a gaff made by the opposing party. The remark has angered a lot of people, especially women. It's coming on now." He turned up the volume on the radio.

"Missouri Rep. Todd Akin, who is running for the Senate against Missouri Sen. Claire McCaskill, stated in a television interview on

Sunday that "women's bodies are able to prevent pregnancies if they are victims of a LEGITIMATE rape."

Sky shook his head. "This is the dumbest statement I have heard a man make about women's bodies since an 18-year-old kid told me once years ago that women can only get pregnant if they have an orgasm during sex….but that was a dumb 18-year-old warehouse stocker…..Akin is a member of the United States House of Representatives and is running to unseat Senator McCaskill of Missouri. What do you think? I'm sure that'll cost Romney the women's vote.

"Here's that recording from the talk show. I went by the name of Steve. Don't put it too close to your ear; I have it turned up loud."

I listened to the recording:

36

"We have Steve on the line. Hi Steve, what would you like to talk about?"

"Hi, I understand that our mayor is interested in saving money on our proposed light rail system. I suggest that we investigate the possibility of a solar monorail, like the one they have in Bologna, Spain."

"A solar monorail? There's just one problem with that, Steve. What do we do when it's dark?"

"We sleep… Actually the solar energy is stored in cells, and is released as necessary."

"They don't have storage cells that big. Steve, have you heard about Spain's financial crisis?"

"Yes, I have. That's the reason they opted for solar power. Energy from the sun is free."

"Steve, I think you've been out in the sun too long. I think your brain is a bit fried.

"Next caller."

Sky said, "Well, so much for that. I still think it's a good idea. With the help of an engineer friend of mine from Newfoundland, we're designing a solar-powered ship. It would be huge, with ballrooms, swimming pools and luxury condos."

"Sounds great, Sky. I wish you all the best with it."

As I was walking up the sidewalk, I saw Serge laying on his side. "Hi Serge, are you alright?"

"I think I passed out, but I'll be alright."

On the curb were Shark and Anastasia. Shark said, "Irene was here earlier, but she had to see her worker, so I'm alone, free and loving it. We got cable and satellite in our new place. Irene is paying for the satellite, I'm paying for the cable. I'm going to drill a hole in the wall of my room, so I can watch both."

"Hi André," I said, "you haven't been fighting with any big natives today, have you?"

André laughed and said, "James and I made a truce. This morning I brought him a bottle and we drank together. There was no point in us hurting each other every day. I'd rather have him at my back than have him facing me. This city can be dangerous.

"That reminds me, Joy, you'll never guess who I saw last night. Sharon, the former girlfriend of Alphonse."

"She's out of prison?"

André continued, "I was panning in front of the coffee shop. Sharon was inside having a coffee. I got Inusik to sit with my cap on the street and I went in to talk to her — I was inside when it started raining, Inusik got soaked — I went back outside, as soon as I sat down, somebody dropped me ten bucks. Inusik was pissed. I saw Maggie walking towards us. Sharon came out to continue our conversation. I knew they both liked to scrap, so I said, 'You're both my friends, I don't want any trouble between you.'

"Maggie was drunk, acting like a smart ass. Sharon punched her right in the mouth. Here I am in the middle. Maggie looked at me as if to say, Who are you going to side with? I said, 'Hold on, whatever you two have to work out, go ahead, but I'm staying out of this.' "

Joy said, "You should have sided with Sharon, she's the better fighter. The last time we got in a fight, I had a broken ankle and was walking with a cane. She kicked my cane and punched me in the side of the head. I took the bus home.

"I told Big Jake about it. He didn't say a word. He walked into the bathroom, took the plastic handle off the plunger and filled it full of dimes. Then, he untwisted a wire coat hanger and wrapped the open end of the handle. He sealed the opening, and wrapped the wire with duct tape. There was quite a weight to that.

"The next day, I was sitting in my usual spot when Sharon came by. She told me to move on. I said, 'Make me!' She bent down to take another swing at my head. I ducked and pulled out the club from my sleeve. I hit her with all my might on each side of her head. She was knocked out cold. I pushed her off the sidewalk, onto the slush of the street, and went home.

"She saw me a while later and said, 'You pack a good punch.' She didn't give me any trouble after that."

Fran rode up on her bicycle. Joy said, "Hi Fran, I haven't seen your dad for a while. Is he okay?"

"He's serving thirty days for a breach. He was panning in front of McDonald's. That's a red zone for him."

Joy said, "They must really have him medicated. He's probably on lithium; that's what they put me on. The last time I was there was for assaulting Big Jake. Mind you, I was on suicide watch. I was kept in observation. They kept giving me cheese sandwiches for breakfast, lunch, supper and snack. I didn't have any appetite, so I made a pillow of them. I said, couldn't you at least give me some soup in a styrofoam cup, or some meat?"

Three men approached. They shook hands with André then Joy, who introduced me to them, "Dennis, this is Tommy. He's Jim's brother, Bettie's boyfriend." We shook hands.

Tommy introduced his two friends, Hank and Dan. "We're all from the same place. We used to call ourselves the 'four horsemen' but one is in jail. Jim is at the West right now. He was sentenced to six months for assaulting Bettie. He'll serve four. I know, he's an asshole."

André said, "So, he got a hundred and twenty days. When I was there last, I couldn't eat. Then I got my appetite back. I was fishing down the corridor for food. I'd pass my paper plate to the guy in the next cell. It'd get passed down the whole block. I'd always get something: fruit, a juice box, a muffin."

André was wearing baggy shorts and Silver noticed what appeared to be claw marks on his upper thigh. "André, did you get in a fight with a cat?"

"No," said Joy, "he got too close to a pussy that he wasn't supposed to get close to. He's lucky that I have my fingernails rounded. When I was in prison, I used to file them like claws. I'm talking flesh tearing claws. That reminds me of my days at P4W (*the Prison for Women located in Kingston, Ontario*)."

Tommy said to Joy, "How old are you?"

"How old do I look?"

"I'd say about fifty."

"Oh, thanks! I'm forty-six."

"It's the lines around your eyes. Are you and André together?"

"No, we've known each other a long time. We're not living together, we're not going out together, he's not fucking me. He tries to touch me and I don't like it. Maybe now he'll learn his lesson."

I said, "I'm her father." Everybody laughed. Tommy winked at Joy. He said, "We have to go now, but I'll see you around."

After they left, Joy said, "Why do guys always hit on me?"

"Because you're pretty," I said.

"It's your charm," said André.

Hope Recovery

23 August 2012

This morning I could barely see Joy's feet beyond the concrete partition. "How's it going today?" I asked.

"Horrible! I've been here since six and I've hardly made a cent. It's worse than Mondays. I guess a lot of my regulars are on holidays.

"Metro's going to get picked off one of these days." We both watched as he walked through the line of cars to hand a driver a newspaper.

I said, "You get a great view of the world from down here."

"Yeah, I see it all. Some men have their flies undone, with their willies flapping in the breeze. If I mention it to them, they say, 'Well, look somewhere else.' I say, 'Hey, man, it's right in my face, and it's not a pretty sight. Where am I supposed to look?'

"Sometimes, I see guys with their shoelaces undone. Sometimes I tell them, but if it's the crusty ones, I just wait to see if they fall.

"Brad was by earlier. He's all stitched up. I asked him what happened. He said, 'Angeline stabbed me with a kitchen knife. She's serving thirty days.'

"'Thirty days for stabbing someone, that's ridiculous. Are you going to take her back when she gets out?' He said, 'Yes.'

"Angeline can be nice, but she's schizophrenic. If she's off her meds, and on the booze, she can't be trusted with kitchen utensils.

"Chester has taken his pennies to the store. They have a change machine that will convert them to bills and other

41

change. Usually, he gives them to one of his French ladies. They donate them to the kid's hospital. This time though, he needs the money.

"There was a guy hanging around this morning, snapping pictures of me. I said to him, 'Hey, I didn't give you permission to take my photo.' He said, 'Well, may I have your permission?' I said, 'No, but it's a bit late now.' I don't want someone I don't know, walking around with pictures of me. It's creepy.

"Outcast is pissed with me because I wouldn't go with him yesterday afternoon. I said to him, 'I distinctly remember you telling me that we were over, which seemed kind of ridiculous since we never started anything. Now, you're pissed off because I don't want to go to your girlfriend's place when she's coming home at five o'clock?'

"I'm going to have to ask the guys to spring for some cash so I can get a bottle. I wonder what I'm going to have to do for that. André owes me money. Little Jake has owed me money for two years. I heard that yesterday Hippo was giving away twenties to everyone, but he didn't give me anything."

At noon, seated on the curb, Jake kept tipping over on his side. André said, " Jake, will you get up. I don't want your nose in my ass."

Joy said, "Jake, you stink. I'm moving away from here." We moved closer to Silver and Hippo, and André followed. Jake had passed out in the bushes.

"Silver," I said, "I haven't seen you in a while. You've lost weight."

"Yeah, I have lost weight. I haven't been eating enough. I've got an appointment with my doctor. I'm having problems with my stomach."

André said, "I made twenty bucks yesterday. Do you want to know how?"

Joy said, "André, I'm sure we don't want to hear about what you did to make twenty bucks. It's probably disgusting."

"No," said André, "a guy bet me a twenty that I couldn't do a one-handed hand stand and hold it for thirty seconds. I did it and that was after eight bottles. He paid me."

Minutes later, three cops on bicycles stopped in front of us. They probably had a complaint about Jake. They kicked the bottom of his foot, trying to wake him. Joy walked over and told the cops that Jake has HIV/AIDS and is very sick. André shook Jake and helped to get him standing and walking. They walked down the street, then sat on a low concrete wall.

The police came over again. The sargent said, "Jake, do you have any place to go? You can't stay here. How much could he have possibly drunk, this early in the day? What's in the bottle, Jake? Hand it over." He opened the lid and took a whiff. '"That's awful! Is that a Jakenator, beer mixed with sherry?"

André said, "You know him well."

The sargent said, "Write him up." André, Chester and I moved away to the other side of the wall. Joy had walked across the street to the hotel to use the washroom.

André, yelled, " Jake, will you learn to shut your mouth?"

Chester said to me, "They're going to write him another ticket that he isn't going to pay. That's what they always do."

I heard one of the cops mention, "Hope Recovery Centre". I expect they've called for the paramedics to take Jake away.

Cops

24 August 2012

Joy had a big smile for me. "How is it going this morning, Joy? Do you mind if I sit down, or will that interfere with your panning?"

"I don't care. It's been a good morning. I'm happy, surprisingly. My legs are sore from the fibromyalgia. My left hip is stiff and it feels hot to the touch. I guess that's arthritis. I wonder if it's the same thing that Big Jake has. Rodent gets his letters from Millhaven. He also contacts him through prison message boards on the internet. He told me that Jake's using a cane. He's having trouble with the same hip I am. Rodent asked me if it's catching."

I asked, "How long do you think they'll keep Little Jake at Hope Recovery?"

"Just overnight, he's probably out now. I remember once, when I was staying at the women's shelter, I got really wasted. I couldn't even ring the doorbell. I did a face plant against the front glass doors. At the desk they said, 'It's Hope Recovery for you tonight, sister.' I said, 'No, just help me to my room and I'll pass out like I do every night; but no, they phoned the outreach workers and they came to pick me up.

"The next morning when I woke up, I couldn't remember anything about the night before. I had $200 in my jeans pocket, three bottles of sherry and a gram of weed in my backpack. I have no idea where I got the money. For days, I was looking over my shoulder. I thought maybe I had robbed somebody.

"I don't know what happened to Jake yesterday. He seemed fairly sober when I went up there in the morning.

Chester went on a liquor run, then Jake mixed one of his Jakenators — beer with sherry. All of a sudden, he was wasted.

"It didn't help that André was throwing his bottle around and making comments to women passing on the sidewalk. They don't want that on their lunch breaks. I've seen some women give him real dirty looks. I saw one stop at the bottom of the hill and make a call on her cell phone. Ten minutes later the police arrived. The last thing we need is someone drawing attention. André has been in town for five years. He knows the rules.

"I'm glad that Shakes is getting treatment. They probably have him on Lithium, Valium and an alcohol drip. That's what I was on the last time I was there. It prevents the shakes from alcohol withdrawal. I was just there for the weekend. I slept most of the time. They just left the jug of tea outside my cell. I had no appetite, all I wanted was something warm.

I said, "Silver's looking awfully thin. He says he has stomach problems and has made an appointment with his doctor. He says that he's not eating enough."

Joy said, "I think he's back on crack. He gets a check every month, but he eats at restaurants. He has a small fridge, he could stock it with vegetables, and in his little freezer compartment he could have frozen meat. He's an alcoholic; he has to eat.

"Chester's coming down later to have a coffee. He was by earlier, but I said, 'Sorry, I don't have a grocery store card yet.' We're going to the food bank later. We need to stock up for the weekend. I always make sure we have lots of vegetables in the fridge. Chester can't carry very much, but I can get a lot in my backpack. Then we take the bus home."

"Was Chester asleep when you left this morning?"

45

"No, I had a coughing fit. I tried to eat, but it came back up. He said it didn't wake him up, but before that, I heard him snoring.

"When I finish here, I have to go wake up André. We both have an appointment at the Salvation Army. My worker is going to look into why it's taking so long to get my identification papers. I'm going to get her to keep a set in my file, for the next time I lose them. She's also going to help me get my meds. I really should be taking them.

"Outcast was pissed with me last Saturday. He got it in his head that Chester phoned Debbie and told her that Outcast and I had been sleeping together. Chester said he didn't call, and Debbie's smart enough to figure things out on her own.

"She also thinks he's been stealing her pot. He said to me, 'Oh no, Debbie keeps that in a safe.' I'm sure that Outcast has watched her open it, and knows the combination.

"Now, he's got no money and he can't borrow any because everyone knows he's a thief – the worst kind of thief, one who steals from his friends."

After I left Joy, I saw Bright Sky at the pay phone in front of the library. He said to me, "Can you believe this, I'm trying to call the University, and nobody's answering. Did you hear that I was on the *Money Show*?"

I said, "You mentioned being on the *Talk Radio Show*. You played me the tape."

"No, this was Wednesday evening, *The Money Show* was on Monday. I was promoting my idea of the solar-powered monorail."

I said, "I read on the internet about the one in Bologna, Spain. It seems like a good idea. I think that's the way we should go."

"I'm glad to hear you say that. Here, I've got something for you. These green and purple ribbons are the colors of my

Peace and Justice party. I'd be honored if you'd wear them. May I take your photo?"

"Sure, " I said.

The usual suspects had met at the park. Wolf was sorting things in Shaggy's canopy-covered cart. When he turned around, I was sitting on the grass beside Joy.

"Dennis," said Wolf, "I didn't mean to ignore you, well, yes I did; I had some things to sort out first. Eventually, eventually, mind you, I was meaning to turn around and say hello to you. So, hello, Dennis."

"Hello Wolf, I was sure you were going to say hello to me."

Willy said, "Dennis, are you really sure that Wolf was going to say hello to you?"

"No, Willy, I'm not sure of nothin'."

Wolf had a bag of treats. Joy asked if she could feed Shaggy. She put one of the treats on the lawn, about three feet from Shaggy, then moved her hand towards it, as if she were going to take it back. Shaggy lunged and nearly bit Joy's wrist.

"Bitch," said Joy.

Shakes had been released from the Detention Center. I said to him, "Hi Shakes, when did they let you out?"

"Yesterday. I was inside for six days. The court screws saw that the sole of my shoe was flapping. They gave me new shoes."

Willy asked, "What were you charged with? Vagrancy?"

"No, it was a breach. I'm not allowed within five hundred feet of McD's on Bank. I'm not sure how far that is, but it's more than a foot."

Willy said, "That was well put, Shakes."

Two bicycle cops, one male, one female, rode up. Shaggy barked.

The female cop did all the talking, "Jake, do you understand the conditions of your probation?"

"Yes, I understand – no panhandling."

"Shakes, I see you have some court documents."

"Yes, I'm now allowed within five hundred feet of McD's."

"You say you're *not* allowed within five hundred feet of McDonalds."

"I am allowed."

"Okay, Shakes."

"The rest of you, any alcohol? Are you staying out of trouble?"

Joy said, "Two of us are just leaving for the food bank."

"What time does that open?"

"1:00."

"Okay, we'll leave you alone then."

They left and everyone breathed a sigh of relief. Willy said, "I had about two inches of beer in my can when I saw them coming. I just turned around and pushed it over the railing. I didn't lose too much."

Wolf said, "I'm glad they didn't check Shaggy's cart. I had my beer in there."

Shakes said, "I've got a gram of pot in my underwear, but I can't find it." He then proceeded to pull down his sweat pants and search for the missing pot.

Willy said, "Shakes, I hope you're not intending to share that with anybody. I don't want anything to do with pot that's been in your underwear. It's going to taste of shit and ball sweat."

"It's in a plastic bag."

Joy said, "Shakes, for God's sake, pull up your pants. I'm seeing way too much and it isn't pretty. The cops will be coming back."

To me she said, "I've seen Shakes down and out before, but never this bad. He's incontinent; he wears Depends. He's so weak, he can barely get up by himself. He's not taking care of his burn scars. He doesn't care. It's sad."

As I was standing with the group — everyone packing their bags, picking up their cushions — I saw Wanda, a woman I work with. I waved. She looked at me with a disapproving look and walked on; she didn't wave.

Sometimes, I question what it is I'm doing. I have arguments with health workers whose job it is to treat people with dementia and Alzheimer's. They say, 'I can feel empathy with people who are sick, not of their own doing, but alcoholics have brought this on themselves. With our health care system, everybody pays for their choices.' I agree, the shelters cost money, welfare costs money, jails cost money, the police cost money, but looking at my friends, in their varying states of ability and disability, their personal motivations to struggle with addiction or give in to it, I know it's more complicated. I don't know the answers; day by day, I'm beginning to understand the situation.

Silver

27 August 2012

This morning I went over to see Silver, panning in front of the coffee shop. He was sitting on a plastic box. When I said hello, he was startled. He may have dozed off. "Hi Dennis, you snuck up on me."

"How are you feeling, Silver?"

"Fine."

"How is your stomach?"

"I'm going to see my doctor on Wednesday. I still don't have any appetite and haven't been sleeping well. Look at my ankles. See how swollen they are. Those aren't my ankles at all. I think I'm getting what my mother had, varicose veins. See, beside my knee and down my calf."

"How did it go panning at the church yesterday?"

"Not good."

"Is that the Cathedral or the small church?"

"The small one, the Cathedral is where I was assaulted last spring. I didn't even have to phone the cops. Two women from church were witnesses and there was a cop right on the corner. I was going to get up and talk to the cop, but the two women said, 'Silver, you stay right here. We'll deal with this.'

"When they came back they said, 'Silver, you need to go to the hospital for stitches.' I said, 'No, just give me a couple of band-aids. It'll heal better that way."

I said, "I see you have a scar on your right eyebrow. Is that where you were hit?"

"That's it."

"So, what happened Sunday?"

"Where?"

"At the church, you said it didn't go well," I said.

"No, I didn't have a problem. I've been taking a bit of a break lately. Trying to catch up on my sleep. On the weekend I watched a bunch of Clint Eastwood and John Wayne movies."

I said, "I've always enjoyed those. 'Pale Rider' with Clint Eastwood is one of my favorites. Another is 'Rooster Cogburn' with John Wayne."

"'Pale Rider' is one of the ones I watched on the weekend."

"I guess you'll be getting your check soon."

"Yeah, Stella will be around with it on Wednesday. I also want to get some laundry detergent and some socks from her. Were you up on the hill Friday?" asked Silver.

"Yes, I was."

"Did the piggies come by?"

"Yes, they did. They didn't give out any tickets or ask us to move. Willy dumped part of his beer and Wolf had his hidden."

"I was in the market. I saw them ride by and decided not to go to the park. I stayed at the loading dock where I often go. I've never been hassled there."

"How are you doing today, Serge?"

"I'm fine."

"On Friday you said you weren't feeling very well."

"When did I say that?"

"You were sitting on the bench with William. I asked how you were. You said, 'Not so good.' "

"I was tired. I went beneath the bridge, where it was quiet, and I slept for a while. I felt better after that. Yesterday, I went up the stairs at the Art Centre and had a sleep there."

"So, you're feeling better now?"

"Yeah, I got my booze," he chuckled.

Bearded Bruce was at the park with the rest of the congregation.

"How are you, Dennis?" he asked.

"I'm fine, how about you?"

"I'm waiting here for my worker. She's taking me to fill out the forms for housing. I'll also have to get my picture taken; my health card has expired.

"Apart from that, it's been a slow day. I was panning since 6:00 this morning and made 87 cents. I'm going to lose the busiest part of my working day getting forms filled out, but it has to be done."

I said, "Joy doesn't do Mondays."

"Wolf," asked Bruce, "can I have a cigarette?" Wolf pulled out a clear plastic bag and threw him a cigarette. Bruce casually caught it in one hand. He lit it and said, "Shakes, can I have a sip from your bottle?" Shakes tossed the bottle and Bruce plucked it out of the air. He took a sip then tossed it back to Shakes who easily caught it in one hand.

Shakes said, "If that had been a sandwich or a ball, I would have fumbled it, but a cigarette or a bottle, I never miss."

I said to Silver, "You mentioned that you didn't have a good day at the church on Sunday."

"Did I say that? I think I meant to say, I didn't make as much money as usual. Normally, I get from thirty to forty bucks. Yesterday, I think I got about twenty. At Christmas, one of my regulars dropped me five twenties. When he gave it to me I said, 'This feels like more than a twenty.' He didn't say anything. I folded it, put it in my pocket. I didn't count it until I got home.

"It has been slow lately. I blame it on the drifters, these people who live with their families in the winter. When it comes spring the parents give them a hundred bucks and tell them to live somewhere else for a while. When winter comes they're crying to their mommies and daddies to let them come home again."

Bruce said to me quietly, "I could never pan in front of a church. I have nothing against those who do, but to me it seems wrong."

Wolf motioned for me to move closer, "Don't worry about Shaggy. She'll be fine as long as you don't touch her or be aggressive.

"I was listening to these guys talking about panning, five or six days a week and getting maybe seven dollars. I couldn't do that. Panning is hard work. Shaggy and I go out maybe once a week.

"I went to court Friday. Did I tell you about that? I was charged a few months ago with animal cruelty. Can you imagine that? Two women — I don't know who they were — reported me to the police. It was just in the parking lot, behind where I live. I guess these women didn't like the way I was putting Shaggy in her cart. They said I was too rough. I was walking along the sidewalk, pushing her cart, when three police cars screeched to a stop. They took my dog.

"You know, that dog means everything to me. I got her back the next day. I talked to my lawyer about it. He said I could plead guilty or ask for a trial date. He recommended going to trial. Friday, they set the date for February 24. He said to contact him about two weeks before the trial. Last time, I got over a hundred signatures, from my friends and regulars, saying that I had never mistreated Shaggy.

"I rough house with her, but she always comes out on top. I've got the scars to prove it."

Bruce's worker came by. "Is Little Jake here?" she asked.

"No," said Bruce. "I don't know where he is."

She said, "If any of you see him, tell him that I'll be by here at noon tomorrow to pick him up. Tell him that it's very important."

"Bruce, are you ready to go?"

"Yeah, just let me refill my bottle."

Silver asked, "With apple juice?"

Bruce said, "Yeah, with apple juice." The worker smiled. He pulled an Old Milwaukee out of his backpack and filled his bottle.

"Is anyone collecting?" asked Bruce.

"I'll take it," said Wolf. Bruce threw him the empty can. Wolf crushed it and threw it in Shaggy's cart.

Shakes Is Sentenced

28 August 2012

This morning, when I approached Joy, I noticed that she had her blanket wrapped around her legs and her hood pulled up.

"Hi Joy, you're all bundled up."

"I'm not feeling well. I was throwing up all weekend. I couldn't keep anything down. Chester asked me if I wanted him to call for a doctor, but I said no. This morning I had toast and tea. I thought that would stay down, but it came back up again. Cathleen was by earlier, she brought me a cup of tea, two cream, three sugars. I only drank half of it and I'm starting to feel queasy."

Alphonse and Magdalene came by, said hello and shook hands, then carried on. Joy said, "I don't like Magdalene. Usually, I don't have anything to do with her. It was weird shaking hands."

Bruce came along, "Hi Dennis, I just wanted to see how grumpy here was doing today."

Joy said, "I'm grumpy alright, feeling sick doesn't help."

"What kind of sickness do you have?" he asked.

"Just nauseous," she said.

Bruce said, "I just saw Alphonse and Magdalene. They seemed happy."

"I've got no use for her," said Joy.

"Why is that?"

"I've got no use for someone who drinks alcohol and smokes crack while they're pregnant. I never did that and I've got five sons. If she'd stayed clean, they'd probably still have their baby."

"Bruce, "I asked, "how did it go with your housing appointment yesterday?"

"Great, they're going to have a list of places for me to look at tomorrow.

"I was panning yesterday and a guy handed me a five dollar bill. He said, 'I guess you're going to spend that on beer, aren't you?' I said, 'As a matter of fact, I'm going to use this to dry my sleeping bag. With all the rain we had last week, it got wet.' Later on he saw me in the laundromat. He said, 'I didn't believe you, but I guess you were telling the truth.' There's nothing worse than trying to sleep in a wet sleeping bag. I probably spend half to two-thirds of the money I make on food. That way I'm not throwing up every morning and don't have the shakes."

Joy asked, "Where's Inuk?"

"I don't know," answered Bruce. "she didn't come home last night. I'm just on my way to have breakfast, then it's to work. Maybe, I'll see you both at noon."

After he left, Joy said, "That's quite a relationship. They've been together three years and he doesn't even know where she is.

"Bruce really does eat a lot. When he was staying at Chuck's, he'd cook huge meals. Two strips of bacon would be plenty for me. He'd put twice as much on my plate as I could eat, but between him and Chuck they finished everything left on my plate. In the morning, I'd see him drinking a glass of milk, then a Pepsi. I'd ask him why he was drinking that. He'd say, 'It's to coat my stomach.' I can see drinking the milk, but the Pepsi?"

I asked, "How are you making out with housing?"

"I find out Wednesday. My worker is going to try to find out what's taking so long to get my identification and health card. My worker asked, 'Do you know who you talked to last time?'

I said, 'No.'

'Can you describe her?' she asked.

'She had an attitude and I didn't like her.'

'That applies to a lot of the staff over there.'

'I can't remember if it was a man or woman, if they were tall or short, thin or fat — they all look the same to me. I see thousands of faces each day. It's hard to pick out just one.' "

A woman dropped some change into Joy's cap. A man, one of her regulars, handed her a five dollar bill."

"Alright!" said Joy. "Thanks!"

To me she said, "Things are looking brighter now."

Chester stopped by. Joy held out her clenched fist to him. He held his cupped hand out. "Pennies!" said Joy. Chester pocketed the pennies and moved on.

Motioning to a woman wearing a black dress passing by, Joy said, "That woman should start thinking of using a dry cleaner or getting rid of her cat. She's covered with hair.

"That guy that handed me the five – I see him most mornings. Usually he says, "Hi!" but if he's with his friends, he just keeps his head down."

"Hi Jacques," I said, "I haven't seen you for a long time."

"No, I've been down by the river. There is always a breeze there, so even on the hottest days it is cool by the water. The cops don't bother me there. I can drink my homemade wine and relax.

"Tomorrow they're coming to spray for bed bugs. I have air conditioning which seems to slow them down, but I pay by the month and I don't want to pay for September. We do get some warm days and there will be the humidity. The bed bugs will be jumping in the carpet then.

"It's so easy to get them; they can jump onto your pant leg, you carry them home, they bury themselves in the carpet and lay eggs. Soon you have thousands of them. I wrap a towel around my pillow. Every morning I unwrap it and find one or two bed bugs. I pick them up and put them in a container.

"I'm looking for a new place. Near where I live, I've seen lots of For Rent signs. Maybe this week I'll take a look at them. The only problem is, if I move, where am I going to make my brew? Another problem in my neighborhood is that there aren't many convenience stores, and no wine stores. The closest wine store is about 12 blocks away – that's a long walk. There are two convenience stores. They make good sandwiches, but I don't buy my bread there; it's too expensive. Also, they're not open late."

"Shark," I asked, "are you all settled in your new apartment?"

"Almost, we've still got some things to rearrange. We found a plastic Mickey Mouse with his hand out. We stapled him to the kitchen wall and put our change in his hand.

"Irene's still at home in bed. I phoned her and asked if she was coming down. She asked, 'Is it 1:00 yet?' She can't get her meds until 1:00."

"So, how long were you able to keep off the booze?"

"About ten minutes. I was down here last week and Shakes gave me a sip of his wine. Then I decided to get a six-pack of beer. What really did me in was the twenty-six of vodka. I'm going to pick up some beer for Irene on the way home. I don't know who I was trying to fool. I am the way I am."

Shark said to Jacques, "That was quite a sentence they gave to Shakes, six months probation. He won't be able to do anything. If he spits on the sidewalk, he could get arrested. If he smokes a cigarette in the park, he could get arrested. That would be a breach on top of a breach. He'd do jail time.

"Danny was with him when he got out. A cop stopped Shakes and said, 'I could arrest you right now.' Shakes asked, 'What am I doing wrong?' The cop said, 'You've been panhandling and you've been drinking.' Shakes said, 'I'm allowed to drink.' The cop said, 'You're allowed to drink inside a house or a bar. You're not allowed to drink outside.' Shakes was ready to argue, but Danny told the cop that he was taking him to the shelter. The cop let it go.

"Friday is check day. We should have that spent by the end of the weekend. I don't know how these people on welfare can live. They get $450 a month and the cheapest price for one room is $400. Landlords prefer to rent to students, even though they make a lot of noise, because their parents are footing the bill and they leave at the end of the school year, which means that the landlord can jack up the rent. Try to pay all your food and other expenses out of the remaining fifty bucks."

I Have to Get Away

29 Aug 2012

This morning Joy's spot was vacant. Hippo was on the west side, Silver was on the east, in his usual spot in front of the coffee shop.

I sat beside Hippo. "How's it going with your housing application?" I asked.

"Great," he said. "I got a place on some street with a French name. Can't remember it. It'll be ready for the first of October.

They're completely renovating the building, including new parquet flooring. There won't be any carpets; I'm glad of that. I won't have to worry about bed bugs. There's a McDonalds near by."

I said, "I was talking to Bruce yesterday. He had to take his sleeping bag to the laundromat to have it dried. Have you had any problems with water seeping in where you are?"

"No, we're just over there, on the other side of the coffee shop, behind the dumpsters. We put up a roof. It's nice and dry. We just pile up the cardboard and go to sleep. I found it really cold last night."

I'm going across the street to talk to Silver. Will I see you at noon?"

"Yeah, I'll be there. I'll see you then."

"How are you feeling, Silver? You have your doctor's appointment today, don't you?"

"Yeah, I'm going to the Community Health Centre at 1:00. That's where my doctor is. I've been going to him for a long time. I asked my worker about him. She said he's a good doctor, so I keep seeing him. It's important to have a doctor that you can depend on. I know a lot of people who don't have their own doctor."

Later, I saw him at the park. I said, "I guess you're getting ready for your doctor's appointment this afternoon."

"No, I got that mixed up. It's tomorrow. Today is ladies day."

"Dennis," said Outcast, "what time is it?"

"It's about five after eleven."

"I don't usually see you here until noon. You've thrown my whole schedule off. Don't do that again."

"Okay, I'll keep that in mind."

I asked Joy, "How are you feeling now?"

"I'm really sick. I've been throwing up blood, and from the other end as well. My poo isn't black; it's red. Don't tell any one." She was near tears. "I feel dizzy and have a full blown migraine. I just want to go home and lie down. I think it may be from the bed bug spray I've been using. I've got some powder now. I'll see if that's any better."

Following are some of the side effects of common bed bug sprays (Pyrethroids):

Inhalation:

coughing, wheezing, shortness of breath, runny or stuffy nose, chest pain, or difficulty breathing.

Skin contact:

rash, itching, or blisters.

Long term effects:

disrupts the endocrine system by mimicking the female hormone, estrogen, thus causing excessive estrogen levels in females. In human males, its estrogenizing (feminizing) effects include lowered sperm counts. In both, it can lead to the abnormal growth of breast tissue, leading to development of breasts in males and cancerous breast tissue in both male and females.

Neurotoxic effects include:

tremors, incoordination, elevated body temperature, increased aggressive behavior, and disruption of learning. Laboratory tests suggest that permethrin is more acutely toxic to children than to adults.

Other:

*A known carcinogen. There is evidence that pyrethroids
harm the thyroid gland. Causes chromosomal damage in
hamsters and mice; deformities in amphibians; blood
abnormalities in birds.*

I asked Joy, "Shouldn't you see a doctor?"

"I can't. I still don't have my health card. I talked with my
worker this morning; the woman I dealt with before back in
April didn't even submit my request. They have nothing on
file. It's been sent now. It'll take about three weeks until I get it
in the mail.

"They may have a place for me as early as August fifteenth.
I told them that I don't want to be in a crack house. I want
someplace safe, with no bugs. An apartment would be ideal.
I'd like to be on one of the lower floors, so I'd be able to climb
over the balcony and drop to the ground.

"If that place isn't available, or if I don't like it, there's
another coming vacant September first. I get to take a look at
them next week.

"I have to get away from Chester. He's a nice man, but I'm
tired of all the noises he makes. He grunts and groans when he
sits down or stands up. I have no time to myself. It used to be
that he'd be asleep when I got up in the morning, then I'd have
peace and quiet while I was drinking my tea. Lately, he's been
getting up when I get up. I don't want to have to talk to people
that early.

"I'm going to leave soon. There are some people here that I
really don't care to be around.

"I have to go by Chuck's old place. My check may have
been left in the mailbox. I'll just sneak up and take a look."

Joy left to talk to Silver, so I sat with Irene. "How is your new apartment?"

"It's great. We're still moving things around."

"Shark said you had a plastic Mickey Mouse stapled to the wall."

"Yeah, that's in Shark's games room. Outcast came over with his tools yesterday to hook up our satellite and the cable TV. He used a three-way splitter so we have TV in the bedroom, living room and in Shark's room. The TV is free."

"How are you feeling today?"

"I feel better than I did yesterday. I just had a couple of beer today. I had a terrible hangover yesterday."

Anastasia came over and sat by me, she said. "Irene was telling me that you live in our neighborhood, Irene's old neighborhood."

I said, "We're just a few blocks away from each other. I'm surprised that we haven't seen each other on the bus."

"What time do you leave in the morning?"

"I leave for work at eight and come home at six, unless I go to the gym after work, in which case I'm home by eight thirty."

"Those aren't my times. They've just sprayed my apartment for bed bugs, but they didn't get all of them. I phoned the exterminator, now he says they might be in the woodwork, or in my books. He didn't tell me that before. He should have given me a full account of what he could do and what he couldn't. He didn't do that.

"I went to the Salvation Army to get some bed bug powder. They wouldn't give it to me. They said that I had to be homeless. Well, I'm the next thing to it. I'm on disability pension. Sometimes, I think I'd be better off to just shut my door and move to the Sally Ann.

"I didn't get to visit my family this summer. The other day I lost my upper front tooth. It just fell out. It was an implant, it cost me a thousand dollars. All my other teeth are fine. They can't put a bridge there, but they can get me a 'flipper'. Some people have told me that it's difficult to chew when you have a 'flipper'. They take it out when they eat."

Crack Haven

30 August 2012

87 degrees at the park today. Sitting on the curb at was Loretta

I said, "You haven't been coming around as much as you used to."

"No, I live way out near the edge of the city. It's hard to get down here sometimes, especially if I've run out of bus tickets.

"Joy's feeling a bit better than she was yesterday. She's with her worker, viewing apartments. There's one she could get for August fifteenth, if she likes it."

I said, "That's great. She'll love having a place all to herself.

"How have you been?" I asked.

"Fine, I've been working."

The sandwich ladies came by offering juice, granola bars, sandwiches and socks. Danny took a peanut butter, Shakes asked for something with meat. Niles explained that he had severe allergies to mustard, mayonnaise and onions. He showed me the EpiPen (*epinephrine autoinjector*) that he always carries.

Niles said, "Did you know that apple juice is poisonous? It contains cyanide and arsenic. Over a long period it can cause organ damage and cancer.

"I just came back from San Francisco. I have my own landscaping business there. When we first moved to the States, we lived in Ocala, Florida. Later, we moved to San Francisco. I got a real break there. I got a job with a landscaping company. There was nobody to look after my daughter, so I brought her with me. My boss really liked my work and would always call for me if she needed something special done.

"One of our clients was Arnold Schwarzeneger. It would take a crew of us about three days to do his property. He would always give my daughter some money. He'd say, 'Don't tell your Daddy.' She's grown up now and has kids of her own. She lives with her boyfriend in Anchorage, Alaska. She's studying accounting, business and something else she won't tell me about. It has to do with the land.

"I have a proposal to build a three floor complex for homeless people. There would be the lower floor with facilities for storage, because that's a problem for the homeless. We'd also have bunks for sleeping on that floor. Food facilities would be on the second floor and the top floor would be for games. My daughter and I would be partners. She would have her own apartment, on the third floor, for whenever she comes to town.

"It would be a safe place for alcoholics and the homeless. Even if people were drunk, we'd let them in, but they wouldn't be allowed to drink on the premises. I estimate the total cost would be about 1.3 million dollars. I even have a location picked out, near the river."

Shakes said, "I'm going to be getting my own place soon."

"Do you know the location, yet?" I asked.

"Right in the middle of 'Crack Haven', behind the Sally Ann. After I've been there for a while, I'm going to ask to be relocated. After I get my place, they're going to take me shopping for clothes. I've got a television set at my daughter,

Bettie's apartment. I also have a DVD player put aside. The guy said, 'As soon as you have your place, Shakes, we'll deliver it.' "

"That sounds great. It will be better than sleeping on the street."

"I think I'll sleep outside, sometimes."

"I said, "At least you'll have the choice of where to sleep."

September 2012

Guitar

"Good morning, Dennis. Did you have a good weekend?" asked Metro.

"It was great. How was yours?"

"Good! Are you hoping to see Joy this morning? I haven't seen her. Maybe she's still recovering."

I didn't see her in her usual spot. I looked across the intersection for Silver, but his spot was vacant also. Pat was nowhere to be seen. I was surprised at how disappointed I felt. I wondered about the results of Silver's appointment with his doctor. I wondered how Joy's viewing of an apartment went on Friday. Even Shakes, who I sometimes see in the morning, is getting a new apartment. I wonder if he's moved yet. Sleeping outdoors is dangerous, I can't help but worry. Hopefully I'll see them at noon.

Later, I saw Silver sitting on the curb near the park, all alone

"Hi," I said, "How was the appointment with your doctor?"

"It was fine. He took some blood tests, but I won't get the results until next week. I have another appointment for a week Thursday. He should be able to tell me something then. I showed him how swollen my ankles were. He didn't tell me what was causing the swelling."

"You were telling me that you had varicose veins, perhaps it's a circulation problem."

"That's what I think it is, but I won't know for sure until next week."

"How are you sleeping?" I asked.

"I've been sleeping okay. I woke up at 6:30 this morning, did what I had to do, then went back to bed and slept for another couple of hours. I didn't bother panning today."

"How was your weekend?"

"It was quiet. My neighbor, Don and I ordered a pizza and watched some movies. That's about all."

"Hi Danny," I said, "I didn't know you played guitar."

Shark said, "Neither did he, but he knows how to hock it."

Jacques said, "Maybe it's not a guitar in the case. Maybe it's a gun, like in a movie I saw a while ago. There was an Elvis convention and these five guys, dressed in Elvis costumes, robbed a casino. Kurt Russell was in it and another guy with long hair in a ponytail. He was a mean one, shooting into the crowd with a machine gun."

Little Jake said, "That was Kevin Costner. The movie was called *3000 Miles to Graceland*."

Shark said, "Dennis meet your new neighbor, Jake. He's moving into Irene's old place, if the landlord ever gets around to fixing it up. He's supposed to change the carpet, but he didn't do that when Irene moved in. He's drunk most of the time. He knows all the people in the building who drink and will come to the door and ask, 'Can I have a beer?' I'll say, 'No, but you can take these empties, since you're here.' Otherwise the maintenance man will go rooting through the trash for them. That makes a lot of noise. You'll see the landlord drinking on the front steps. If not there, he'll be on the back steps. The maintenance guy moves things from one apartment to another. When you view the place everything looks all nice and new, then they switch the nice furniture for crap.

"It took Irene ten months to get out of that place. The landlord said that she would be on probation for the first three months, then he was supposed to have her sign a lease, but he never brought it around. When she was moving out he said, 'You know you're breaking your lease.' I said to him, 'She never signed a lease, you drunken bastard. There's no lease to break.' He said, 'You don't have to get nasty about it.'

"Eventually, we're going to get all new furniture. Irene and I have a difference of opinion when it comes to buying things. She always wants to buy what's cheap; like her mattress, she paid $125, I paid $300, but mine is twice as thick as hers. I don't want to be sleeping on something that has pieces of metal sticking out. If I want something, I pay for it, I don't care what it costs."

"So, when are you moving, Jake?"

"They're supposed to get back to me, but I think it should be next week, or the week after."

Jacques said, "Those shelter people, they don't look very hard for an apartment for you. It's okay if you find one yourself, then they'll help you with moving. Otherwise, they're useless."

Danny said, "I nearly had a place lined up last week. I told the landlord that my disability pension would cover the first $450 of the rent. If there were any extras, my mom would pay them. He could just give her the bank information and she would deposit a check every month. She's an elder and a Clan Leader. She's been handling my finances for the last twenty years because of my addiction problems."

I asked, "André, how was your weekend?"

"The weekend was pretty wild, but I'm trying to keep it cool today. I have to see my worker to arrange for my identification and my health card again. This time I'm going to have them keep a copy on my file in case I lose them.

"Here are my workers now." Two women walked into the park and André met them.

Jacques said, "Who are those two? I thought it was a big guy and a girl who came around. Maybe they fired him because he wasn't doing his job."

I asked, "Jacques, did you hear if Joy got her place?"

"I saw her Saturday, no it was Friday. She went with her worker, then she was going to pick up an air mattress."

"Yes, she didn't want to bring bed bugs into her new place."

"It's best if you don't have carpets. They make nests everywhere in carpets. I found a big spider web with lots of dead bed bug husks. I love the spiders, me. I don't mind how many I have of them as long as they keep eating the bed bugs."

Jake said, "I saw Chester having breakfast at the shelter, but Joy wasn't there."

Shark received a telephone call, "Yes, Irene?" he said. "What's Hippo doing there? Tell him to get out. Tell him anything — tell him you and Kat have to go out. Tell him you have to go to the doctor. That's what we had to do last night. We were at Buck's playing Bingo. Trudy wanted to wash the floors, so Buck said, 'Okay, Hippo, time to go.' He left with no problem."

To me he said, "We've got Kat with us now."

"You have a cat?"

"No, Kat is a person, a friend of Irene's. She's over there now. She's small, doesn't take up much space, not like Hippo. When we sweep, we can just ask her to lift her feet, there's no problem.

"Silver hasn't moved in the last twenty minutes. Is he okay? I don't think he's drinking today, is he?"

"Yeah, " I said, "he has a beer on the go. He's not feeling too well."

"I know he went to the doctor last Thursday. Irene said to me, 'Make sure he goes to his appointment.' Our doctors are both in the same direction. He goes to the Community Health Clinic, my doctor is further up, but my appointments are Mondays and Wednesdays. Thursday he's on his own.

"I want to go visit my son, but my dad said, 'It's not a good time.' I'd like to go for two weeks but I have to arrange it with my doctor. I said to him, 'You phone my dad and arrange it. I can't get anything out of him.' "

Look at Me!

5 September 2012

Sitting on the curb was André, more sober than I've ever seen him. He'd also shaved recently. "André," I said, "I see cheeks and a chin that I've never seen before."

"I've got an appointment with my worker, she's meeting me here at 1:00. She's going to check on my ODSP (*Ontario Disability Support Program*) and my OW (*Ontario Welfare*). Every time I go there, they tell me it's in the works, but I never get a check. Then I need my drug card and my social insurance card. I'll just leave it on file with the pharmacy. That way I don't have to worry about losing it or having it get soaked in my backpack.

"You should have seen the bullshit I had to put up with this morning. I went to the pharmacy to get some emergency medication. They wouldn't give it to me without a prescription. I said to the pharmacist, 'You mean I have to walk a quarter of a mile to pick up a prescription, then walk a quarter of a mile back here to get it filled? Can't you see it's an emergency! Isn't it obvious! Look at me!'

"I got lucky this morning. I was talking to a guy who had to go to court. He said, 'I need a cap to go to court. If you can get me a cap, I'll split a joint and a cigarette with you.' I walked into the restaurant, looked around and saw these two guys sitting at a booth. There were three caps in front of them. I asked, 'Does this cap belong to anyone?' They said, "No, but it's yours now.' So, I give the cap to the guy outside, we split the joint and the cigarette and I got the edge off. No more shakes. I hardly had to do anything.

"Do you smell Listerine? Is Serge nearby? I stay away from that stuff now. I hate the headaches, the throwing up, the stomach pains and the smell that comes right through your skin.

"It really pisses me off when I share a bottle, or a couple of beer with a guy, and he says he's going to get the next bottle then he brings back Listerine or rubby. That's not right! You don't replace a bottle of sherry or a couple of beer with Listerine or rubby. Mind you, if that's all you got, then that's what you drink.

"I met this guy on the weekend who I haven't seen for, must be, fifteen years. We grew up together in Cornwall. I was at this apartment building. I have no idea how I got there. I missed my appointment with my worker yesterday because I had no bus tickets and no way to get downtown. Even if I had bus tickets, I wouldn't have known which bus to catch.

"Anyway, Timmy says to me, 'André, I want you to meet a good friend of mine. We looked at each other. I said, 'Steve?' He said, 'André?' Timmy said, to me, 'André, you know everybody.' It seemed I knew everybody in the apartment building, but I don't remember meeting them.

"I'm glad that Rodent left. I was about ready to punch him. He thinks he's being funny, just like my uncle Roscoe; but then the comments get personal and it's not funny any more. I was getting really pissed off. I think he could sense it."

I said, "I'm going to the park to see who else is up there."

Silver said, "I'm staying away from there because Shaggy is barking her head off."

André said, "I'll just wait here with Silver until my worker comes."

"I'll see you on my way back then," I said.

I sat with the group of ten. Chasing each other around and through the circle, back and forth, were Wolf's dog Shaggy and Buck's dog Dillinger.

It was all Anastasia could do to sit upright as she ducked the dogs or watched them tear around. As she was trying to light a cigarette, she kept tipping backwards. "I'm an otter," she said, "swimming on my back, looking at the clouds." I was closest, so I offered my arm to pull her upright, all eighty pounds of her.

As Wolf sat down on the blanket beside Shaggy's cart he said, "I've got a stiff back. All I've done for the past week is take Shaggy for her walks, lay on the couch, read, watch TV, get up for a beer and lay back down again. It's good to make the effort to come down here and socialize a bit. Shaggy's having fun with Dillinger. Did you see that, she actually gave up her spot so Dillinger could lay down?"

I asked Wolf, "What are you reading now?"

"I just started this book. It was given to me by a lady who gives me books all the time. I was reading the back cover and it seemed to be some kind of romance novel, so I put it at the back of my pile. When I started reading it, I found that it was all about spies and espionage. Four of them get shot in the first few pages, a real shoot-em-up, just the kind I like to read. If I had known what it was about, I would have started it a month ago. It was nothing like the Harlequin romances my mother used to read."

It was time for me to head back to work. Irene asked, "Dennis, would you walk me to the bus stop?"

I said, "Sure, are you ready to go now?"

"Where?" she asked.

I said, "Don't you want me to walk you to the bus stop?"

"No," she said, "I don't want to take the bus anywhere."

Couch Surfing

7 September 2012

Today at the park the weather was pleasant, but the mood was tense. Sitting on the curb was a group of six. Facing them on the sidewalk were André and Clint.

"André," I asked, "How did it go with your worker on Wednesday? Did you get your papers signed for housing?"

"I got a lot of things sorted. They set me up with a street allowance because I said, 'Hey, I sleep behind a dumpster, or if I'm lucky, I do some couch surfing.' So, on Monday I'll be able to pick up a check for $200.

"I'm 46 years old; I can't be on the street like Weasel and Jake. I'm going to get on the ball, go to my appointments. They're giving me a monthly bus pass, otherwise I'd have to go there to pick up bus tickets every time I have to see somebody. With ODSP (*Ontario Disability Support Program*) alone, I have to go nine times a month. I have to go to the doctor twice a week, then there'll be visits for housing.

"I'm staying at the Sally Ann right now. That's good, because that's where my workers are. If I need to contact them, after hours, I can just slip a message under their door. If they need to contact me, they can come to my room or leave a message for me. I know they're going to work really hard to get me settled."

Clint said, "The best fish and chips I've ever had were at the Sally Ann in Halifax. Every Friday they'd serve them. It was a great big plate and the fries were just like you'd get at a fish and chip shop — hand cut, crispy.

"I got in trouble at a dance there. I was dancing with a woman; I didn't know she had a boyfriend. It turned out that he had boxed for ten years in prison. He broke my nose, broke my jaw; I had to have it wired shut. Now, if I yawn, sometimes it'll lock open."

André said, "That's why I don't go to dances. I was at a dance one time. I was drunk. I started dancing by myself, I turned around and, you know how it is, I was dancing with three women. I was having fun, clowning around, then three guys showed up. They'd been there all the time, but they didn't want to dance, that's why the women were dancing together.

"The first guy caught me with a left hook. It was a good left hook, flattened my nose to one side. The next guy hit me with a right hook, flattened my nose to the other side. By this time my white tee-shirt was red. I said to the third guy, 'Bring it on, let's see if you can get my nose straight again.' "

"I've had my jaw broken," said Joy. "Isn't it great having to get all your nutrition through a straw?"

Joy kept scowling down the line at Raven. André said, "Just take a few deep breaths and count to ten."

Joy was punching her fist into her open palm. "You don't know the half of it. That Chester is so stupid. It was Raven's old man who stole Chester's bank card and drained his bank account. And how did he get in? Raven! Now he wants to invite her over to where I'm staying. Over my dead body!

"I'm feeling really pissy today. I didn't get much sleep last night. I was awake chasing cooties most of the night. I've found out that the mature bed bugs have a numbing agent, so you can't feel when they bite, but the young ones don't seem to know about that. You can feel when they bite. They start out kind of colorless, then turn orange when they suck your blood. When you crush them between your thumb and finger, they have a rotten wood smell about them."

I asked, "Do you sniff every bug you crush?"

"Every one. See all these bites I have below my knees? I've got them all over my body. They're either from the bed bugs or from the spiders I bring in from the balcony to eat the bed bugs."

André said, "I remember going to visit a guy in Guelph, at the Redbird Hotel, I think it was. It was a long time ago. Anyway, we were going to go to his room. He couldn't get the key in the lock, he was that drunk. So, I had to unlock the door for him. I turned on the light and there were thousands of roaches everywhere. The walls looked alive with them scrambling away. He asked, 'Do you want to sit down?' I said, 'No way, man! I don't want to be carrying those things to the next place I go.' "

Joy said, "I think my lungs are worse since I moved into Chester's place."

I asked, "Is it because of the bed bug spray, or are you using the powder now?"

"The powder is better, but I've run out of that too."

André asked? "Do you dust it over all the carpets?"

"I sprinkle it only in the area where I sleep. Chester is on his own. I wash and dry my clothes, cook them, powder them, bag them and put them out on the balcony. Chester takes his clothes out of the bags and puts them in his drawers. He won't listen to me.

"Now he says he's broke. I gave him money for food, but that's not what he spent it on. At least I have a grocery store card if I get hungry. Last night I made spaghetti sauce. Tonight I'm turning it into chili. I've got it in the crock pot now. Chester asked, 'Can I still put it on noodles?' I said, 'Do anything you want with it.'

"I'm going to go home now, before Chester gets there, so I'll be able to watch English television. Sometimes, I'll be in the middle of watching a movie and Chester will say, 'I don't like this,' and he'll switch over to one of his French channels.

"He gets up so early. This morning he got up just as I was falling into a deep sleep. First thing, he goes to the fridge for a beer, then he lights a cigarette. As soon as he does that, I start coughing, and I have to use my inhaler. I wish there was a door he could close. At least he doesn't smoke in bed. That would really scare me.

"André, can I ask you something that I never thought I'd ask?"

"Sure."

"Will you come sit between me and Jake? He's driving me nuts with his babbling. It's all I can do to keep from punching him."

To me she said, "The only reason I don't punch him is because he's HIV positive, or has full-blown AIDS for all I know."

André said, "Jake, will you wipe your mouth? You're drooling."

To Joy he said, "If he needs straightening out, I'll do it."

Chester came over to Joy. She said, "What is it, honey? Do you want to sit on your blanket?" She pulled it out from under her and handed it to him. "Come sit down."

Chester took the blanket and went back to sit with Raven. André said, "I thought he was going to sit with us."

"So did I," said Joy. "I think part of the reason I feel so schizoid is because of menopause."

I asked, "Are they any closer to getting your health card and other identification?"

"Yeah," she said, "I just have to go in and fill in some personal stuff about my parent's birth dates and my mother's maiden name. I have all that. They were both born in 1944. My father was such an asshole." Joy was weeping as I left.

Stolen Boots

10 September 2012

I wore my Fall windbreaker today. The sky was overcast and there was a cool breeze blowing. The congregation was at the far end of the park. Joy walked toward me and we met at the sidewalk.

"I didn't know whether or not you'd be coming," she said. "I was about ready to leave when I saw your head above the bushes. I'm feeling sick. I cooked some chicken from this store in my neighborhood and I've been throwing up all night. It didn't affect Chester, but it's the second time I've gotten sick after eating their chicken. I'm always careful to cook it thoroughly, same with pork, I know how sick it can make you. I'm going to leave now. I just want to lie down and take it easy today. I can't even drink.

"You wouldn't happen to have some extra bus tickets for Chester would you?"

"No, I'm sorry. I'm all out. I'll have to get more at the convenience store."

"I just thought I'd ask. I'll see you tomorrow."

"Take care, Joy. Get lots of rest, I'll see you tomorrow."

"Hey," said André to Joy, "Don't I get a hug?"

"If I bend over, I might puke all over you."

André put his wide-brimmed hat upside down on his head and said, "Okay, I'm ready. How about my hug?"

The grass was still wet from the overnight rain Shakes, as usual, was lying on his side, resting on one elbow.

"Shakes," I said. I haven't seen you for a while. How are you?"

"I just got back into town from Kingston. I spent the last week there. A friend took me. He wanted to get out of town for a while, just to have a change of scenery."

"Did you enjoy yourself?"

"The first day was awful. A dog died, some women were fighting and one guy tried to commit suicide. But that was just the first day."

"Were these friends of yours? Did the dog belong to one of your friends?"

"No, I didn't know them. I spent seventy dollars on food, but mostly I had meals home cooked by friends I met.

"Since I got back, I lost my wallet. Could you give me another of those grocery store cards? The one you gave me before was in the wallet I lost."

"Sure, Shakes."

Timmy put some tissues in Andre's wide brimmed hat. "That's for Shakes; he's drooling."

"He's just drunk, that's all."

"André," I said, "you've got a couple of fancy hats since I saw you last."

"Yeah, I'm starting to get a collection. This one has feathers around the brim. If I ever get lost in the woods, I can use them to tie flies for fishing. I lost most of my clothes at the shelter. A friend, who'd been sleeping at the hut with us, was leaving town. He made a pile of all the stuff he couldn't carry with him. There was a pair of size twelve work boots. I was going to bring them to Clint. There was also a pair of size ten, Gortex winter boots with kevlar toes, heels and shanks. They were insulated and Thinsulated — do you know what I mean? Two layers of insulation. They came up to my knees. I'm guessing they were worth about $400. I stayed at the shelter one night. The next day, I left my things in storage. They were locked and were supposed to be secure. I stayed at Katrina's for two nights.

"When I came back to the shelter, I went to bed 245, where I thought I had slept, but the locker was empty. It looked like my bed, same color blanket, made up like mine. I always make my bed after I get up in the morning. I went to the desk and asked the guy, 'What bed was I sleeping in? I thought it was 245.' He checked and said, 'You were in 295.' I checked that bed and again, an empty locker. I was really pissed off. I figure the guys at the desk cut the lock and took my stuff.

"I went down and yelled at them, 'I had two brand new pairs of boots in there, and a bottle and a half of sherry.' One guy said, 'André, are you ratting yourself out, telling us you brought liquor on the premises?' I said, 'I'm just being truthful.' They said, 'It shows on our record that the contents of that locker were signed out.' I said, 'Well, I didn't sign anything out. I don't believe that. You guys cut the lock and took my new boots. They were so new they didn't even have dirt on the treads. You don't want to see any of us building up a stock of anything.' I stormed out. I was living outside for four months and after one night at the shelter I've lost everything.

"I've been getting these bites all around the waistband of my track pants." He pulled his pants down to expose his hip and to show the red marks. "They're some kind of mites, I think. I threw all the clothes I was wearing in the garbage, then took a shower. When I came out, all I had to put on was a towel. The guy at the desk asked, 'Why are you walking around like that, André?' I said, 'I need new clothes. My old ones were full of bugs.' He said, 'We can't help you with that until 7:45.' 'Well,' I said, 'I guess I'll be walking around in this towel until 7:45.' "

I said, "I haven't seen Hippo for a while."

André said, "You're not likely to either. He's probably in hiding. Little Jake was drunk, Hippo came up and punched him four times in the head for no reason. Then he was causing trouble at the coffee shop. They called the police. The police knew we were staying out back. Bruce said the police ripped down our hut and threw all our stuff into the dumpster. Later, someone set fire to it."

Shakes said, "I lost my brand new sleeping bag."

André said, "Those women at the Homeless Hilton are really saints."

Clint asked, "Do you mean at the shelter?"

"Yeah," said André. "They all know me there. It's funny though. I went downstairs and they said I was too drunk, so I went upstairs and they said I wasn't drunk enough. One of them even asked me, 'André, do you have any more booze? Go out, have a few more drinks, and we'll let you in.'

"I went out back to what we call the pig pen. A street sister came by and asked me, 'Do you want to buy a twenty-six of rye for thirteen bucks?' 'Yes,' I said. 'That's a pretty good price.' I just happened to have $13.70. I'd already drunk two and a half bottles of sherry. A guy sat next to me, pulled out a fancy crack pipe and put a forty in it. His buddy, sitting next to him, said, 'Be careful.' The guy looked around for cops then lit his pipe. I drank more and more of the rye, straight up. Then I smacked the guy in the back of the head. The pipe flew out of his mouth, the forty went rolling across the parking lot. Some sisters picked the stuff up, but the pipe was fucked. The guy's buddy said, 'I told you to be careful. When André gets into the hard stuff, he gets crazy, especially around crack smokers.'

"I went back upstairs and they let me in."

Timmy said, "That reminds me — we should have walkie-talkies. Then I could six you if I saw the cops coming from my direction, and you could six me if you saw them coming from where you were."

André said, "They've got this new fangled invention now. It's called a cell phone. That's what people use them for."

Clint said, "You know, one time a cop was really nice to me. I was up in North Bay. I asked him if there was any place I could set up a tent. He said, 'Sure, get in.' He let me sit in the front seat. He didn't pat me down or anything. He took me behind this gas station, where some empty rigs were parked. He said, 'You should be safe here.' Then he left."

Timmy said, "I've been given rides by the cops before, but they always frisked me. They even apologized, said it wasn't anything personal, it was regulation. If a guy was in the back seat with a gun, he could shoot the cops and steal the car. They left the sliding window open so we could chat back and forth. I've never ridden in the front seat of a cop car. Sometimes, they even have console mounted shotguns on a swivel."

Sweet Grass

11 September 2012

André came staggering up the sidewalk. The sides of his track pants were unsnapped, his shirt was off. He had a four-foot length of gold chain with two-inch links, a padlock attached to the end, wrapped twice around his neck.

He, Debbie and Little Jake immediately started arguing "What do you mean I'm acting like an asshole?" asked André. He started swinging the chain. Joy said, "André, if you hit Jake in the back of the head with that padlock, I'm going to kill you. You know I mean it."

André sat down, "I'm sorry for being an asshole. I'm just waking up. I passed out in a park last night. You all know what that's like."

Joy said, "Been there, done that, couldn't afford the tee-shirt."

Shakes, who was surprisingly sober, said, "I think Andre's still upset about being rolled last night."

I asked, "Is that right, André? How much did they take? Was it a gang?"

"No," said André, "it was just two guys. They got 140 bucks, but I did quite a bit of damage to one guy. I had him in a head lock and was punching him in the face, when the other one kicked me in the side of the head. Things are a bit confused after that."

Shakes asked, "Do you have my radio? I lost it twice yesterday."

I said, "That means you must have found it once."

"Yes, I did."

Debbie asked, "Have you seen Jake's new apartment? I was there last night. It's gorgeous. The walls are freshly painted, the floors have been varnished. Jake's bedroom is as big as his living room."

Jake said, "They gave me fifty bucks for groceries. Tomorrow they're going to see about getting me some furniture, even a television."

Joy said, "I've got an appointment to see an apartment. It's $600 a month."

I said, "You saw one a few days ago, didn't you?"

"I had an appointment, but my worker cancelled at the last minute. They wanted $795 for that one. I'd only have $50 left after I cashed my check."

Two workers from the Outreach Program came by. One said, "Shakes, can we meet with you tomorrow around 10:30?"

"Sure."

Joy said, "I'll make sure he's here, because I have an appointment with my worker tomorrow at the same time."

After they left Joy said, "I got 4 bucks. Has anybody got any change? André, in the mesh pocket of your backpack I can see some change." André threw over two quarters and a dime.

Joy said, "Okay, I've got $4.60. I still need forty-five cents." Everyone checked their pockets and came up with the needed change.

To Chester, Joy said, "Honey, would you mind going to the store and picking me up a bottle?"

"Sure," said Chester, "and if they don't have Imperial? I've been there sometimes when they've been out."

"If they don't have it, don't bother getting anything. It would only make me sick."

"Jake," I asked, "Are you moving into the apartment that Irene moved out of?"

"No, it's nearby, but different apartment, different building. I'm really going to make it work this time."

Joy said, "Every Fall the workers try to get us off the street and into apartments, that way they don't have to bury so many of us."

Shakes pulled a new bottle of sherry out of his backpack. He cracked the seal, poured some into the cap and threw it over his shoulder. Then he handed the bottle to Joy, who poured some into her coke bottle, then passed it back to Shakes who took a sip from the bottle. Joy then reached into her backpack for a large Sprite bottle of partly frozen water. She added water to the sherry then took a drink.

Jake said, "I'm going to get some sweet grass to smudge my apartment."

Joy said, "Sweet grass has a beautiful smell, especially when it's mixed with sage, burnt properly and wafted with an eagle feather. It's so relaxing and peaceful."

Seizures

12 September 2012

The sun was shining and Joy was in good spirits.

"Hi Joy, you have an appointment with your worker today, don't you?"

"Yeah, I'll be meeting Janice and Darla at the park at 10:30. I have the same workers as André."

"What will they be talking about today?"

"Just details of the place I'll be moving into."

"You must be excited. This is the first time since I've known you that you'll be having an apartment of your own. You've always shared with somebody."

"Yeah, it's exciting and scary. It's been so long since I've lived alone, I'm not sure how I'll cope."

"It has to be better that living with bed bugs, and you won't have to put up with Chester's noises. You'll be able to watch English television, whatever programs you choose. There'll be no one to beat you."

"Yeah, that'll all be good. I just worry about my mind. The last time in prison I was in the psych ward, under suicide watch because I kept stabbing myself with pencils. That was when they put me on Seroquel, it's an antipsychotic for schizophrenia and bipolar disorder. When I'm on that, I don't hear the voices. Lately, it's been television commercials that are going around in my head, like the one for Yop. It has kind of a reggae beat:

When I wake up in the morning I'm still asleep

I really don't want no toast

I want no water, no tea, no cereal

give me a yogurt drink I'm wanting first.

Ooooooh! Give me Yop! me mama oh

Yop! me mama when the morning come.

Give me Yop! me mama

Yop! me mama

Yop! for when the morning come...

I said, "André was really wild yesterday."

"Yeah, he was being a real asshole."

"He said he got rolled. Where did he get $140?"

"The workers arranged that for him. It was his street allowance. On Monday he got a check for $150. With the last of his money, he bought three bottles. Jake invited him over to his new place. André didn't even have bus fare. Jake, of course, is all proud because he has a bus pass.

"Hippo is going to get the shit kicked out of him, or else he'll be exiled. I'd rather take the beating. Being exiled is hell.

"I saw him this morning. He's been hiding out with Jacques near the river. He's afraid of Bearded Bruce."

I asked, "How did that all come about?"

"Hippo was drunk. He was ten feet tall and juiced to the gills. He was in the coffee shop, performing, when someone called the cops. They knew where he was staying so they went back there. They recognized Bruce because of his record, and were holding him up against the fence. Bruce was upset with Hippo. He said, 'I could have been breached.'

"The exterminators are coming today. I just hope that Chester remembers to tell them about the day bed. The stuff they spray will completely soak the mattress. I've been sleeping in the middle of the room on an air mattress. I was thinking, there's no way they'll be able to hold onto plastic, but sure enough they were there. I could feel a bump in my sheet, and it moved, so I squished it and smelt my fingers. It had that rotten wood smell of a bed bug. In the morning, I saw a streak of blood where I squished it."

As soon as I sat down at the park, Shakes asked me, "Dennis, how do you like my shades?"

"Very nice Shakes! Are they yours? I guess they're yours now."

"My worker took me shopping for clothes today. They didn't have everything I wanted, but I did get a nice winter coat and a belt. Now, I don't have to wear this dog leash to hold my pants up. When we got to the cash, the guy said, 'Shakes, you need some sunglasses, don't you?' I asked, 'Can I have these?' He said, 'Go for it, Shakes.' "

Joy sat next to me. I asked, "How did it go with your worker today?"

"Really great! Friday I go to see a place. Janice said it was the biggest bachelor apartment she's ever seen. The guy who owns the building is friendly to homeless people. I guess one of his family was homeless and died on the street."

I asked, "Are they any closer to getting you a health card?"

"They're going to take me to a doctor at a clinic tomorrow. I said to her, "Things aren't right in my head. I hear voices and they keep me awake all night. With them and the bed bugs I'm not getting much sleep.

"I told her that when I pee, there's blood. I cough up blood, then my nose starts bleeding. I'm bleeding everywhere. That's not right. I've got no energy. I can't keep food down.

"If I get this place -- it could be as early as September, 20th -- I'm going to cut back on the drinking. She asked me, 'Why do you drink?' I said, 'I drink to pass out, to get away from the pain in my legs.' My hip feels like it's burning. I'm having seizures. I'm glad I haven't had any here. Yesterday, I had two at Chester's place. He didn't even notice. My eyes just rolled back in my head and my mind went blank for a while."

Jacques answered a call on his cell phone. He handed it to Joy. "Chester," he said.

I heard Joy ask, "Did the Health Department guy come by to spray. He said he would... You told him what? I'm going to be coming home soon."

Joy handed the phone back to Jacques. She said, "That stupid, stupid man." Then she started sobbing. The sobbing turned to gasping. She reached into her backpack and pulled out her inhaler. After four puffs, the gasping stopped. Tears were still falling from her eyes.

I asked, "Did something go wrong with the exterminator?"

"Chester wouldn't let him spray. He said it would be an invasion."

"It is an invasion," I said, "An invasion of bed bugs."

Joy said, "After we sprayed Chester's room the first time, they don't seem to have gone back there. We found their nest under his bed and we soaked it with spray. Maybe they bite him and he doesn't react, but I see him scratching. I'm going to have to sleep on the balcony. That's the only way I can get away from them. They don't like the cold.

"That really pisses me off. I paid him $400 for rent, I filled the fridge with groceries. He was supposed to buy more but he hasn't. He says he has no money. He shouldn't be spending it on the muk-muks. I clean, I cook, I just can't take it any more."

Bed Bugs

13 September 2012

This morning the sun was shining and Joy seemed in good spirits.

"How did you sleep?" I asked, "Were you outside on the balcony?"

"No, it was a bit too cool for that, but I slept okay. I took the sheet off my air mattress and made sure that none of me touched the carpet. The bed bugs didn't seem to have been able to climb up the shiny plastic. I didn't get any bites during the night. I have a chalk line of powder around where I sleep.

"When I was in the bathroom, I saw something move. I squished it. Sure enough, it was a bed bug. I could tell by the rotting wood smell. I've never known of bed bugs to crawl across tile."

I said, "I'm still pissed off with Chester."

"Why is that? What's he done now?"

"I just think it's very selfish of him to turn the exterminator away. He knows how much the bed bugs bother you. Just because they aren't bothering him, that's no reason to turn away the exterminator. It's not a safe, healthy environment for you."

"Yeah, I was pissed off about that, alright. I stayed out until 9:00 last evening. He was upset that I came home so late. I said, 'I'm 46 years old. Are you saying I have a curfew? I wasn't planning to come back at all.' I told him, 'I can't live like this.' He said, 'I'm sorry. I'll phone the Health Department and have them come another day.' I said, 'They're not going to drop everything and come here, when they've already been turned away once. They may charge you for the visit.'

"I do the cooking, the cleaning. Before I moved in, he said he kept his place very clean. It was a mess. It took me an entire day to wash the floors, the fridge. There was some kind of dairy product that had gone bad in the sink. That nearly made me sick. I bought groceries. He was supposed to buy some, but he hasn't. We're down to our last slice of bread.

"He doesn't do anything but make messes after I've cleaned up and piss on the toilet seat. He said that if I'm concerned with the bed bugs, he'll share his bed with me. 'No, thanks!' I said. I have no interest in sleeping with any man.'

He said, 'Oh, Joy, I would never touch you. You don't have to worry about that.' I said, 'I've heard that before.'

"I wish Chester would bathe more often. I have a shower every morning. He has one a week. All the guys are smelling a bit ripe now.

"I've heard from Rodent that Big Jake wants me to write to him. Why would I do that? I still love him, but I don't have a death wish.

"I heard that Silver is at the Mission Hospice recovering."

I said, "I knew that he had an appointment with his doctor last Thursday, to see about the swelling in his ankles. I haven't seen him since."

Joy said, "Chili may have to have both of her legs amputated. I'm so angry with her. I told her months ago to have the swelling in her knee taken care of. She's been smashing cocaine into her arm and it's become infected. The infection has spread to both legs as high as her hips."

Joy was meeting sith her worker when I arrived at the park. They were together for about twenty minutes.

Jacques. said, "I'm looking for a new apartment also. They raised my rent in June by three percent. It was $685, now it's $710. I can't afford that. I've had to cancel my cable. I tried to fix up an antenna using wire, but now I only get a few channels and they aren't very clear. I saw an ad in this newspaper. I can get an antenna for $7. That's not too bad if it works. I'm going to go there this afternoon to talk to them about it."

"You're going to miss living by the river," I said.

"Yes, it's a great bachelor apartment, but it has bed bugs. I've told the landlord about them. I suggested that he remove the carpet. It doesn't matter what kind of floor is underneath. He isn't interested in having it removed. I'm not paying $710 for a place with bed bugs. I hear that Chester has them too. They're everywhere.

"I talked to Serge yesterday about us sharing a two bedroom apartment somewhere. He seemed interested, but today he isn't here. I think he's staying at his friend William's place, while he is away. He has his own key."

When Joy came back she said, "That was a waste of time. I still can't see a doctor until they get my identification sorted out. They've moved the viewing of the apartment to 2:00 tomorrow. At least that's something to look forward to."

Native Cigarettes

14 September 2012

This morning was pleasant. Metro greeted me waving a newspaper, "Good morning, Dennis. Are you going to keep out of trouble this weekend?"

"Not if I can help it, Metro. Have a good day."

"Joy's down there."

"Great, thanks Metro."

"Hi Joy, how did you sleep?"

"Great, when I woke up I thought it was 5:15, my usual time, but it was 6:15. I really had to scramble to get everything together. When I got outside the door, I realized that my keys were at the bottom of my bag. So, I just left the door unlocked. We always used to leave the door unlocked. We never had any problems."

"Weren't you afraid that someone would steal Chester?"

"They can have him. He was all pissed off last night because I came home late."

"Why on earth should he care what time you come home?"

"Ever since he fell down the stone steps, backwards, he hasn't been right in the head. Every woman he's been involved with, in any way, he falls in love with. Sometimes, I hear him talking in his sleep, 'Joy, I love you.' "

"Has he made any arrangements with the Health Department for an exterminator?"

"Yeah, somebody is supposed to come by on Monday, but I told Chester, 'I don't care. If everything goes well at my appointment this afternoon, I'll be out of here soon, maybe even next week.'

"He may come by later. He's out of cigarettes, so he'll probably be doing a butt run. He'll be wanting to bum a cigarette from me as well, but I smoke natives; he prefers a stronger cigarette."

"What are natives?" I asked.

"They're made from the scraps of what they use to make tailor-mades. The tobacco is supposed to be for ceremonial purposes. It's not meant for human consumption."

"Who makes them?"

"Natives."

> At $20 a carton, some young entrepreneurs from the Kanasatake reserve near Montreal are selling a lot of cigarettes. The brands they are pushing may be unfamiliar to most people – Native and Mohawk Blend – but they come from a manufacturing plant on the American side of the Mohawk reserve in Akwasasne. Making cigarettes has become an important business in Akwasasne. There are two manufacturing plants employing a couple of hundred people. The cigarettes are sold in native communities all across the United States, and now in some Canadian communities as well.

Joy said, "I was talking to Timmy the other day. He said that smoking them gives him the dry heaves in the morning, and he's been coughing up blood. He figures it's not the liquor that gives him a hangover, it's the native cigarettes.

"On the bus last night I saw Kit's brother, Ronny. He must live near where Little Jake moved in, and where Irene moved out.

"I don't want to live near any of those people. My worker was surprised that I wanted to live at the place she showed me. She said a lot of hookers are moving there. I probably know them all. Jacques won't live there, but I've never had problems."

I said, "I've lived in that neighborhood. I liked it. I never had problems.

" I couldn't believe how quiet Shakes was yesterday."

Joy replied, "Yeah, that was something, wasn't it? I think he's still upset about being robbed. I've told those guys that sleep at the shelter, 'Don't store money in your socks.' I said, 'Put it in a plastic baggie and stuff it in your underwear. If someone touches your crotch, you're going to wake up.' "

"It's strange that Shakes and André were both robbed within days of each other."

Joy said, "I think it was Sharon who got Andre's money. When she was at the park, I saw her rearranging her bra a few times, as if something felt uncomfortable. I think that's where she hid André's money." André said, 'I had my hand down her top a few times. I'd have noticed if it was there.' I said, 'If she had it right at the bottom of her cup, you'd never know it.'

I said, "André told me that he was robbed by two guys and one of them kicked him in the head."

Joy said, "He put up a fight when the money was taken from his sock, but I kicked him in the head. He kept touching me. I warned him, 'Next time you do that, you're going to regret it.' He put his hand on my thigh. I stood up and kicked him in the head. He tried it a second time, I kicked him again. You'd think he'd learn. He put his hand right on my crotch. I got up and kicked him with all my might. The third kick was the best. It connected with the back of his head, his head snapped forward and bobbled, just like one of those bobble-headed figures. He was out cold. Chester and I left shortly after that. He said, 'Do you think he's okay? Maybe he has a broken neck.' I said, 'I don't care if he has.' Then we left.

"He was by here this morning; he's okay. He was hanging around. I finally had to tell him to move on. This is Friday, it's government pay week. I've got to make some money."

Apartment Hunting

17 September 2012

I was greeted this morning, as usual, by Metro and Two-four.

"Good morning, Dennis," said Metro. I think Joy's there this morning."

"Thanks guys, have a great day."

I saw Joy talking to a woman, who handed her a package in a gray plastic bag. The woman smiled at me. I said, "Bless you!" She winked at me and left.

I asked Joy, "Was that your worker?"

"No, I ran out of tampons. That lady was kind enough to buy me some."

I asked, "So, how did it go Friday, with your viewing of the apartment?"

"It was good. The place is different from what I imagined. It's at a good location for me. My worker said it was a large bachelor. I was expecting one large room, but the kitchen is separate. It's the same size as the living room. The place is rather narrow, so I'll have to get a futon, or something that folds up. A mattress would take up too much space. I wouldn't be able to move around.

"The guy's daughter was with him. She had all sorts of questions like, 'Will the shelter pay for any damages?' My worker, Janice, had never been asked that before, so she has to check with her office and get back to them.

"I think if it was just the father I had to talk to, there wouldn't have been any problem. Maybe if I'd been dressed as a skid it would have gone better. As it was, I wore a dress and makeup. That's what Janice told me to wear. I don't know what's going to happen. She's coming to see me at noon, so then I should know for certain.

"They keep asking me why André misses his appointments with them. I don't know. She asked if they should keep wasting their time on him if he isn't that interested. I said, 'If I were you, I'd drop him.' "

I said, "André will be happy as long as he can find a woman who will take him in for the night."

"Exactly! Are you going to be at the park at noon? How be I see you then? I haven't made a cent so far. I'm PMSing, and Menopausing, just generally pissed off."

"I'll be there. I didn't come Friday because of the rain. I didn't think anyone would be out."

"We were there, huddling around."

This afternoon at the park was interesting, as in the Chinese curse, 'May you live in interesting times.' The weather was pleasant, everyone was cheerful.

"Hi Joy," I said, "How are you doing?"

"A lot better than this morning. I actually made some money."

André said, "I nearly had a job this morning. A guy came by the Sally yesterday and asked a bunch of us if anyone had experience raking asphalt. Inuvik said, 'I've never done that kind of work, but I can learn.' He's from Baffin Island, what would he know about asphalt? All they have there is ice. Are they going to pour hot tar on ice?

"I told the guy, 'I can do anything you want. I've worked hot tar, cold tar and cement.' The guy said, 'Fine, meet me here at eight tomorrow morning. I'll drive you to the site.' I said 'Great, I'll see you here tomorrow morning.'

"I even went to a construction site to steal a cooler, so I'd have water to drink throughout the day. This is it here, I'm sitting on it.

"This morning I was on the steps at 8:00, right where I was supposed to be. I waited two hours. The guy was a no-show. I heard that he picked up some other guys at the Mission. So, here I am, gave up my morning… and now I don't have a plan for the rest of the day."

Shakes said, "Hey, do you want to know what I did today? This morning, after I got out of bed at the Shep, I had a shower and shampooed my hair."

"What did you use on your hair, Shakes?" I asked.

"Finesse."

Joy said, "A shower and using designer products on your hair. I bet that doesn't happen very often. Shakes, some of us do that every morning."

The Outreach worker came by. Joy asked her, "Has there been any word on my apartment?"

"I'm going to be checking on that this afternoon. I had to make sure all the paperwork was filled out and signed."

Joy said, "I don't think I'll get that place. Do you?"

"I don't see why not," said Janice.

"I got the feeling that the daughter didn't like me."

"I didn't get that impression, but we should find out for sure this afternoon. I think the daughter was just being cautious. If we can't get you in there under the Salvation Army, we can submit the application through the city. Don't worry, you did fine."

"I wish they would tear that wall down between the kitchen and the living room."

"Yes, it does seem odd, but don't start thinking about tearing walls down. We don't want that."

"Have you been able to make any headway with my identification. I really need my medical card to have this pain in my legs looked at."

Janice said, "You had arranged that through the Womens' Center, hadn't you? Maybe we can put some pressure on them. Do you know who you were dealing with there?"

"It was a white chick with blue eyes."

"Well, that covers about half the city. Do you know anything more about her?"

"I think she was married to a black guy, because her kids, in the photo on her desk, looked mulatto."

"Anything else?"

"I think her last name was something like Havasaki."

"Joy," I said, "that sounds more like a drink order."

"That's all I know. She gave me a card, it may be in here somewhere. I know I have an appointment with her on the 26th, but I can't remember if that's August or September."

"Can I give you this card? I've been trying to contact the health center for over a month. They're either on lunch, or they don't return my messages. It's my probie who wants me to contact them. It's about anger management, but I'm not angry. I get angry about having to see my probie every ten days. I get angry when people don't phone me back, but I'm not angry about Big Jake. That's all in the past."

Loretta said, "Way to go girl. I'm glad to hear you say that, Joy."

Joy asked, "How about the check for my street allowance? Do you know when and where I'll be getting that?"

"I'm not sure what the date is for check disbursement. You guys would probably know better than I would. I'm pretty sure that we made application for your street allowance. I'll have to check. That was somewhat dependent on whether or not you get this apartment. When it comes in, we'll let you know. You can pick it up at our office."

André said, "When I was at the office last, I'm pretty sure I saw a sign that said that checks were going out on the 27th. Do you know anything about how my place is coming along?"

Janice said, "You're on the list."

André said, "I was talking to Little Jake, and he said there were some places vacant where he's living now."

"You'd be content living there? The reason I ask that is we took some people there the other day. They looked at it and said they weren't interested. I told them, 'We'll cover the rent.' It didn't make any difference. You've seen the building? It wouldn't bother you?"

"I'll go anywhere, that place is fine. It has to be better than living in a box behind a dumpster."

Janice said, "Okay, we'll see if we can set up an appointment."

Shakes said, "Hey, does anybody know about my apartment? Hey, Chesty, do you know about my apartment?"

Janice asked Joy, "Did he just call me Chesty?"

Joy said, "Can you imagine what he'll say when you take him to view an apartment. 'I want a fuckin' apartment, right now!'

"Shakes, this isn't your worker. You'll have to get in contact with the people you deal with."

"Shakes," said Janice, "Do you know the name of your worker?"

"No, she wrote it on a card, but I lost it."

"I'll try phoning a few people and try to get you sorted out."

"Okay, thanks."

After they left I asked André, "How was your weekend?"

"It was good, what I can remember of it."

I said, "Maybe it's better not to remember too much."

"Yeah, you're probably right there. I remember getting in a fight with Little Jake and Weasel, both at the same time. They were drunk and talking stupid, so I threw Little Jake down, then I threw Weasel down. Somewhere, in all that, I twisted my knee. I jumped down from that concrete wall, across the street, and I felt a sharp pain going through my knee. Maybe I broke it."

André Shaved

18 September 2012

As I approached Joy's spot, I recognized Luther standing, André squatting and Joy sitting cross-legged on the sidewalk. A lady stopped and handed Joy a folded five dollar bill.

She said, "This is for yesterday — remember, I said I didn't have anything with me, but would catch you tomorrow? Well, here I am."

"I remember. Thank you so much."

"Bless you," I said.

Joy said to André, "This is kind of embarrassing, but yesterday that lady stopped by. She asked if I'd like a coffee and, maybe, a bagel with cream cheese. I said, 'What I really need are tampons.' She was kind enough to get me some."

"That was nice," replied André.

I asked Joy, "Have you heard anything more about your apartment?"

"Today is the day. They've sent the faxes. I find out at noon what the verdict is."

"Congratulations!" I said.

"We'll see."

"André," I said, "you shaved."

"Yeah, it happens."

"Have you heard any more about getting an apartment near Jake's place?"

"No, but I'd sure like to. They have some nice units there."

Sun Car

19 September 2012

I wore my leather jacket this morning. I regretted not wearing a sweater underneath and a pair of gloves. Joy was huddled in a winter coat, wrapped in a blanket, wearing mitts.

"Hi Joy, how's it going?"

"I'm freezing."

"Any news about your apartment?"

"Janice left a phone message with Chester yesterday. The guy wasn't able to bring the contract at noon, but said he'd be there later. So, everything's still looking good. I'm supposed to meet with Janice at noon.

"Dennis, I just have to get out of that place." She was near tears. "This morning I found six bedbugs in the bathroom. I saw one walking up Chester's back towards his neck. I squished it. Now, he has the heebie jeebies about them. See the marks on my wrist. Someone told me that was a spider bite. They're supposed to be eating the bedbugs, not me. They seem to have their wires crossed.

"The exterminator is coming today, but I said to Chester, 'You could have had this problem cleared up weeks ago.'

"He finally put Anne's clothes in a bag on the balcony. They'll be infested with bed bugs by now. She's probably the one who brought them in. When I moved in, there were no bugs, but Anne and Trudy had been staying at Nick's and he has bedbugs.

"Can you watch my stuff for a while. I'm going to try to slip into the pizza place to use their washroom. I'm usually good for once a day, before they start giving me dirty looks."

While Joy was away, André arrived. He said, "I had a bad start to my day. It was raining. I was panning at Shakes' office when a patrol car pulled up. The cop said, 'What are you doing, André?' I said, 'I'll be honest, I'm just trying to get some money for food. I haven't even been drinking.' The cop said, 'Would you do us a favor? Would you have a look at this building and tell us the number?' He wrote me a ticket. He said, 'Since you've been honest with us, and since we haven't seen you panning here before, the ticket is just a warning. We know you guys don't pay these tickets, and when they go to court they're usually thrown out, but the law is changing. People with unpaid tickets are going to be doing jail time.'

"That's just great! I wouldn't be panning if I had enough money to eat, let alone pay a ticket. If I had money, I'd have a roof over my head. I went to the hut yesterday and Weasel told me that only he and Bear are allowed to stay there now; as if he has a lease on a space behind a dumpster."

On my way down the street I came across Bright Sky. "Hi Dennis, did you hear Rick Mercer's rant last night?"
"No."
"Have you got a minute to listen to it?"
"Sure."

"So Parliament is back and we learned this week that the cornerstone of Stephen Harper's fall agenda will be yet another big budgetary omnibus bill. Well, of course it will.

Prime ministers, they love an omnibus bill. Government tables a budget, they know every member of their party has to vote for the budget or they lose their jobs. And let's face it – a lot of these characters don't have that many options in this world. And seeing as they know that everyone is going to vote for it, instead of just putting budgetary things in the budget, you know – math, they fill it full of goodies no one's even heard of before.

In the last budget, in the 'jobs budget' there was a provision that allows the CIA and the FBI to come across the border and arrest Canadians on Canadian soil. And I know I sound like a conspiracy theorist with a tin foil hat just saying it out loud but it's true. It happened and there was no debate. And that's just the tip of the iceberg.

Even some of Harper's own MPs will admit privately that they had no idea what was in that last budget. Just that it was 400 pages. You know how you and I just click "accept" when entering into an iTunes contract? That's how MPs vote on the budget. And now we find out we're getting another omnibus bill. Aren't we lucky? In North Korea they only get one every year.

And listen don't take my word for it. One of the most elegant pleas ever made against omnibus bills was made not that long ago in the House of Commons by a handsome young man by the name of Stephen Harper. He said it, omnibus bills are anti-democratic, they're a slap in the face to MPs and voters.

See, this fascinates me. Because it's one thing if you don't know any better, but he clearly does, he just doesn't care. Who does that? I wouldn't want to spend five minutes in that guy's head for all the money in the world. Because he knows right from wrong here, he's on record, but he has decided it's okay to do wrong in order to advance the right. And democracy no longer enters into it."

Sky showed me a picture of a Sun Car, a solar powered car. "How would you like to have one of these parked in your garage?"

"It's beautiful, how much does it cost?"

"As far as the cost is concerned, they will be less expensive per capita than the nine billion that the government is spending on sixty-five fighter planes to bomb other countries and take more lives.

"A friend and I want to start production of these at the GM Auto Assembly Plant in Oshawa. Have you heard that they're shutting that down? They're also closing down plants in Windsor and Ottawa. The reason is higher gasoline prices. Unemployment will rise by thirty-seven hundred.

"Dennis, the cops stole all my gear. I just left my cart for a minute to get something to eat, when I got back, it was gone. I'd just stocked up for winter. I talked to the cops, they said it wasn't them. I don't believe that. I've sent emails to the Mayor and the Councilman for my area. Could you help me to get my stuff back?"

"I don't know what I can do, Sky. I'll look into it and do whatever I can."

"Thanks, Dennis, anything you could do, I'd really appreciate it."

Noon at the park was alternately warm and cool; warm when the sun was shining, cool when clouds obscured the sun.

I asked Irene, "How do you like your new apartment?"

"It's beautiful. It's above a Vietnamese Restaurant. You should come over for supper. I made stew. Outcast was over last night.

"We've got a huge king size bed. I hardly even know that Shark is there."

Shark said, "I know Irene's there every time she punches me in the stomach."

Shakes was quiet, wearing a button on which was stamped 'Stephen Harper Hates Me', referring to our Prime Minister's policies concerning the homeless. These buttons were made by the Public Service Alliance of Canada, the largest union representing federal public servants. Employees who wore these buttons to work were asked to remove them. This was considered by employees as a violation of their freedom of expression.

I said to Shakes, "Where are you staying now?"

"I'm staying at the Shep. They won't let me in at the Sally. I still haven't heard anything about them getting me an apartment."

Outcast said, "Are those the jeans you got from Zellers? I hear that you didn't pay for them."

"These are the jeans I got from Zellers. My worker gave me the money to pay for them. I had it with me, but there was nobody around, so I just walked out with them."

Lucy came by in her electric wheelchair. She pulled out her change purse and gave everyone a one dollar coin. James, from the Native Canadian Center, handed out energy bars. He advised everyone of locations where they were providing meals, socks and underwear. He also asked if he could take a group photo for publicity purposes. Everyone obliged. The Center is a non-profit organization that provides services to the Aboriginal Community.

Outcast said, "I'm not exactly homeless, I have a roof over my head, but I'm just staying with a friend. She could kick me out any time. We're just barely scraping by."

James said, "That's okay, we also provide services for those at risk of being homeless."

Miigwech

20 September 2012

I didn't learn my lesson yesterday. It was so cold this morning that my hands were balled in fists and, like a turtle, they were trying to pull themselves into my sleeves. I was eagerly anticipating Joy's news of whether of not she was accepted for her own apartment. This is something I have wished for her since December 2010 when I first met her. Now, it seems near to becoming a reality. The system may move slowly, but at least it moves.

I crossed the street and in front of the Coffee and Donut Shop I met Bearded Bruce.

"Good morning, lad," he said, "How've you been?"

"Great, Bruce. You're looking well. I haven't seen you at the park lately."

"I'm not like some of those people who pan until they have enough for a bottle or two, then sit around for the rest of the day. Noon is my work time, the best time to pan. I like to make enough to carry me over the weekend, or for a rainy day. We have lots of rain this season; when there's raining, there's no panning."

I said, "I was hoping to see Joy this morning. Yesterday she was to find out if she was accepted for an apartment of her own. I don't know if she's absent because she is celebrating or depressed because she didn't get it."

"I hope she gets it. She deserves a place of her own, where it's quiet. She's good people. I've known her a long time."

I said, "I hear that Hippo is in hiding."

"He should be, the lazy asshole."

"I heard that you guys lost a lot of stuff. Shakes said that his new sleeping bag was taken. I also heard that there was a fire."

"The fire was nothing. There was a lot of exaggeration."

I said, "So, where are you staying now, Bruce?"

"Same place, in behind here."

"Does Weasel let you stay there?"

"I let Weasel stay there. That's been my place for the last year and a half."

"André told me that Weasel said only he and Muff were allowed to stay there."

"I know, I told him to say that."

"It's good seeing you, Bruce. You're looking great. I won't keep you from your work. Have a good day."

"Thanks! Bye, lad."

At the park I met Joy and Steve.

"Hi, Joy, do you have any news about your apartment?"

"My worker called this morning. They're still sorting out the details of the contract — who's responsible if I cause damage, that sort of thing. It's the daughter that wants all this contract bullshit."

I said, "If they're working on a contract, that has to be good news."

"I guess so. I'm just tired of waiting. I asked my worker if I could get a sleeping bag, and she said, 'We'll see what we can do.' You know, whatever."

"So how long has it been since you've had a place of your own?"

"Big Jake and I lived above a restaurant for five years until he started beating me and the cops kept coming over. I had the place with Roy for nearly a year until he stopped paying the bills and the rent. This past year has been the worst. I've been all over the place."

I said, "I'm sure it will all work out. I watched the documentary, 'Life on the Heater'. It was really well done."

"Yeah, I missed out on that one. I think they filmed Jacques. I know he has a copy of the video. It was mostly about Rip and Faye."

Steve said, "It was Faye that stabbed him, wasn't it? No, It was Theresa — got him in his junk."

Joy said, "Rip and Faye were both crazy. I think they're both still alive. I haven't seen them for a long time. Most of the others are dead. It was really wild to see Star as a puppy."

Steve and I were comparing scars and broken knuckles. Steve said, "I've got a lot of scars from Winnipeg. This one on my middle knuckle was where I caught a guy's tooth. My hand got infected and swelled up like a grapefruit. He must've had rabies. I don't know how many times I've broken this outside knuckle on my right hand. I had to learn to hit with my left hand.

"One time I was in a fight with this guy. I can't remember his name. He tried to rape my street sister and ripped her off for a $150 to boot. I remember her name. I didn't know it at the time, but he was a Dilaudid (*a narcotic pain reliever*) dealer. After I beat him, a big native and a black dude came looking for me. Luckily for me, I was sitting in a bar with about thirty bikers.

"I talked to these two guys. I said, 'Hey, what would you do if somebody tried to rape and rob your sister?' They understood that. They said, 'We'll let it slide, but don't let it happen again.'

"A while later, my real sister got in a fight with this same guy. This lady is over six feet tall and knows how to fight. I guess the guy tried the same thing with her as he had with my street sister. She beat the shit out of him. The same two guys came after me. I said, 'Hey, I didn't have anything to do with it. I wasn't even there.' I told them that it was my sister who punched the guy out. They couldn't say much about that.

"I remember when I was a kid in Mississauga. There were three of us. We called ourselves the 'Three Musketeers.' If you saw two of us, you could be sure the third wasn't far away — Dave, Dennis and myself. Dave's been dead thirty-two years now. I still have his picture. If there was a fire at my place, I'd grab that picture and jump out the window. I don't know what I'd do if I lost that. It's irreplaceable. Dennis is around somewhere, but I've lost contact with his parents and I don't know how to use a computer."

I asked, "How did Dave die?"

"Dave was nineteen. He and his brother were joyriding in a stolen car. They crashed it. It was such a mess, they couldn't tell who was driving — it was that bad."

"Were you born in Mississauga?" I asked.

"Yeah, then I moved to Barrie. The cops were hassling me a lot, so I moved to Winnipeg. I was there for fifteen years. I have a son there. It's hard to panhandle in Winnipeg."

"I know," I said, "It's cold."

"It's cold and the welfare system is really hard to deal with. Believe it or not, as bad as it is, it's better in Ontario."

Shakes said, "Joy, can I bum a cigarette?" She opened her white plastic case, secured with a rubber band, and threw one to him and Curt.

"Miigwech," said Shakes.

Joy said to me, "That means *thank you* in Ojibway."

Rain, Rain Go Away

21 September 2012

Rain started falling Thursday afternoon and is expected to continue through the weekend. I had my umbrella and leather jacket, so I decided to venture to the park.

Huddled in a covered doorway to the underground parking lot were Wolf, Shaggy and four other friends.

I went to shake Wolf's hand; he waved me away. "Fuck off, Dennis. I'll say hello to you later. Right now I've got Jacques leaving. I didn't even shake hands with him. Joy just stepped on Shaggy; I've got to get her settled and out of the rain. I've got to find some way of keeping her dry on the way home. All I have is this small umbrella."

"It's okay, Wolf, I can see you're busy."

Joy said to André, "He's got no right to talk to Dennis that way."

André said, "Joy, just take it easy. Take a few deep breaths and count to ten."

"Everything's fine, Joy," I said, "Don't worry about me."

I asked her, "Any news about your apartment?"

"My worker phoned Chester earlier. She said nothing is definite. It could be good news, it could be bad. I have

Chester's phone now. I tried to call them, but they must be at lunch. I'm just waiting for her call now.

"At 2:00 I'm going to meet a friend I haven't seen for over twenty years."

"Jake," I asked, "how is your new apartment?"

"The apartment is great. I've got lots of space, now I need furniture. All I have is an air conditioner, still in its box. That's what I use to sit on, sometimes to eat at. I just slide it around wherever I need it."

"André," I asked, "How is it going with your apartment application. Have you had any news?"

"I phoned my worker this morning. She wanted me to come in, but I said to her, 'We're talking now, just let me know what's going on. There's no point me coming in if there's no need.' The only really positive thing is that on September 27th, I get to see a doctor. I'll have a family doctor of my own. The one I had was from Cornwall, but he died.

"The doctor can verify that I need medical attention and that I need appointments at least six times a month. That way I qualify for a yearly bus pass. He can also sign the papers for ODSP *(Ontario Disability Support Program)* and all the other stuff, so I'll be able to get started on that. Right now, I got nothing."

"Okay, Dennis," said Wolf, "Now, I can say hello and shake hands with you. Shaggy is out of the rain and taken care of. This morning I got a new book and three new dvd's. After I get home, I have enough to keep myself entertained all weekend."

"What book did you get, Wolf?"

"I can't remember. It's all wrapped in plastic in the bottom of Shaggy's cart.

"What do you think of this weather? It's really coming down now. This is the worst it's been and it's going to keep up like this for three days, so we better get used to it. I brought my umbrella, I'm wearing a raincoat, I've got proper shoes on, but I'm still soaked from the crotch down.

"I had a proper cover for Shaggy's cart, but I lent it to Weasel for Bear — anything to get rid of him."

Joy answered Chester's phone. I couldn't hear the conversation. I saw the tears running down her cheeks. She dabbed at them with paper towel from her pocket.

"Was it bad news, Joy?" I asked redundantly.

"It's a no go. Even with that fuckin' twenty page contract, they've decided they don't want to work with our program."

"The father seemed in favor of it, didn't he?"

"Yeah, it was just the daughter who didn't want anything to do with us. I don't know why my worker didn't have anything else lined up, in case this fell through."

"She'll have other places to show you, won't she?"

"Yeah, it's no problem."

"Everything will work out, Joy."

"Yeah, I know." She put on a brave face, but another hope was dashed. For now, it's back to Chester's place and bedbugs.

I'm presently reading , *The Art of Happiness at Work,* by His Holiness the Dalai Lama and Howard C. Cutler M.D. When asked about self-understanding he said:

> "Humility is a good quality, but there can be too much humility. This kind of low self-esteem will have the negative effect of shutting out any possibility for self-improvement, almost by default, because the tendency of such a person would be to automatically react to the event with the thought, No, I cannot do this.
>
> "In addition, I would also list an agitated state of mind as another obstacle for greater self-understanding. Since self-understanding demands a certain ability to

focus on one's own abilities and personal character, a constantly agitated mind simply will not have the space to enter into any serious self-reflection.

"...when you have low self-esteem, then you underestimate your actual qualities and abilities. You belittle yourself, you put yourself down. This leads to a complete loss of faith in yourself."

In the same book, Dr. Cutler states, "Low self-esteem and underestimating of one's abilities can be paralyzing, stifling personal initiative and inhibiting the individual from exploring new opportunities. Ultimately, it can obstruct the realization of one's full potential, preventing the achievement of one's goals."

What I have observed, over the past two years, is that what may seem no more than an inconvenience to myself or other employed people — such as obtaining a birth certificate, a health card, applying for available government assistance programs — may be an insurmountable obstacle to those with mental conditions, alcoholism or other substance dependencies.

Exterminator

24 September 2012

From the corner, I looked for Joy in her usual spot. I could see a folded blanket on the sidewalk, but no Joy. I waited to see if she had perhaps gone into the coffee shop or the library to use their washroom. A large truck stopped at the traffic lights, blocking my view. When it moved ahead, I saw Joy. I walked over to her.

"Hi Joy, I was looking for you, but didn't see you here."

"Weasel and Bear passed by the corner, just before you got there. I didn't want him to see me."

"Why didn't you want to see Weasel?"

"Not just Weasel, any of the guys. They make more money than me, sometimes they're out panning all day and evening. I'm only here for four hours. First thing in the morning, no matter how much they collected the day before, they come to me for a cigarette. Chester had a carton and supplied me all weekend because I ran out, but that's rare. Usually, he'll come by in the morning on a butt run and will bum off me."

"How was your weekend?" I asked.

"Fine, quiet. I've got to get out of Chester's place by Christmas."

"Did the exterminator come to spray?"

"Yeah, he sprayed alright. We could smell that stuff for three days. It's really powerful."

"Are there any bedbugs now?"

"I only saw one in the bathroom. I watched it for a while. It didn't move, so I threw it in the toilet."

"Did you squish and sniff it first?"

"I squished it, but I knew what it was. I didn't need to sniff it. Jacques got me started sniffing bugs I'd squished. He still has bedbugs. I didn't know about the rotten wood smell before then, but that's how dogs are able to sniff them out. I saw it on television. They had a beagle sniffing around a hotel room. He could direct the exterminator to the exact location of the bugs."

"I've seen that too. Do other insects have a distinctive smell?"

"No, just bedbugs. The guy is supposed to come back in two weeks to a month. I told Chester to make sure it's two weeks. There's a final spraying after that.

"Chester's still putting his clothes back in his dresser drawers. I told him not to, but he wouldn't listen to me. Last night he offered me a blanket that had been on his bed before they sprayed. I said to him, 'Thanks, Bud, but no thanks.' He said, 'It's cold, Joy, you should have more to keep you warm.' I said to him, 'I'd rather be cold than have to deal with those bugs again.'"

"Has your worker contacted you about any available apartments?"

"Not yet, but she's working on it. I have an appointment with her Wednesday morning. It has to do with the anger management course I'm supposed to take. She's going to escort me to every meeting, so I don't get breached. My probation ends November 2nd.

"Guys, like André, keep asking me if I want to share a place with them if they get one before me. I told him, 'For one thing, my name's higher on the list than yours; I've been waiting longer than you have. For another, I just want to be alone.' "

1000 Ways To Die

25 September 2012

I saw Joy briefly this morning. Already packed up, she asked me to watch her backpack while she went into the Coffee and Donut Shop to use their washroom. When she returned, she said, "They were mopping the floor in there. They've got to change the brand of their cleaner. It smells like wet dog, even worse than Bear. It's horrible. The stuff they use the first thing in the morning is even worse. I could never eat there with that odor in the air.

"Weasel was by earlier with Bear. Because of that dog, he collects more money than any of us. Now he has Little Jake caring for the dog while he goes off someplace. He's always getting somebody to stay with Bear: Wolf, André, Hippo. And he never pays them, not even a beer. There's no way I'd look after that dog. For one thing, you never know when Weasel's coming back, it could be days. Then you're stuck with feeding a dog, cleaning up after him."

I said, "I'm sorry I didn't make it to the park yesterday. I had a dental appointment that took longer than I expected."

"What did you have done?"

"I got a partial plate, to replace three missing molars."

Joy said, "I don't have any back teeth. It makes chewing difficult. I have my boyfriends to thank for that."

"Yesterday, everybody was asking, 'Where's Dennis?' We thought that maybe you had been in an accident, or that something had happened to you. You've hardly ever missed being at the park at noon."

I asked, "What did I miss?"

"Not much, the usual. Jacques was there, Chester, Shakes and Serge. André and Little Jake weren't there, thank God. I guess Shakes and André were together on Sunday. Shakes lost his backpack. He's hoping that André has it. Shakes said to me, 'Without my bag, where am I going to put my booze?' I said, 'Shove it up your sleeve, where you usually put it.' "

This afternoon, as I was approaching the group, I saw Hippo standing head and shoulders above everyone else. I gave him a wave and he waved back.

"Hi Hippo!" I said, "I haven't seen you around much."

"I haven't been around. I fucked up again."

Joy and André were discussing the television program '1000 Ways To Die' — the ways that people have accidentally killed themselves.

Joy said, "This one woman was masturbating with a carrot. It tore her vaginal wall, she developed an air embolism and died. The title of the video is 'kill-do', that's hilarious. You'll never see me masturbating with a carrot."

André said, "I saw a television program about the stupid ways that some people have died. This one guy accidentally touched his crotch with a live cable from a battery. He liked the feeling, so he wrapped his penis in tinfoil and plugged it into a live socket in the house. He was electrocuted and died."

Joy said to Jacques, "Have you got any wine ready to be turned?"

"I don't have any wine. Oh, you mean at the house? Yes, I have one batch ready to be transferred. I like to transfer a little at a time."

Steve came over to Jacques and handed him a ticket, probably a liquor violation. "Another one for my wall?" asked Jacques.

"I must have over a hundred stapled to my wall now, and I have two stuffed envelopes to be put up. I want to take them to my new place. I hope I can get them all down."

André said, "What you need is one of those special staple removers. You're going to need to fill a lot of holes in your walls before you move out. You can fill the small holes with a bar of soap or a stick of deodorant. It can even be painted over. You've got to use the chalky stuff, not the gel."

Joy said, "The last time I was over at Jacques', I tried to find my name on that wall. I'm sure I must be there a couple of times."

"André," I said, "you've shaved again."

"Yeah, I'm trying to clean myself up a bit. Nothing too drastic. I want to set little goals for myself. If I meet one goal, I can set another. If I try to do it all at once, I'll screw up, for sure."

I asked, "Did Shakes find his backpack? Did you have it?"

"No, I was on the opposite side of town to where Shakes was. I noticed earlier in the day that he seemed to be having trouble carrying his bag. Me and some others offered to carry it for him, but he said, 'I can carry my own damn bag!' You know Shakes. When you sleep outside, people will just come by and help themselves to your stuff. I know, it's happened to me."

André asked Hippo, "Where are you staying now."

"At a hostel. I'm going for a butt run now, then I'm going back across the bridge."

To André Joy said, "He said they were feeding him well over there, but he's lost weight."

André replied, "It's probably all the walking he's been doing. It's a long way from that hostel to here."

"Joy," I asked, "Did you mention to me this morning that you don't have any back teeth."

"Yeah, that's thanks to boyfriends. My teeth got punched out or broken. When I was in prison, the broken half teeth got infected. It was considered an emergency, so I had them extracted right away."

"How are the dentists in there?"

"Some are good, but you can get some real butchers. I love the drugs you get when they put you in the medical ward. I was high all weekend."

André said, "I'll be able to get all my teeth extracted. I'm just going to get them to put me out. They're going to help me get some dentures, upper and lower. Most of mine have been knocked out in fights."

Joy said, "Tomorrow, my worker, Angie, is going to be meeting me, to take me to anger management class. She apologized that she couldn't get the Salvation Army van. We'll be taking two different buses. I prefer her to Janice — she seems afraid of me, she's so uptight. It's probably because I say it like it is. I don't pussyfoot around. I'll tell you what time it is.

"They're going to be escorting me to every class, usually with the van, so I don't get breached. That's the only way I would go to that course. I shouldn't even be required to take anger management.

"André, you and I are going to have to chip in and buy Dennis a new pair of shoes. He could give you the ones he's wearing for panning shoes."

"Hi, Jake," I said, "how is everything at your new apartment."

"Fine, but I still don't have any furniture.

"When will they be getting you furniture?"

"Around the first of November, that's what my worker said."

"So, you'll be without any furniture for over a month?"

"That's the way the system works. Yesterday, my worker — you've met her before — took me to the doctor. I've been having raging migraines, ringing in my ear, pain in my sinuses and behind my eyes. When I try to roll a cigarette, I notice that the skin on my fingers is very dry. I think I'm a bit dehydrated. The doctor had me close my eyes, stand with my feet together with my arms straight out at my sides. I nearly fell over. He's going to send me for a CAT scan to see what's going on in my head. I hope it's not a tumor."

"Did the doctor suggest to you that it might be a tumor?"

"No, he wants to see some pictures first before he tells me what's wrong. Yesterday morning I took a Seroquel (*a drug used to treat severe mental disorders like schizophrenia*). It was a drop. This guy said to me, 'I'm sorry, I don't have any money, but here's three Valium and two Seroquel'. Joy and I shared the Valium, I took the second Seroquel before lying down for the night. That knocked me right out."

"I wouldn't jump to any conclusions about having a tumor." I said, "There may be a lot of reasons for balance problems. Perhaps you have an ear infection. It may be something simple that can be treated with antibiotics."

"Shakes," I asked, "Did you find your bag?"

"No."

"What did you have in it?"

"My clothes, my bottle, my cigarettes, my weed, my house — everything."

Andre said, "This is kind of an off day for me. I was drinking last night, then at 3:00 I was wide awake. I drank a couple more bottles and slept until 5:00. I came down here and haven't moved more than six feet since. See that sweater on the curb? That's mine. It's there in case anybody wants to sit down. That's where I started this morning. I've been watching and thinking about people. I try to figure out where they're coming from, what their motives are.

"Joy said to me yesterday, 'If you point your finger at someone, you have three fingers pointing back at you. So, you shouldn't point at people.' By the way, do you know where Joy is today?"

"She had an appointment with her worker." I said, "They were going to take the bus to Joy's anger management course."

A woman walked by. André said, "Hi darlin', blue really works well on you, it brings out the color of your eyes."

"André," I said, "her eyes were brown."

"Doesn't matter. This is what I do all day long. Sometimes it works, sometimes it doesn't."

A soldier in uniform passed by. André said, "Thank you sir, for protecting our country." The soldier waved.

To me André said, "I really mean that. I have a lot of respect for the military."

Lucy passed in her motorized wheel chair and waved. We all waved. André said, "Hi, sister, take care."

Shakes reached for Andre's insulated travel mug. "No, you don't," said André. He threw Shakes an unopened bottle of sherry. A few minutes later he asked, "Did you honor it before you took a drink?" (*Honoring means to fill the cap of the bottle with liquor and to throw it over one's shoulder*)."

"Yes, I did."

"Good, " said André. "I don't know where I slept last night, but I have green stuff all over my pants. I've been picking it off all morning."

I asked, "Did you sleep outside?"

"Yes."

Jake said, "I'm going home now."

I asked, "What are you going to do, Jake, watch your air conditioner?"

"I don't know what I'm going to do."

André said, "I'm just sort of floating right now. Everything is mellow. I don't have a plan. I don't know what I'm going to do for the rest of the day.

"Shakes, I'm going to take you someplace where we can get something to eat."

"That sounds good."

"Eating is good," I said.

Shelter

27 September 2012

"Dennis," said Outcast, "before you sit down, here's a newspaper to keep your cheeks dry."

"Thanks, Outcast."

"How's everything going, Hippo?"

"Great, I get the keys to my new apartment tomorrow."

"Where will it be?"

"Not far from here. It's really nice."

Outcast asked, "It's in one of those projects, isn't it?"

"Yeah."

"Where did you sleep last night, Hippo?" I asked.

"We all slept behind the coffee shop, the old place."

"Were Bruce and Weasel there?"

"Yeah, and Bear. I slept next to the dumpster, nearly underneath it. I was the wind break."

André said, "You should have seen it, Dennis. Bear's nose was about an inch from Hippo's."

To Hippo he said, "It's a good thing you didn't make any sudden movements in your sleep. You could have lost part of your face. I don't know how you could have put up with Bear's breath, or how he could have put up with yours."

"Bear and I are good," said Hippo.

"Don't get too friendly," laughed André.

A female police officer, followed by a male, rode up on bicycles.

"Hello gentlemen, does anyone have any open liquor?" Outcast had kicked his can over the railing. She noticed an open can of beer between Hippo and André. "Who does that belong to? Is that yours, Hippo?"

"Yes ma'am." He held up the can. "If I dump it, do I still get a ticket?"

"If I don't see anything, you don't get a ticket" André put his cap in front of the can and took a swig.

Hippo said, "This is my last beer. I'll take the ticket."

The ticket was written and handed to Hippo. He took it, folded it and handed it to Jacques. "Another one for your wall, Jacques."

André said to the police officer, "You guys know that we don't pay these things. Does that bother you at all?"

The officer said, "We do our job, the courts do their job. We'll be back in fifteen."

After she left, André said, "She's my cousin."

Outcast said, "That's the second beer I've kicked over the rail today."

André said, "I'm just glad they haven't changed the law, so we'd have to do jail time for unpaid tickets. I know I'm over eight thousand bucks."

Shakes said, "I'm over ten thousand."

Outcast said, "It would be ridiculous to have us do jail time. It costs over seventy thousand a year to keep a man in jail. We've got no houses, no cars, no jobs. There's nothing they can take from us."

Rodent

28 September 2012

When I arrived at the park I could see that Joy was upset. Sje said, "I'm so pissed off. I'm drunk too. My check hasn't arrived yet. I phoned Janice, my worker, and she said that because information arrived after September 16th, some checks would be delayed until Monday. I said to her, 'Look, I owe one guy $200. I owe another guy $250. What am I supposed to do?' She asked, 'How did you get so far in debt?' I said 'I'm an alcoholic and a pothead. What do you expect?' Right now I'm kind of in hiding. I guess I will be all weekend.

"Chester is supposed to buy groceries, but I know that isn't going to happen. He ate this morning, so I won't be eating. He was drunk for two days. He is sober today and drank about a dozen cups of coffee. He'll probably be awake all night.

"Outcast is picking on me because I had some of the guys over."

"He picks on a lot of people," I said.

"He thinks that he's so superior. I'd like to walk over there and punch that smug grin right off his face. Of course, then he would go over the railing backwards. He'd probably break his neck, or his back, and die, or he'd be severely fucked up. He had the nerve to ask me, 'I suppose that means you're not coming over to my place?' I'm never having anything to do with him again.

"I think, right now, I'd just like to be alone for a while."

I walked across the sidewalk and sat beside André. I asked, "How did you sleep last night, André?"

Gotta Find a Home 2

"I was cold. I passed out across the street for a while, then I went downtown. Some guy was mouthing off to me, so we got into it. He kept poking me in the mouth. When I didn't get up, he went away. After that I went back to the hut. These other guys have been at it since this morning. I just woke up."

I noticed that he was drinking a Smirnoff vodka cooler. "You've changed brands, haven't you, André?"

"These were given to me."

He rolled one across the sidewalk to Hippo, who said, "Thanks, man."

Little Jake said, "I think that I lost the master-key to my apartment. I don't know how that happened. Sometimes I black out. I guess I'll have to have the super buzz me in."

André said, "They're probably going to charge you for a lost key, especially if it's one of those electronic ones."

Danny said, "Joy just gave me the finger. She shouldn't treat us like that. We're family. You don't give the finger to family. I haven't done anything to her."

Shakes said, "Just leave it, man."

Joy asked, "Has anybody gone for a run yet?

André said, "As soon as I finish this, I'll go. It seems odd, me being the soberest one here."

I asked Hippo, "How is it going with your place?"

"I'm all moved in."

"Do you have a bachelor apartment?"

"No, I've got a one bedroom, with kitchen, living room, bedroom and bathroom. It has hardwood floors."

"Do you have any furniture?"

"I got a few bits of stuff, the rest I'll have to wait for."

Rodent went back to talk to the other group. As he was coming back he said, "Wolf, if you ever talk to me like that again, I'm going to punch your face in."

125

Joy said, "Rodent, I'd really like to see that. I've never seen you go against anybody in my life."

"Is that so?"

"Yeah, Rodent, that's so. Go ahead, prove me wrong!"

October 2012

Skinny Minnie

I walked toward the park. I recognized Jacques' bushy white beard and waved to him. While I was still about a dozen feet from the group, an attractive young woman with long black hair approached me.

She said, "We haven't met before. My name is Doreen."

"I'm Dennis," I said.

"Do you happen to have a cigarette?"

"No, sorry, I don't smoke."

"Good for you. I wish I didn't smoke. It's bad for you and it smells bad." Doreen then sat on the curb.

I sat between Shakes and Doreen.

"How was your weekend, Shakes?"

"I'll tell you in a minute." He was counting coins and putting them in a plastic pill bottle. "My weekend was good, except for the rain on Sunday. I was walking in that. My leathers didn't dry until about 3:00 this morning."

"Have you been sleeping behind the coffee shop or inside somewhere?"

"Both, it all depends on who kidnaps me, ha ha ha ha."

"I guess you mean that in a good way?"

"I stayed at Danny's place last night. He lives in Little Italy."

Doreen asked me, "Where did your family come from?"

"My grandparents came from Iceland in 1902."

"I know people from Iceland. I'm from Baffin Island, not far from Iceland."

I said, "My mother didn't learn to speak English until she went to school."

"Where I went to school," said Doreen, "if we spoke Inuk to anybody, we got a slap on the head. When I went home, if I spoke English, even to someone who spoke English, I'd get a slap on the head. I got it from both sides.

"Do you know whose land we're on?"

I said, "I was told it was Algonquin land."

"There is a dispute about that. It's Huron and Algonquin land. It makes me so mad to think about it, but this land was a native burying ground. How would you like it if they built over the place where your grandmother was buried?

"I may live in the city, but I still make my stamp on the ground." She demonstrated by hitting the sidewalk with the side of her fist.

To some women passing on the sidewalk, Doreen yelled, "Will you please give me a smile?"

The women turned and smiled. Doreen, replied, "Thank you, you did give me a smile. That makes me so happy."

To me she said, "I just want to be happy. I think that is what most people want, just to be happy."

I agreed, "If everybody expressed love to each other, the world would be a happier place."

I could see Joy walking up the sidewalk. She didn't look happy.

"Hi Joy, how was your weekend?"

"It was okay — quiet. I'm so fuckin' pissed off right now. I haven't been able to get my check yet. It was supposed to be ready Friday, but my worker said that because I switched to the Salvation Army, it was going to be delivered to a different office. I phoned this morning. They said, 'Your check will be

ready any time you want to come down and pick it up.'
'Great,' I said. I used my last bus ticket to come down to the office. When I got there they said, 'Come back at two o'clock.' What a run around."

Jenny stood up and tried to give Joy a hug. Joy said, "Jenny, I've had a bad day and I'm not in the mood for a hug. I just want to be left alone for a while."

Jenny said, "Joy, don't be like that. I just want to be friendly."

"Jenny, what did I just say? Now, sit down or I'll knock you down."

Danny said, "Joy, that's no way to talk to your friends. Whether you've had a bad day or not, there's no excuse for taking it out on the rest of us. I've talked to you about that before."

"Danny, keep your mouth shut before I come over there and smack you."

"Come on over. I'll smack you right back."

Joy was quiet for a while, then she said to Jenny, "I'm sorry for talking to you like that. I had no right. I apologize."

"It's alright, Joy, I understand."

"Danny, I apologize to you too."

Minnie, walking with a cane, stopped and asked Doreen, "Aren't you cold with bare arms?"

Doreen said, "Since the accident, I've lost all feeling of heat or cold in my arms and legs. If I wear too many clothes, I get itchy all over (*major spinothalamic or spinal cord injury*)."

"Let me give you a hug," said Jenny.

Doreen stood up and they hugged. Jenny said, "Can I have a hug too, Skinny Minnie?"

Minnie hugged her and said, "Jenny, you're skinnier than I am."

It was nearly time for me to go. I walked over to Jacques to shake his hand. He said, "You know, I woke up in the middle of the night with such a sore throat. Then I had to go to the bathroom. An hour later I had to go again. It was back and forth, back and forth, all night long. You better not get too close to me."

I said goodbye to Joy, she said, "Do you have to go already?"

"Yes, but I'll see you tomorrow."

"Not in the morning. I have a meeting with my PO, but I'll see you here at noon."

Dennis, I'm Losing It

2 October 2012

It's 12:00, Tuesday, in the park. The regular crowd shuffles in.

The first person to greet me was Serge, He said, "It's my old friend, Kenny Rogers."

"Hi Serge, how are you feeling today?"

"Not so good. I have an appointment with my doctor this afternoon at the clinic."

"What are you seeing your doctor about? Are you having problems with your stomach again?"

"Yeah, it's my stomach, and I have a pain in my shoulder."

"What's caused the pain in your shoulder?"

"The cops came by. I smashed my bottle so I wouldn't get a ticket. They put my hands behind my back, put handcuffs on me, then pushed me to the sidewalk. It hurt something in my shoulder."

"I know what those cuffs feel like. They always put them on too tight, don't they?"

"I don't know why they did that. I didn't get a ticket."

"This morning a guy saw me drinking out of my Listerine bottle. He said, 'I'll give you twenty dollars if you throw that bottle away.' 'No way,' I said. 'Keep your money.' He gave me the twenty anyway."

"So that worked out well for you. I hope everything goes well at the doctor's office this afternoon. I'll see you later."

Shaggy was barking non stop. "Don't pay any attention to her," said Wolf, "she's just saying hello. She doesn't make much of a guard dog; she barks, but she's too lazy to lift her head off the sidewalk."

"How's everything going today, Joy?" I asked. She gestured with her head toward Chester and rolled her eyes.

"Dennis, I'm losing it. I met with my PO (Probation Officer) this morning. I didn't think that I was talking loud. All of a sudden two cops came in. They said, 'We thought there was a disturbance.' My PO was upset. She said, 'There's no disturbance. If there had been, I have a buzzer to press, or I would have called you.' After a while, I had to pee. When I got outside her door, sure enough, the two cops were on either side. They followed me to the bathroom and waited outside. I stayed an extra long time, just to piss them off. I also had a drink.

"When I was finished my appointment, I took the elevator down. The two cops went with me. I said to them, 'What is it with you guys? Is it that you just don't like me? I wasn't put on this earth to be either liked or disliked by you.' I said to the big one, 'I remember you. You're the one who smashed my cheek.'

"He said, 'You didn't lodge a complaint.'"

"I know better than to charge one of the city's finest. I learned that lesson in Montreal."

I asked, "How did he smash your cheek?"

"Feel both of my cheeks. See if you think they feel the same." I noticed that the bone structure felt different. "Part of my cheek bone was broken off. They were called to our apartment, when I was still with Big Jake. One cop was talking to him outside, the big one was with me in the kitchen. He opened the fridge and started taking out beer. I said, 'Excuse me.' Notice that I was being polite. I said, 'Excuse me, but those are my beer. You've no right to be taking them.' That's the last I remember. I woke up in hospital. I still have a scar, but it's nearly faded now.

"I also met with my worker this morning. She may have an apartment for me to see tomorrow. I just hope I get it. Chester is driving me crazy. I'd never hurt him, but I just don't know what I'm doing some times. I think I freaked out my PO this morning. Hopefully, she'll get me back on my anti-schizoid medication. I haven't had it since I was in hospital last January.

"Last night, I was at a party at Chuck's place. I was having a good time. I'm entitled to have a good time, once in a while, aren't I? I'd been there about an hour when I got a phone call from Chester. Even though I told him not to, he invited Loretta over for some muk-muk loving. I don't think it worked out the way he planned. He was drunk and she gets crazy when she drinks. Chester said that she was hitting him and he didn't know how to get her out of his apartment.

"I said to him, 'Chester, go over to the fridge. The number for security is on a card there. Phone them and tell them you want someone removed from your apartment. They'll take Loretta out. If you don't want to do that, dial 911 and the cops will deal with her.' I must have gotten half a dozen calls from him. I phoned security, told them that my father was having trouble getting someone out of his apartment. I said, 'I've seen you guys, you're big enough to handle a hundred pound woman. I've also seen that you have handcuffs, if she gives you any trouble.'

"Chester called back again. He said that security had gotten Loretta out of the apartment, but later he heard a knock and opened the door. It was Loretta. She barged back in. Who in their right mind opens a door when they don't know who's on the other side? It could have been thieves, ready to invade his home and take all he's got.

"I came home and Loretta was passed out on the couch. That's my home. I saw red. I really laid into her. I'm not exactly sure what happened, I was fairly wasted at the time. I know I threw her out. This morning, I saw that there was blood on the couch. My knuckles are sore. My foot is sore, there was blood all over my white shoe, and I found teeth prints in the leather. Loretta doesn't have teeth, but whoever removed them did a lousy job. She still has nubs. I don't know what kind of shape she's in.

"Tomorrow, I go for my second anger management counseling session. I'll have someone messing with my head. I just can't take much more. I feel like I'm dying from the inside."

Death in the Family

3 October 2012

As I got off the bus this morning, I was approached by Metro. He had a grim look on his face. "Dennis, someone just told me that Joy is in hospital. I'd like to visit her, but I don't know her last name."

I told him Joy's last name.

"Thanks, Dennis, I'm not good at hospitals. There are too many sick people there, but I'll try to get over to see Joy."

"Thanks for telling me, Metro, I really appreciate it."

"No problem."

Nearly beside me, sitting at a patio table outside the coffee shop, drinking coffee from a paper cup, was Deaf Donald.

"Dennis, something really bad happened to me. I just got out of jail. The police, all they say is lies. My landlord phoned them last night. He said I was making too much noise. I wasn't making a lot of noise. It's just that my landlord doesn't like me. The police say I assaulted them. I didn't do that. They came to my door, and when I opened it, they grabbed me, put me in handcuffs and pushed me to the floor. I spent the night in jail. My mother posted bail for me. I have a ticket for disturbing the peace. It says I have to pay $350 within fifteen days, or I go to jail. On top of that, I'm not even allowed to go back to my apartment. My rent is paid until the end of the month, but my mother and some friends are going to have to move my things. I'm not allowed. That's not right.

"I've stopped taking drugs. I can't go to jail again. Do you know the name of a good lawyer?"

I wrote down on a piece of paper the name of a lawyer I've used in the past, and handed it to him. I said, "Contact this person, if she can't help you, she'll refer you to someone who can. She's very pleasant. There's no charge for the introductory visit. She will explain the charges to you and what your rights are. Any information needed for your court appearance can be collected by her office. If you want, she'll represent you. Don't worry, you won't go to jail."

"Thanks, Dennis, I'll walk there after I go for my methadone treatment."

"Take care, Donald. Everything will work out."

At noon I was relieved to see Joy. I said to her, "I'm so glad to see you. Metro said that you were in hospital. He said that someone gave him the message to pass on to me. Are you alright? Metro didn't know your last name, but wanted to visit you in."

"I'm fine, thank him for me when you see him next.

"We did get some bad news," said Joy. "Silver died on Monday at the Mission Hospice. He and Chester were really close. Silver checked himself into the Mission, then they moved him to the Salvation Army, then he was moved to the Hospice. There's something not right there. He should have gone to the hospital, not the Mission. They have no trained medical staff there."

Jacques pulled out a photo of very healthy looking Silver, sitting by the canal. "I must have known him for ten, twelve years, maybe. It was strange. He had a swollen ankle, then his belly swelled up, his face became skinny. He died so soon. I think he must have had some sort of virus or an infection. I wonder if they'll do an autopsy. I'd like to know what he died of.

"We were just talking about all the people we know who have died. Just in one year, Rip died…"

Shark said, "Rip's still alive."

"Oh, I meant Tim, he died at Easter, Digger died on Canada Day and Hobo died on Labor Day, all in the same year."

I said, "I saw some of those people in a video."

Shark said, "It's called *Under the Bridge*. Most of those people have left town or are dead."

Jacques said, "I had an uncle. He retired and stayed home with his wife. He had nothing to do, nothing to keep him busy. He died within two weeks of retiring. Me, I don't have to worry about that. I've never had a job, so I'll never die from stopping work."

I said, "That's good preventative medicine, Jacques."

André said, "I out drank Hippo; he's gone. I outdrank Shakes, see he's going fast. He's giving me the evil eye, pretending he's not falling asleep. He's gone."

"Where is Hippo?" I asked.

"He's at his apartment," said Jacques. "Didn't you know? I saw his place. It's a one bedroom, the size of a bachelor. The bedroom is so small there's only room for a single bed. When they brought it to him he said, 'Hey, I wanted a double bed.' They said, 'There's no room.' I was there but I don't know what street he's on. It goes in this way, out that way, before you know it, you're lost."

Joy said, "That's the place I should have gotten. I know why I didn't get it; my worker told me. They thought I was a hooker. If I was a hooker, I wouldn't have been wearing that cheap, polyester dress.

"I told Chester I wouldn't be coming home tonight. Last time, he waited up for me. I said to him, 'Chester, I'm 46 years old, nobody has to wait up for me. If something is going to happen, it'll happen. If I'm not home by 8:00, figure that I'm going to be gone for the night.

"He's invited Raven over, can you imagine? She's worse than Loretta. At least I won't have to deal with getting her out of the apartment."

I asked, "Have you seen Loretta lately?"

"Not since I threw her out Monday. I took her down in the elevator, bounced her around the walls a bit. Nothing was broken. She was able to walk away from the building."

We saw a fire truck pull up. Jacques said, "We better leave, soon the police will be here."

Firemen came over to Shakes and tried to wake him up. Shortly after, a paramedic truck pulled up. I expect that he will be taken to the detox facility at the Shepherd. He'll be allowed to sleep the night and will be back in his usual place tomorrow.

I Killed a Pumpkin

4 October 2012

"Does anybody know any details about Silver's funeral?" I asked, " I'd like to attend if I can."

André said, "From what I've heard, it's at the funeral home down the street. The viewing of the body is at 10:00, and the service is at 11:00. You won't see me there. I've been at too many funerals, dozens of them. I want to remember Silver the way he was, not the way they'll have him in his casket. I can't take that."

"Shakes, how are you today? You didn't look too good yesterday when the fire truck and the paramedics arrived."

"I'm fine, I'm just tired that's all."

"How are you, André?"

"Last night Joy, Jake and I were drinking at Jake's new apartment. Joy and I got into a little tiff. We were both drunk. I decided to leave and I woke up in somebody's garden. I was eating carrots, some kind of squash. I used a grocery store card to slice a tomato. That worked really well. I killed a pumpkin, a big sucker. I just wound up and 'kapow'. Now, I got all these stains on my pants.

"I'm just waiting for my worker, she's supposed to be here at 12:45. She's going to take me to see an apartment. Next week she'll take me to see a doctor. She asked me, 'Do you have any medical problems?' I said, 'How much time do you have? I can keep you writing for an hour with all my medical problems.'

"I walked into a clinic one time, there were all kinds of people in the waiting room. I walked up to the counter and said, 'I'm in the middle of one of my mood swings. I want a doctor, NOW! I guess I looked real freaky. The doctor saw me right away and gave me some medication. It was potent stuff. I felt like a zombie for three days. I didn't want to take that again; I couldn't do anything but sleep. When I was awake, it was like I was in a fog. I smoke pot instead. It keeps me mellow. If I don't have any for about three days, I start to get wired up.

"One time the cops were chasing me and I pulled myself over a five foot fence. What I didn't realize was there was a thirteen foot drop on the other side. I broke some ribs that time. I had a floating rib for a while. That really hurt. Sometimes, I wouldn't be able to catch my breath.

"Another time I jumped out a second story window. There was a wooden shed below that broke my fall and my ribs on the other side."

Wolf said, "Did I tell you that Shaggy bit me this morning. That's why she's over there in front of Nick. She started the

138

day well, she walked all the way down here on her own. For a thirteen year old dog that's pretty good. These guys got her all wound up. I reached in front of her and she chomped down on my wrist. It didn't break the skin, but it's so sore.

"That's all I got to say to you.

"André, can I have a drink from your bottle?"

André said, "Yes."

"You know, I don't often ask you for anything, do I?"

"No, you don't, Wolf. I don't remember the last time you asked me for something."

"Alright then, just so we have that straight."

A skateboarder went by and Shaggy started barking and chasing him. André grabbed Shaggy's leash just in time. He said to the frightened kid, "She doesn't like skateboards."

André said to a woman passing by, "That's a beautiful shawl you're wearing, sister. Has anybody told you today that you're beautiful too?"

To me he said, "See how tall she is, she must be six one or two. I love tall women. They can wrap their legs around you twice."

Nick was chattering away to nobody in particular, mumbling something about, "I know how to survive. I've even slept in a snow drift with a piece of cardboard and newspaper inside my pant legs and in my sleeves. I was fine until the cops kicked me in the face.

"Can somebody throw me that bottle?"

Wolf said, "It's not mine. I'm not going to throw it to you."

The Funeral

5 October 2012

At 10:15 this morning I entered the funeral home to attend the viewing and memorial service for Silver. Most of the viewing rooms were empty. I heard voices and walked into one of the rooms. I didn't know if I was in the right place until I saw, at the front, two boards of photographs with Silver lettered on top. There must have been a dozen photos on each board. Many of the photos I wouldn't have recognized. They were from Silver's childhood, teenage years and as the adult that I had considered my friend for the past nine months. As I was looking, I was approached by a woman with blond hair and a welcoming smile.

She asked, "Did you know Silver well?"

"Yes," I answered, "I sat and talked with him nearly every day. In the mornings, in front of the coffee shop, and at noon at the park."

"I'm Silver's sister, Cathy, by the way."

"Silver spoke fondly of you," I said.

"Did you also know that he has three brothers, a son and a grandchild? Did Silver mention that? I'll introduce you to them when I see them."

"Silver may have mentioned the rest of his family. The last time I saw him was about two weeks ago. He showed me the swelling of his ankle and varicose veins he was worried about. He said he had an appointment with his doctor that same day. Jacques mentioned that Silver's stomach was swollen. We all noticed that he had lost weight, especially in his face, and were worried about him. Sometimes, he would sit alone and just gaze into the distance. It just seemed to be his way. It was a great shock to hear that he had passed away.

"What was given as the cause of death?"

"Liver failure. Swollen ankles and abdomen are symptoms of liver failure. Luckily the whole family was able to be at his bedside for the last week; his son and granddaughter, of course, his mother and father, his brothers, his nephew. We all had lots of stories. It was good to see Silver laugh."

"Here's Cody now, Silver's son, and Cody's daughter Jennifer, Jenny for short."

"Hi, Cody and Jenny. I knew your father well. I'm so sorry for your loss. You have a striking resemblance to your dad."

"I know. I'm proud of it," said Cody.

Cathy said, "Dennis, have you met Steve and Dave?"

"Hi Steve. Hi Dave."

Linda said to Dave, "You saw Silver fairly regularly too, is that right?"

"Every day or so we'd go for a beer together. I lived next door to him."

Cathy said, "We'd lost contact with Silver. We didn't know he was so close. He didn't have a phone. If we'd known where he was, we would have whisked him away."

"Steve, how long was Silver staying in the same building as you? About four years?"

"Nearly five years."

"Dennis," asked Cathy, "what was your impression of Silver?"

"He was the sweetest, kindest, gentlest man. He always had a smile to greet me. It was always a pleasure talking with him."

Cathy said, "He was a glass-half-full kind of person, wasn't he?"

"Yes," I said, "He was always cheerful and optimistic."

Outcast walked over to the photographs and said, "Here's me with Silver, this other one is of me also, but my head is cut off."

I said, "Outcast, I'd recognize your crotch anywhere."

Shark said, "We're not staying for the service. We just came to pay our respects to Silver's family, then we'll cross the street and raise a few glasses to him."

Irene and I walked over and signed the visitor's book. I saw Danny sitting down, so I went over and sat with him.

"I'm just on my way to Thunder Bay," he said. "After I leave here, I'm going to the bus depot to pick up my tickets."

I asked, "Is that where you're from? Do you have family there?"

"My mother's in hospital, so I want to spend time with her. She's had part of her colon removed. Now they've found more polyps in the remaining colon. Doctors want to remove another two inches. She doesn't want to go through that again. She said, 'I'm ready to go. Why won't they just let me die at home?'

"She's had a hard life. My dad passed away a while back. He was on life support. The family was asked for permission to stop the machines that were keeping him alive. I was talking to my mom, on my cell phone, when they pulled the plug. I heard laughing in the background. The family thought that after he was removed from life support that he would die immediately. He drifted off to sleep for about ten minutes, then he awoke. He said, 'I must be in heaven, I see all the angels of my family around me.' Everyone laughed. I think he was trying to hold on until I arrived, but he didn't last long enough for me to see him. At least I got to talk to him and tell him that I loved him.

"I met Silver's brothers and his nephew. I also met Spike. I introduced myself. I said, 'I think we've met before at the benches, or at the heater."

"Maybe," he said, "I go to those places."

Shark asked Spike, "What do you think of this place?"

Spike said, "It's within walking distance of three beer stores."

It was time to go upstairs for the memorial service. I'm guessing there were about fifty to seventy-five people in attendance. The minister, who hadn't met Silver, started the service with a reading from the Book of John:

> "Do not let your hearts be troubled. You believe in God[a]; believe also in me. My Father's house has many rooms; if that were not so, would I have told you that I am going there to prepare a place for you? And if I go and prepare a place for you, I will come back and take you to be with me that you also may be where I am. You know the way to the place where I am going."
>
> "Thomas said to him, "Lord, we don't know where you are going, so how can we know the way?"
>
> Jesus answered, "I am the way and the truth and the life. No one comes to the Father except through me. If you really know me, you will know[b] my Father as well. From now on, you do know him and have seen him."

The minister added a personal note. "I am getting on in years. I know that when my time comes that my Lord will have prepared a room for me, even though in my life I have made mistakes. I am human. We all make mistakes. The dead are not gone, they live on in our hearts and memories, and in the genes of our children.

He then went over and blessed Silver's cremation urn with holy water.

A family member read a poem she wrote for Silver.

Cathy talked about stories from their childhood, stories that they had recounted at Silver's bedside:

"In the winter, Silver loved 'bumpering'. To go bumpering, you grab the bumper of a moving vehicle and allow it pull you as it careens along the icy roads. This is dangerous and not at all recommended.

"Silver enjoyed board games such as *Monopoly* and *Clue*, and playing cards. He and his older brother, Don, played a game called *Hi-Lo*. The loser of each hand would have to do push-ups. What Silver didn't know was that Bob was stacking the deck against him. Don was ahead in the short run, but Silver developed massive shoulders that gave him an advantage in wrestling.

"Our father died when Silver was nine years old. The three oldest siblings had to take turns minding the two youngest. Silver wanted to go riding on his bike, but it was his turn to care for his younger brother. He found a way to do both things at the same time. He tied his brother to the front stair railing and hopped on his bike. He rode around and around the block, waving at his brother each time he passed."

Cathy read the poem *Do not stand at my grave and weep* by Mary Elizabeth Frye,

> Do not stand at my grave and weep,
> I am not there; I do not sleep.
> I am a thousand winds that blow,
> I am the diamond glints on snow,
> I am the sun on ripened grain,
> I am the gentle autumn rain.
> When you awaken in the morning's hush

I am the swift uplifting rush
Of quiet birds in circling flight.
I am the soft star-shine at night.
Do not stand at my grave and cry,
I am not there; I did not die.

The service ended, and as the congregation arose and left the chapel the following song was being played:Spirit in the Sky by Norman Greenbaum.

When I die and they lay me to rest
Gonna go to the place that's the best
When I lay me down to die
Goin' up to the spirit in the sky
Goin' up to the spirit in the sky
That's where I'm gonna go when I die
When I die and they lay me to rest
Gonna go to the place that's the best

Prepare yourself you know it's a must
Gotta have a friend in Jesus
So you know that when you die
He's gonna recommend you
To the spirit in the sky
Gonna recommend you
To the spirit in the sky
That's where you're gonna go when you die
When you die and they lay you to rest
You're gonna go to the place that's the best

Never been a sinner I never sinned
I got a friend in Jesus
So you know that when I die
He's gonna set me up with
The spirit in the sky
Oh set me up with the spirit in the sky
That's where I'm gonna go when I die
When I die and they lay me to rest
I'm gonna go to the place that's the best
Go to the place that's the best

At the door leaving the building, I had a chance to speak
with Stella, who has known Silver and the rest of his friends
for the past sixteen years. She said, "I met Silver at the
beginning through Tom, who used to pan at the corner. They
both decided they would hitchhike up to Timmins for some
reason, but only got to Carp and came back. Guess there
weren't many beer stores along the way. Very funny. Tim
passed away a few years ago."

This was a very emotional service. Over the past nine
months Silver had become one of my family — my street
family. It filled a void in me where my own family once was.
They have all passed away, or are living in different parts of
the continent. I too am a father and a grandfather.

Loretta and Vance

9 October 2012

Joy was huddled in a blanket with her hood pulled close to her face. She was rocking back and forth. When I came closer, I could see that she was shivering.

"I'm freezing," she said. "I didn't see you on Friday."

"I was at Silver's funeral. I met his sister, his three brothers, nephew, son and granddaughter. She's a little sweetheart, just four years old."

"I know that Outcast, Shark and Irene went."

"Yeah, I saw them there. They didn't stay for the service. Stella was also there."

"We were too bummed out. Chester was crying. He got me crying. He took it really hard. He said, 'What am I going to do with the dvds that Silver lent me?' They'd often get together to watch movies, game shows, eat pizza and drink beer."

"How was your weekend?" I asked.

"Quiet, I went to visit Loretta for the weekend. She's renting a room in a house. It's out in the country overlooking a conservation area. Her landlord doesn't like her boyfriend, Vance. He's been really ignorant on the phone when the landlord has answered. He said, 'Why the fuck are you answering Loretta's phone?'

"The landlord was away this weekend. Vance came to visit. I hardly saw Loretta at all. When I woke up Sunday morning, they were gone. I had no bus fare because I'd given tickets to Loretta. I had no cash because I spent the last of it on a bottle for her. So, I was stuck. The landlord had change in a dish near the door. Without that I wouldn't have been able to get home."

"So, you and Loretta are friends again?"

"Yeah, we're fine. It's just when she gets drunk that she acts crazy. When she's relatively sober, she's okay. She has to go into rehab sometime soon. She'd previously said that she was going to come back to the house after she finished. Vance gave her an emerald ring on Friday. I could see that it was an antique ring. I talked to her landlord on the phone yesterday and he seemed really pissed off. Now, Loretta is saying she's going to find a new place to stay after rehab. I wouldn't be surprised if Vance had stolen the ring from her landlord.

"Irene was really upset Friday after Silver's funeral. She had been going out with Silver for about six years. She dumped him for Shark. She and Shark have been together now for about five years."

I said, "Silver mentioned that. When I told him that Shark and Irene were going to share an apartment, he said, 'He'd better have a place to hide when she gets crazy.' He also mentioned that Irene was the reason he started smoking again."

"It hit Silver really hard when Irene left him. He hadn't gone out with any women since her. He'd say, 'I still love Irene, I have no interest in other women.' "

Downtown Charlie Brown

10 October 2012

This morning was even colder than yesterday. I gave Metro a picture of Silver from the funeral. He would have seen him every morning for nearly eleven years. Joy was wrapped in her blanket, rubbing her legs. "I wore the wrong shoes today.

These Pumas, given to me by Wolf, are worth about a hundred and fifty bucks. People look at me and they figure, 'Why are you panhandling if you can afford shoes like that?' I try to hide them, but I have to straighten my legs out to rub them every once in a while. They're really bad today."

"How are you and Chester getting along these days?"

"He got shitfaced last night. I gave him some money and asked him to buy a bottle for me. He used my money to buy himself more beer. He went through an eighteen pack yesterday. Usually, he'll be asleep after six.

"He was saying to me, 'Joy, I love you. I won't mind if you stay after Christmas. Then he touched my leg. He hasn't done that for a while.

"I said to him, 'Chester, you don't like to be touched. I feel the same way, so keep your hands to yourself.'

"Later, he was banging around in the kitchen stark naked. He said, 'What's for supper?' I told him, 'I'm having this box of Kraft Dinner. I don't know what you're having. When are you going to buy some groceries?' I've spent a lot this month supplying him with cigarettes — he chain smokes, one right after another — and I've bought all the food. He hasn't bought any.

"Well, I don't think I'm going to be making any more money this morning. I had a good day yesterday."

"I'll see you later, Joy. Stella will be bringing pumpkin tarts."

"I'll give mine to Chester. I can't stand pumpkin. I don't mind the seeds, but that's all."

Later, at 10:00, I went to the park. Stella and her husband Tim were there. Stella loves to walk Weasel's dog, Bear. She's known him since he was a pup — at that time he was owned by Andre, who has since passed away. Stella had brought pumpkin tarts with whipped cream for everybody. She brought me a package of photos and a photo copy of a newspaper article entitled, 'Street Sister.' The article was about her work with the homeless, collecting clothes in her neighborhood and delivering them to people forced onto the streets.

Joy said, "Janice, my worker, is meeting me here to take me to my anger management appointment." She poured some wine in her water bottle, added water and placed it in her bag.

Little Jake, asked, "Can you roll me a joint?"

Janice arrived and said hello to the people she knew. André asked, "We're meeting tomorrow, right? You're coming here?"

"That's right, André."

Joy asked, "How many buses do we have to take, and how far do we have to walk?"

"We walk a few blocks then board the bus. That will take us right there."

Joy asked, "Can you just wait until I finish this joint? Then I'll be ready to go."

"Sure, we have time."

Joy hoisted her heavy backpack onto her shoulders and they walked down the sidewalk towards the bus stop.

I said hello to everybody I knew. Shakes introduced me to Clifford.

He said, "So, you're Dennis the Menace! I'm Downtown Charlie Brown. I've been on the street for the past few days. Before that I was in a recovery program. I'm native Algonquin. I was born, on the Madawaska River, near Algonquin Park. My father is a millionaire, but he won't even answer the phone to me. He won't give me fifty bucks; won't even give the price for a bottle. My sister is the same, she has a great big house; I sleep on the street. She says, 'You got yourself this way, you get yourself out.' "

I said, "I'm really interested in learning about native culture. Is the Center a good place to go?"

"Yes, every Wednesday the native ladies host a meal, storytelling, chanting and drumming. You'll get to see Shakes dance, sing and play guitar."

"Shakes," I said. "I didn't know you sang and played guitar."

Clifford said, "Shakes and I used to sing in the park. He taught me some boxcar Willie and other blues songs."

> *Boxcar's my home, railroad my friend*
> *It's been that way since I don't know when*
> *I'm here today, tomorrow I'm gone*
> *Where I hang my hat is where I call home*
> *Stars at night my roof over head*
> *The ground below where I make my bed*
> *Horizons you see, well that is my walls*
> *When the sun comes up my hobo blood calls.*

Clifford said, "When I think of native culture, I get so angry. In school the nuns forced us to speak English. They called what we spoke, 'the devil's language'. If we were ever caught speaking Algonquin or any other native language, we would be beaten with the edge of a ruler or a leather strap. Can you imagine if something like that happened today, especially to the children of white people. The nuns would be arrested.

"Most native people would rather sleep outside, than in one of the shelters. Last night the guy in the bunk on my right kept saying, 'six, six, six, six, six…' all night long. He never stopped. The guy on my left was a crack head. Every twenty minutes he'd get up and walk around. I didn't trust him, so I was trying to sleep with one eye open. Whenever he got up, or went back to bed I woke up."

Back from the Garden

11 October 2012

I could see my breath this morning. Joy was wrapped in her blanket sitting next to André. I asked Joy, "How did your appointment go yesterday?"

"She was messing with my head. She said, 'You've had quite a life, haven't you?' I said, 'It started with my grandfather, then my father, then his younger brother. I got into drugs, was kicked out of my home, joined a biker gang, was into prostitution, jail, then ended up on the street, sleeping behind a dumpster. So, yeah, I've had quite a life.' "

"Is she any closer to getting you in to see a doctor, or at least get you back on your previous medication?"

"She's working on it. I see her again next Wednesday. I'm just tired of this runaround. It's been going on since January."

I said to André, "I see you've shaved again."

"I'm trying to look respectable for a while." To Joy he said, "I guess I look better than I did last weekend. I still can't figure out how I ended up in that garden. I sure didn't get far from Jake's place."

Joy said, "The last time I saw you, you were sitting in the middle of somebody's lawn. I told you to come, but you said, 'I'm staying right here.' "

"I guess I can get pretty stubborn sometimes."

"Sometimes?" I asked. "When aren't you stubborn?"

"That's more like it," said Joy.

"So you left me there?"

Joy said, "I saw the bus coming from one direction, so I figured the one going the other way would be along soon. I wasn't going to miss my bus arguing with you. Yes, I left you there."

André said, "All I know is, I woke up with watermelon and squash all over me. I had tomato dripping down my chin. I was a mess."

I said, "You told me you remembered slicing a tomato with a coffee shop card."

"Yeah, I remember saying that."

Joy said, "I remember one time, sitting here, a guy wearing a $600 suit and an even more expensive overcoat, threw a full cup of coffee at me. It burnt my face. I went after the guy with all I had. Some of my regular ladies came by and asked what happened. I said, "Look at me. This jerk threw a cup of coffee at me. They started hitting him with their purses."

"Did anyone call the police?" I asked, "That's assault! He shouldn't get away with that!"

"Somebody may have called the police. I didn't stick around. What I did to the guy probably would have gotten me charged. Can you imagine, a person going into a restaurant, buying a coffee with the express purpose of throwing it on somebody? He must be one sick fuck. It's not as if I even ask for money. I just sit here. I say, 'good morning' to some people who I know, apart from that I'm quiet as a mouse."

I asked Joy, "How are you and Chester getting along?"

"Last night we had another big argument. He slammed the door in my face. I said, 'Chester, I'm moving out. I can't put up with this bullshit any longer.' I packed my bag, put it out on the balcony. It must have weighed more than me. I didn't have money for a cab. I had no place else to stay. I thought about going to the dumpsters behind the coffee shop, but they've moved them close to the wall now. Nobody is staying there anymore. I don't know where Bearded Bruce is. I think he's with Weasel.

"Chester said, 'Please Joy, don't leave. I love you.' So I stayed the night. He was a little better this morning."

André said, "Bruce is trained as a chef, isn't he?"

Joy agreed, "Bruce is a good cook, but he serves beans with everything. He filled my plate until it was heaping. I couldn't finish half of it. Chuck took some, but he couldn't finish his either."

I said, "I was talking to Charlie yesterday. He was mentioning the Native Center. He was saying that every Wednesday there is a free meal, storytelling, dancing and drumming. Do you know anything about that?"

André said, "I went there once. A guy said to me, 'This is for native people.' I'm part Ojibway. I said, 'Who are you to say whether or not I'm part native. I see a guy over there that looks white, and another over there. Did they have to prove they were native?' The guy said, 'I know they're native. You're lucky you got a bowl of cereal. Don't come back again.' "

Joy said, "I've had the same problem, my father was Ojibway, my mother was English. I'm Metis, but I look white. I don't fit in anywhere."

At noon I was leaving work and ran into Buck and Dillinger. He said, "Joy, André and Shakes are together, sitting in the middle of the street." I had no idea what that meant. I found them sitting on the concrete island with the elevated flower garden.

Joy said, "We're just trying to stay out of trouble. The cops were by earlier. They can't say anything about us sitting here.

We're not talking to anybody, we don't have any alcohol visible." Then she looked at Shakes.

"Shakes, for Christ's sake, will you put that bottle under your coat or something. You don't have to advertise that you're drinking." Just then a police car passed.

"Just watch, he's going to turn around," she said. The car continued on and didn't return.

André said, "I haven't seen that big cop lately. The one with the muscles and all the tattoos."

Joy said, "I heard that he got promoted. He works in the building now."

"He sure doesn't like Little Jake," said André. "I remember the last time; Jake was sitting on the ground, and that cop was bending over him saying, 'Why don't you learn to shut up. If you say one more word, I'm going to take you behind that electrical shed and beat the shit out of you.'

"The other cop looked at me and said, 'If he gets into it with your friend, I'm not big enough to do anything about it. If you can talk reason to Jake, now would be a good time.' I bent down and said to him, 'This guy is the size of a tree. There's no way out of this. Just keep your mouth shut.' He said, 'Okay.'

Joy started sneezing, over and over again. She said, "I heard that a sneeze is like one tenth of an orgasm. I usually sneeze ten times. I don't need men at all.

"I'm not looking forward to going home. Chester is still acting pissy. He went to the Mission for lunch and was complaining about the food. He said, 'They were serving grilled cheese sandwiches. I told them it was garbage and threw it in the trash.' I've seen Chester cook a grilled cheese sandwich. He didn't throw it in the trash; he ate it and didn't complain."

"Is Chester still upset about Silver's death?"

"I guess so, but he has to move on. I have.

"I need to be on my medication and I'm having a real problem with menopause. I've got more zits now than I've had at any time in my life. I like my face. I don't want to look like this. I'm whining, aren't I?"

I said, "You have good reason to be upset."

A police car pulled up. The cop asked, "Are you guys waiting for your meal?"… I'll hear the rest of the details tomorrow.

Curly Water

12 October 2012

The mornings are getting ever colder. Joy was wrapped up, rubbing her legs. André was sitting on a cushion. He said, "This cushion keeps me dry, but it sure doesn't keep me warm."

Joy said, "I'm going to get one of those plastic storage boxes and stash it behind the coffee shop when I don't need it. This cold really causes my legs to ache."

I asked, "What happened when the police came by yesterday?"

"Nothing much — the usual. They sent the Shepherd van for Serge. He was sleeping at the heater. I didn't like the way they were treating him. I said, 'Hey, be careful with him. He's my friend.' One of them kept waving her hand in front of her face. I know he probably doesn't smell that good, but they must have dealt with worse than him. I found it disrespectful."

"How has Chester been?"

"He was better this morning. Mind you, I bought him a gram of pot yesterday. When I came home he said, 'Joy, I saved you a joint.' I said, 'That's okay, Chester, I have my own.' "

I asked, "Do you have any plans for the weekend?"

"No, I'll probably be doing laundry. Some clothes I had just thrown on top of the bags I moved out to the balcony. They'll have to be washed and Asshole probably has things he wants washed.

"At noon we'll probably be at the corner or under the bridge. We're getting hassled too much at the park, especially if there are more than four of us."

It was snowing at noon. I passed André on my way to the park. He said, "Hi Dennis, I'll be back in a few minutes. I just have to get something."

I could hear Shaggy barking long before I could see anyone. It brought to mind a comment that Silver had made a while back, 'I don't want to go up there, Shaggy's barking his head off.'

Hippo said, "My parents visited yesterday and brought some DVDs, but they took them home with them. My dad brought a tape measure last week, but he took it back yesterday. I don't know what all that was about. I wish they'd left the DVDs — there were some good movies there. I have cable now. I just plugged it in and it's working."

Joy said, "He's been complaining like this all morning."

Hippo said, "I turned my TV on full blast this morning. It'll serve the crack heads right for keeping me awake all night."

Joy said, "André's gone to get a bottle of water for me since he drank most of mine."

André returned with Joy's water, did a little dance then sat next to Jake. A woman was passing. He said, "Hey, beautiful, did you wash your hair with curly water today?"

Wolf said, "This is only my second time out this week. I was here Tuesday. I haven't got my clothing figured out yet for this weather. I'm warm on top, but I need warmer shoes. Can you believe this snow? Shaggy doesn't know what to make of it either."

Chester went on a run for Joy. After he left she said, "I bought a dozen eggs last night; I had one. I checked this morning, there were only five left. Chester ate six eggs in one day and he goes to the Mission for meals. I also bought some bologna, but I stashed that away.

"This afternoon I'm going to Chuck's old place to see if my checks are there. I'm expecting one for a hundred bucks and one from GST (*Goods and Services Tax*) for sixty. I'll check the mailbox, or if someone is at home, I can ask if any mail is there addressed to me. I'll just tell them that I was slow in getting my change of address filed. I hope they don't ask for identification because I don't have any. Last time the crackhead gave the letters to me."

Depression

15 October 2012

It had rained during the night, sidewalks were wet. Joy was protected by a plastic cushion. I sat on the cold, damp concrete. "How was your weekend, Joy?"

"It was quiet. I went out Saturday night and hung out with Little Jake and André. When I got home I got a frantic phone call from Toothless Chuck, 'V's dead. He was hit by a car.' I'm not sure how the accident happened, but Chuck has broken bones in his foot and refuses to go to the hospital.

"This may sound unkind, but V's better off dead. Chuck didn't train him properly and would kick him if he misbehaved. That's no way to treat a dog."

I asked, "Do you have any appointments coming up to obtain your identification?"

"My regular appointment is Wednesday. I'm so frustrated that I've started cutting myself again. I was so proud that I had gone almost a year without doing that. I need my medication. They say the most common reasons for cutting are Attention or Depression. My reason is definitely Depression. Chester makes it worse with all his noises. He had the temperature way up yesterday, to the point I was sweating, but do you think he would put it up this morning when I said that I was cold? No!"

I said, "I was thinking back to this time last year. You were so happy. You'd received all your identification and your health card. You had moved into that nice house with Roy. You had your pet snake, the lizards and Roy's dog, Harley, but you were stressed about the cop car parked in front of your house. That was before your kidneys failed."

"Yeah, no chance of that now. Mind you, we had three cop cars in front of the apartment building yesterday. Chester said, 'Are they here for you, Joy?' I said, 'No, Chester, they're here for you.' He said, 'Me? I don't do any bad stuff.' I said, 'I don't either.' They were probably called because of the crackheads down the hall."

I said, "Even a place like Hippo's would be better for you. He has to deal with crackheads, but he has his privacy. He has cable, the choice to watch any programs he wants -- and in English too."

"Yeah, my worker is coming to see me and André at noon about two apartments she's found. I sure hope that works out. I'm overdue for some good news."

"I asked, "Did you get your laundry done?"

"Yeah, most of it. I washed all Chester's winter clothes. There wasn't enough room for mine. Chester's going to give me his winter pants. They go with this parka. Hopefully, I won't get too cold this winter. My arthritis and fibromyalgia just won't take the cold."

"Chester isn't in the cold that much, is he? He doesn't pan."

"No, he just comes to the Mission for meals and visits with the guys for a while. If he's cold, he goes home."

At noon the temperature was a balmy 63 degrees. I felt too warm in my down filled winter coat, so I sat on it instead. Shaggy greeted me at the sidewalk, licking my hand and barking.

"She's okay," said Wolf, "Go ahead and pet her. That's what she wants."

Sitting on the curb were the usual suspects. I was sitting on the sidewalk facing Joy. Loretta was fidgeting, standing beside me. At one point she draped her coat over my shoulder while she rooted through her purse looking for change to buy a cigarette.

I said, "Hey, what am I — a coat rack?"

Joy said, "I wish that dog would shut up for a while."

I asked, "How did the rest of your morning go? Did your worker come by to show you the apartment?"

"Today is a typical Monday, although it is payday for the government. My worker should have been here hours ago, but I know that Friday she had a lot of shit on her plate. She'll come either later today or tomorrow."

"Have you heard any more from Chuck, about his broken foot?"

160

"No, I didn't go over. When I talked to him on the phone, he said something about community service. He's not going to be able to do much with a broken foot."

Jake asked, "Is Chuck still living in the same place?"

Joy said, "No, he has a really nice apartment. I'm sure he won't have it for long. He has too many people living there. Every night there are twelve to fifteen people. They're loud, drunk — the police get called there a lot.

"He says, 'I can't let people sleep on the street!' I said to him, 'Dude, yes you can! They aren't your problem!' It was the same when I lived with him. People would eat all our food, there was hardly any place to sleep. It was doing my head in. I had to get away from there.

"Saturday he had a party with a lot of muk-muks. Magdalene brought Ruby, a friend of hers. This Ruby chick got in my face as soon as she arrived. Within a few minutes I was on my feet. Chuck had to hold me back. Somebody was holding Ruby back. I said, 'Let her go. I can deal with her.'

"Today Chuck mentioned that Ruby had phoned and asked him to apologize to me. She said she was out of control. I said, 'It's all water under the bridge to me.' The thing is, I'm sure she doesn't remember what I look like, but I sure as hell remember her. The next time I see her, I'll just walk up behind her and give her a snap at the back of the head. She won't know what hit her."

There was a demonstration taking place in the park. André said, "The RCMP (*Royal Canadian Mounted Police*) are there and some natives with a red flag, a yellow sunburst in the center, and the silhouette of an Indian brave on that."

Joy said, "André, you're part native, you don't recognize the flag of the Mohawk Nation? Don't you know about the land grant, from Queen Victoria, that gave the land we're sitting on to the Seven Nations of the Iroquois Confederacy?

That included the Mohawks of Akwisasne, Kahnawake, the Hurons of Wendake and the Anishinabegs."

"Well, I'm sorry," said André, "I must have been sick when they taught that history lesson."

I noticed that Shakes was very quiet.

Joy said, "He didn't get up until 8:00. He's sober and he doesn't have any pot. Usually by this time he's been panning long enough to get a couple of bottles."

I walked over to him, "How are you feeling, Shakes?"

"I'm broke," he said. "I stayed at the Shep last night. Somebody stole my bottle, my mary-jane and my money."

"Make sure you eat, okay, Shakes," I said.

"I will. Thanks, brother."

Bed Bugs Again

16 October 2012

This morning, as I approached Joy, I could see that she was shivering, even though she had her blanket wrapped around her legs.

"Hi, Joy," I said, "don't you have any warm, winter clothing?"

"I'm wearing two pairs of long underwear under my jeans. This coat is warm, it's just sitting on the concrete that's making me cold. Chester is going to give me his winter pants. He doesn't want them anymore. I said, 'If you're going to throw them out, I'll take them.' "

"I asked, "Did your worker come by yesterday?"

"No, she said she'll come today or I'll see her for my regular appointment tomorrow.

"Yesterday I hung out with André, Jake and Shakes. I went at André; he just won't get the message. I said to him, 'We've been through this before. I don't want you touching me.' 'But, Joy,' he said, 'I'm clean now!' I said, 'André, you've got five days dirt under your fingernails. Don't tell me you're clean. Even if you were, I haven't been with a man for the past year. I don't intend to start with you.' Still he kept putting his hand on my thigh, as if it were some kind of joke. Even Shakes and Jake yelled at him, 'André, for Christ's sake, leave her alone, she's family!' Again he put his hand on my thigh and started moving it up, so I punched him in the side of the head. I said, 'Next time, I'll stand up and kick you in the head.' Can you believe it? He started crying. His eyes welled up and he said, 'Joy, I love you. We'd be good together.' I said, 'No, I don't think so.' I just want to be left alone.

"This morning, when I was in the bathroom, I saw a red spot on the wall. I thought to myself, that spot shouldn't be there. I took a piece of toilet paper, wiped the spot, sniffed it — sure enough, it was a baby bed bug. Next time the guy comes to spray, I'm going to be there. I'll make sure he douses the carpet, the baseboards, anywhere else they like to hide.

"It was just getting to the point where I was sleeping through the night. Now, I have to worry again about whether or not the sheets and covers on my air mattress are touching the carpet. Besides that, I think that the tube shaped air chambers are affecting my fibromyalgia."

Teeth Returned

17 October 2012

This morning, as I approached Joy, she was doing a jig and smiling with her teeth clenched.

I said, "Don't tell me, Joy. You have to pee."

"Like ninety," she said. "I'll be right back."

When she returned she said, "This morning, when I got to the coffee shop, I had to get them to unlock the security washroom because the ladies was being serviced. I told the woman, 'Either you unlock that door now, or I'm busting into the men's room. I really have to go."

"How are your kidneys now?"

"Good, obviously, although, sometimes in the night, I have to get up and only a dribble comes out. That worries me.

"Chester was saying that he thinks he has Alzheimer's. His memory is really bad. He fell backwards, down fourteen concrete steps. He was with Outcast and Jacques. One minute he was there, the next minute he was gone. He was in a coma for five days. That was two years ago. Sometimes, he thinks that he just recently got out of hospital.

"He was mad at me yesterday. I guess he expected that I'd join him at the shelter for lunch. I don't go into those places. People often ask me about that. There are too many people and a lot of them I just don't care to see. There are a lot of crackheads. You never know what they're going to do.

"Even at Thanksgiving I didn't go for the meal. For one thing, I don't like turkey; for another, I don't like crowds. I barbecued some ribs, roasted veggies and baked a potato. It was the best Thanksgiving meal I've ever had.

"Last year, Meg was working with the church ladies. She brought me a frozen turkey for the Christmas season. In fact, she brought something different for each of the twelve days of Christmas. She isn't there anymore. I don't know what the church ladies will do this year.

"Chester should be by soon. I want to use his phone to cancel my appointment with the lady from the anger management program. My legs are so sore, I just can't take that much walking today. She's good that way. I've already had five appointments, probably more time than I would have had if I'd gone through the group program.

"Which reminds me. I got a letter in the mail from Big Jake. That really freaked me out. He wasn't supposed to know my address. I phoned Rodent, sure enough it was him that gave it to Jake. I said to him, 'I've told you before that I don't want Jake knowing where I am.' He said, 'But Joy, he wanted to write to you and didn't know where to send the letter. If you write him back, I can tell you the prison code the inmates use if you want him to phone you.' I said, 'Rodent, I don't want a letter, I don't want a phone call. I don't want anything to do with Jake.'

"Half the things Rodent said to me were in prison code. He said Jake was teaching some kind of course to get points. He hasn't been on a detox program. I didn't know what he was talking about, or when Jake will be getting out. He hasn't been penetentiarized long enough to know all that stuff. One time he said he'd served twenty-five years; another time he said it was twelve. He said when Jake gets out, he's going to be staying at his place. I wish them well with that. It sounds a little too cozy to me.

"I've served more time than most of the guys put together. I served three out of five for something I didn't even do. I just happened to be in the car.

"Here's Chester now. Chester, can I use your phone? This looks really great, doesn't it? A panhandler using a cell phone."

I said, "A friend of mine mentioned that to me yesterday. He said he saw a panhandler at the corner talking on a cell phone. He said he wouldn't give money to the guy, and any he'd given to him, he wanted back."

It's 10:00 Wednesday, the day that Stella usually comes to the park for a visit. Everyone was hoping she'd come.

Outcast said, "Dennis, what are you doing here this time of day? Are you playing hooky from work?"

"Yeah," I said, "I'm confusing everyone. I was hoping to see Stella."

Joy said, "She has a coat for me."

"She hasn't been here yet," said Outcast, "Maybe tomorrow, but they're forecasting rain for tomorrow, so maybe not. I haven't been here because I've been sick. I'm on a massive dose of antibiotics. Nearly everyone in my building is coughing and sick."

"Do you have pneumonia again?" I asked.

"Not pneumonia, emphysema. My lungs are full of infection."

Shark handed Outcast a sealed clear plastic bag.

"Thanks Shark!" said Outcast. He held up the bag and said, "My teeth! I was wondering whose house I had left these in. When I drink beer from cans, I like to take my teeth out. Usually, I put them in my shirt pocket, sometimes they fall out. I lost my original teeth playing hockey."

Joy said, "It freaked me out the first time I woke up to find a set of teeth on the bedside table looking back at me."

Jacques handed me a copy of the newspaper to sit on.

"Don't you need this, Jacques?"

Joy said, "Jacques always has lots. He needs two copies for his fat ass."

"That's right," said Jacques, "I need two copies for my fat ass.

"I heard that they are changing ODSP *(Ontario Disability Support Program)* to separate the sick people from the addicts and alcoholics."

Outcast said, "I qualify on both counts."

Jacques asked, "What's going to happen when we get a new Premier of the province now that Dalton McGinty has resigned?"

"He's the one who signs our checks. The next guy might cut us off completely.

"Jacques, are you moving?" I asked.

"No, that fell through. It was $850 a month. I can't afford that. I called Shark's landlord; he has buildings all over the city. He's going to try to find me a place. I'm not sure if I believe him too much. He said he'll have something for me. I'll see. I've got 'till the end of the month. Otherwise, I sleep on the street, or at the shelter."

Outcast said, "You're not going to find much for under $850."

Joy said to me in a whisper, "All of these guys have had apartments before, but they were kicked out. I'm pissed off that Little Jake got a place before I did. Even Weasel has a nice apartment. The last place he was in, they condemned; it was that nasty."

Why Don't You Just Kill Him?

18 October 2012

The weather at the park was a balmy 65 degrees. Joy walked toward me, "Dennis," she said, "we were so worried that something had happened to you. I didn't see you this morning and now it's 1:10. We always expect you at noon."

I looked at my watch, "Joy, it's 12:10; this is the time I usually arrive. I was running late this morning because it's garbage day. I came by your spot at about 8:50, but you weren't there."

"We must have just missed each other. I was probably in the coffee shop, I had to pee."

Outcast said, "All of us thought it was 1:00. Yesterday you came by early to see Stella, but she didn't come. Today she came by, but you missed her; you arrived late."

I wore a sweater, but after sitting in the sun for a while, I took it off. With the sun shining on the back of my black shirt, I felt so hot I moved to the shade.

Joy said, "I didn't like the way that Weasel was snapping his fingers at Stella. If she wants to come over to see Bear, she will. That Weasel is such an asshole."

Jacques said, "Stella has always been nice. She's been coming around for a long time, fifteen years maybe."

"Crash was around then," said Joy. "A lot of people have come and gone. Jacques, it's only you, me, Shark and Irene who are the originals."

Somebody asked, "Where's Shakes?"

Joy said, "He's gone to his office."

There were three bees flying around Jacques. He said, "What do you want from me? Is it my beer you're after? I may be stupid but not as stupid as that." As he was swatting at the bees, he knocked his beer over with his knee.

"This morning," said Jacques "the cops came by. They ask me to pour out my beer. I tip it upside down and say, 'It's empty. I just save the can for recycling.' They didn't even check my travelling mug. It was full of beer."

Outcast said, "I'd just opened a fresh beer, I took one swig. The cop said, 'Take one swallow and pour the rest out.' He still gave me a ticket."

Joy said, "Rodent was by earlier. What a piece of work he is."

Outcast said, "I don't like him either."

Jacques said, "You guys! Nobody likes him, so why don't you just kill him?"

I said to Jacques, "That's a straight-forward, simple solution. Why didn't anybody else think of that?"

Joy said, "That asshole, Chester, really gave me a hard time yesterday. He was drunk. He always gets abusive when he's had too much to drink. I phoned him this morning and asked him, 'Is everything alright with us? You were so angry last night.' He said, 'Everything's fine,' but he just walked by and waved. He said he's going to pay ten per cent on the hydro bill, so they don't turn the power off. I gave him money for hydro; he spent it all on beer. He's going to Rodent's place now. Usually when he goes out, he leaves me the electronic key so I can get into the building, but this time he didn't. I have my own key for the inside door."

I said, "Couldn't Chester have a copy made for you?"

"He could, but I don't even want to go there. I should be able to get in. I'll just have to wait until someone unlocks the door; I'll slide in behind them. I hate doing that. I feel like a thief.

"Next week I go to see my worker, it's about getting my identification. I said to her, 'Little Jake, André and Hippo all needed their identification replaced. They only had to wait a few weeks. Why is it that I've been waiting since January?' She couldn't give me an answer. She said that she'd look into it."

Just Asking for Trouble

22 October 2012

When I arrived at Joy's spot this morning, she said, "Man, am I glad to see you. Have a seat on my cushion, it's warm. I'll be back in a few minutes."

When she got back I asked her, "How was your weekend?"

"It was quiet. I don't know what was going on with my stomach, but I couldn't keep anything down. I made some really good soup in my crock pot. We had leftover chicken, I added veggies, rice and noodles, but I couldn't even keep that down. Most of the weekend I slept or watched TV from my bed."

"How has Chester been?" I asked.

"He was okay Saturday, until he went to the Mission for his supper. When he came home, he started coughing. I said to him, 'Chester, now is the time to cut back on the cigarettes for a while.' He chain smokes, one right after another. When he coughs, he makes a really loud noise, like a dog barking, so I didn't get much sleep last night.

"This morning, he got up just after I did. First thing, he had a cigarette, then the coughing started again. I said to him,

'Have some chicken soup and rest for the day.' He said he would. He may come down and visit with the boys for a while."

"Did anything happen after I left Friday?" I asked.

"Not much, I got into it with red-haired Debbie. It was funny — some of the government ladies, who come out for a smoke, saw us. They were talking to me today. They asked, 'What was going on between you and that woman? We thought you were going to kill her. It was hilarious.' I said, 'I'm glad I was able to provide you with some entertainment. I wouldn't have killed her, but I would have come close.' They asked, 'What did you have against her?' I said, 'Do you mean besides the fact that she's a fuck puppet for all the guys and has a big mouth?' They asked, 'What do you mean by that?' I said, 'She's slept with Chester, André, Little Jake – I don't know about Jacques — anyone else that's been around. She has HIV/AIDS and doesn't use condoms. Little Jake had HIV, but he must have full-blown AIDS by now.'

"I said to the ladies, 'You should see me with the guys. I don't take shit from anybody. If someone gets smart with me they'll get either a punch or a kick in the head. I can take care of myself, believe me.' They said, they thought I could.

"By the way, André may be in jail now. Chester saw him coming out of the liquor store. As soon as he cracked his bottle, two security guards grabbed him. I've asked him before, 'If you boost a $7.45 bottle of sherry and lose your freedom, is that a good trade?' "

I said, "He told me he never boosted from liquor stores, well, only once."

"It was more than once, believe me."

At noon the curbs were crowded. There must have been close to a dozen people. Joy made room for me and Jacques gave me a copy of the newspaper to sit on. Joy was talking to

171

Dennis Cardiff

the group, "I was told by a lady cop that, in their opinion, one of the city's finest is a serial killer, responsible for the murders of prostitutes over the last ten years. It would make sense — a person with power and authority, armed."

"How about the cop that beat you up, Joy?" asked André.

"I didn't report it. I went through that in Montreal, I didn't want to go through it again here.

"I grew up with this guy. His name was Luke. He was a handsome guy, but he became a tranny — called himself Lucy. He made a gorgeous woman, but a guy can never hide his Adam's apple. He was out with a guy who thought he was a chick. When the guy found out, he killed him.

"I knew a lot of transvestites in Montreal. They were really nice to me, invited me to all their parties. I was a fat chick, but I was cute. The apartment they lived in was beautiful, draped fabric in the living room, like a tent. It was really over the top, but nice. Someone handed me a pellet shaped lump of hash. I said, 'What do I do with this?' The guy said, go into the bathroom and take it like a suppository, up your ass. It will give you a body high as opposed to a head high.' I went into the bathroom, but I put the hash in my purse. I didn't want to be any more fucked up than I was. When I came out of the bathroom the guy asked me, 'How does it feel?' I said, 'It feels a little uncomfortable.' He said, 'You must be a virgin.' People kept handing me this stuff. They were stoned, but I put it all in my purse. By the end of the evening I had a half ounce of hash. I didn't need to hook at all."

Weasel said, "Do you remember that cop we called Sasquatch? I met this woman at the Mission; we started getting it on, then she invited me over to her apartment. A while later we heard a loud knock on the door. I'm standing in my underwear. She opens the door and it's Sasquatch, all seven-foot two of him. The woman was his former girlfriend.

172

When he got through with me, even my socks were soaked with blood. Has anyone seen him around?"

André said, "He's in Cornwall. He's my uncle. I can remember we were at a party one time. He leaned on the apartment door — the whole thing came down and went through the door opposite. He was standing there looking sheepish. The people from across the way were dumbfounded. He said, 'I guess I shouldn't lean on doors anymore.'

Joy yelled across the sidewalk to Glenda, "What are you drinking?"

"Wiser's, Devil's Cut."

Joy said, "Would you mind keeping it under your sweater, or in your bag. The cops come here regularly. I wouldn't want to see you to get a ticket and have to pour out your whiskey."

To me she said, "Look at Shakes, he's laying in the middle of the sidewalk. This crowd is just asking for trouble. In a few minutes, I'm moving down about twenty feet to where the benches used to be.

"Glenda, Debbie and Gnome drank all Shakes' sherry, smoked all his cigarettes and all his pot. Now that they have whiskey, do you think they're going to share with him? No way! Glenda asked me where the liquor store was. I told her. She asked, 'Will you come with me?' I said, 'No, for one thing I'm barred, for another I have everything I need, besides that, I don't know you.' With her size she'd be slow getting up. I should be able to get a few shots in, but if she caught hold of me, I'd be in trouble. What do you think?

"Actually when I look around, there aren't too many people here I would trust. Little Jake may remember something, sometime, and just blurt it out. Hippo is too soft. André and Jacques, I don't know. Shakes, I'd trust him with my life, in fact I have. He stood up to Big Jake to protect me, until I told him to just stay down. There was no point in both of us taking a beating. Nobody could take on Big Jake."

To Chester Joy said, "When you leave, I'm going to give you my cigarettes to take home. Andre's been bumming off me all day, so has Shakes."

Serge in Hospital

23 October 2012

This morning, André was standing at Joy's spot. I said to him, "Don't tell me; Joy had to pee."

"You got it."

"How's your morning going, so far, André?"

"Lousy — twice, while I was panning, the cops pulled up and told me to move along."

"How about trying someplace near Shakes' office?"

"That's where I was."

"How about Silver's old spot?"

"Jake's there." Joy returned. "I guess I should move along, let Joy get to work."

After he left, Joy said, "That's the third time he's been by here. I finally had to tell him that he was interfering with my business."

I asked, "Did he tell you when he'll be going to court?"

"No, he didn't show me the paper. He has two charges against him. One for the bottle of sherry, and one for three hundred dollars worth of meat from the grocery store. They found it in his backpack. He could hardly carry it.

"Have you heard about Serge?"

I said, "No, I haven't seen him lately."

"He fell and hit the back of his head. I told him that he should go to the hospital to get it checked, but these guys are stubborn. The same with Silver, he had a swollen leg — instead of going to a hospital he went to the Shepherd, now he's dead. Anyway, Serge had another fall. This time he hit his forehead. One side of his face is all bruised. He's in Intensive Care at hospital."

"Are you sure it wasn't a beating?"

"That was my first thought, but Chester was in contact with his workers at the Sally. The medical staff at the hospital say that blood from his forehead is pooling in his cheek. The only thing keeping him alive is life support. They don't know how to contact his family. There are so many Serge Roberts' in the phone book."

Chester came by, but didn't stay long. He saw a bag of mini chocolate bars that somebody had dropped for Joy. "Are those for me?" he asked. Joy just scowled. He left to talk to Jake, in Silver's old spot.

"That asshole, yesterday I came home to find that he had invited Sylvain and Yves over. They had eaten all the soup. I had half a roast beef sandwich from the coffee shop that I put in the fridge. Chester asked, 'Is that my supper?' I said, "No, dude, you get your own. I'm tired of buying all the groceries for everyone else to eat.

"Last week, I bought a dozen eggs, I got two. Of the pot of soup I made, I got one bowl. I stashed some bologna, Chester found it and ate that too. I said to him, 'Chester, I haven't eaten for days. Do you think of me at all?'

"I'm feeling so frustrated, and with Chester coughing all night, I'm not getting any sleep."

I said, "You have an appointment with your worker tomorrow. Do you think anything will come of that?"

"Yesterday she was supposed to meet with André at 10:00. She didn't show. I'm going to ask for a new worker. Janice is teaching this new girl. I thought they'd know what to do before they hire them. The time she's taking for training is time she's not working on finding me a place.

"Pat and Chantal are the ones who found places for Hippo and Jake. I don't like Pat, but if he can find me an apartment, that's all that matters. Otherwise, I'm thinking of asking them for a sleeping bag and go back to sleeping behind the coffee shop. I'd leave my stuff at Chester's.

"Sometimes, I just don't want to be here."

"Do you mean panhandling?" I asked.

She said, "I used to be able to take a break when I got my check, but now I can't. I just don't want to be on this earth."

I phoned the hospital to enquire about Serge's condition. Telling them that I was his brother, I was able to speak to the nurse in the Intensive Care Unit. She said, 'He was doing okay, but he kept losing consciousness, so we brought him into ICU to keep an eye on him. He has a breathing tube now. He's suffered a cerebral hemorrhage — bruising and bleeding to the brain. We're hoping to take the breathing tube out tomorrow, see how he is then. We'll just take it one day at a time.'

"Dennis," said Luther, "I told you I'd get my guitar back, and here it is. I had an electric, but I sold it.

"Do you know what happened to my baby? They chopped her up. I saw the body. It was her sixteenth birthday party. They got out of control with booze and drugs. That's why I drink. How do I forget about something like that?

"I'm also evil, especially when I drink, that's what my girlfriend says. The doctors say I have psychotic tendencies."

I said, "Don't worry, Luther, that can be treated. I know you're a good man."

"I'm not Ojibwa," he said, "I'm Dene. Do you know many Dene people?"

"Some," I said.

"Do you know them to be honorable people?"

"Very honorable."

"Would you give me money to buy a beer?"

"I don't carry cash, but I can give you a card for a sandwich."

"Okay," he said. I handed him the card.

"Actually, I have another of these. I could sell them for $2.50 each, enough for a bottle."

"It's your choice, Luther."

"No, I'll give it back to you. Give it to someone who is hungry."

"What was that all about?" asked Joy.

Luther said, "I don't mind accepting money, but I don't want to be told what to spend it on."

I asked Joy, "How have things been since this morning?"

"Okay — I'm not too happy about Luther and Gnome being here."

André said, "It wouldn't take much for me to ask them to leave."

"I don't mind asking him to leave, don't worry."

Luther said, "Ugly Rambo sitting with the pretty Indian woman."

"Luther," said Joy, "I don't appreciate you making remarks about my friend, Dennis!"

"Joy," said André, "he's referring to my uncle. They used to call him Rambo. He was going out with Luther's sister. It's a long story."

"Well," said Joy, "I don't want to hear it."

André asked Joy, "Can I bum a cigarette?"

"Okay, this time, but that's it. I appreciate you getting the bottle of water for me and doing a liquor run before that, but you're becoming too much of a burden to carry. That goes for all these guys."

André said, "I understand, Joy."

Later in the day I phoned the Salvation Army. They had taken Serge to the hospital. The outreach workers had already left for the day, but I left my phone number in case I could be of any help in finding Serge's family. The hospital was having trouble contacting any relatives. There are so many Roberts in the phone book that it would be difficult to phone them all.

I visited him tonight, but he was asleep the whole time. He is under light sedation and is being administered Tylenol for pain. His head has been shaved, he has a bruise on his forehead and his right eye is black, apart from that he appeared to be resting comfortably. They don't have plans for any surgery. He has been admitted previously for falls. I was surprised that they had his age listed as 55. He looks much older.

Bear's Birthday

24 October 2012

This morning, as I approached Joy, she waved, got up and headed towards the library. When she returned she said, "I've been waiting for you. I had to pee so bad. I slept outside last night."

"Why?" I asked.

"Chester's drinking again. When he does, he gets all touchy feely. I'd had enough, so I packed my bag and slept behind the dumpsters in back of the coffee shop."

"Do you have a sleeping bag?" I asked.

"No just this blanket, it was cold." It was 35 degrees last night.

"You have an appointment with your worker today, maybe she could get you a sleeping bag."

"I'm just so fed up!" she cried, "My legs are aching. I'm half in the bag. There is a commercial on TV that says, 'It's now time for that second talk' — referring to menopause. I need to have that second talk, but I have nobody to talk to. I remember my mother going through it. She was all over the place. I'm just losing it, man!"

"Perhaps you could talk to your worker about that. Also, Stella is coming down this morning."

"I sure hope so."

"She sent me an email. She wants to celebrate Bear's fifteenth birthday. She has a card and a big bone for him."

"I hope she brings the coat she promised me."

"I saw Serge in the hospital last night. He was asleep the whole time I was there. He had a breathing tube in his throat and oxygen going in his nostrils. The nurse said they may take the breathing tube out either today or tomorrow, depending on how he responds. He had a slight fever so they had a cooling blanket that looked like an air mattress on top of him. That's common with head injuries. He sure looks younger with his head shaved."

Joy said, "They would have done that for the lice. When he was picked up last time, by the outreach workers from the Shepherd, they shaved off his beard. I'm glad it's not more serious. I can't take any more deaths right now."

André stopped by and said to Joy, "I see Jake is at Silver's old spot."

Joy said, "Jake is family. I had to kick Al out of there this morning. Later I saw his girlfriend, Angeline. Her arm was in a make shift sling and was all purple. She said, 'Bo did this to me.' I said, 'I hope you got him back.' She said, 'After he had punched me three times in the head, I stabbed him in the side. That slowed him down.' Bo is going to be on a lot of shit lists. These guys got to learn not to treat women that way."

I said to André, "How's your day going so far?"

"Lousy, I'm barred from every McDonalds in town, the liquor store, and both grocery stores. The list of places I can go is getting shorter and shorter."

"What happened at McDonalds?" I asked.

"I was panning out front of one and the district manager was there at the time — he barred me. He said, 'I never want to see you in front of any of our stores. If I do, or if any of my staff does, the police will be called immediately.' That was a good spot for me.

"I stole a cooked chicken, and some other meat, from the grocery store. I was hoping to have a real feast. So much for that idea."

Joy started getting restless. She said, "I've had about enough of this place, and I've got to get my legs moving. I want to get drunk."

I had agreed to meet Stella at the statue of the soldier, near where the group usually meets. All the regulars, including Bear the birthday dog, were there. Jake and Weasel were near coming to blows.

Shakes said, "Will you guys keep the noise down. Soon the cops will be coming."

"Shut up, Shakes," said Weasel.

"I won't shut up. I'll talk as much as I want to. Nobody's going to stop me."

I said, "I'm glad we got that settled, Shakes!" He laughed.

Loon was drunk, has no teeth, and was talking nonstop over the din of the arguing.

Outcast asked me, "Do you understand a word he's saying?"

"No," I said.

Outcast said, "I've just come from Shark and Irene's place, I think Loon was there earlier. They were nodding off, so I left. Give it a few minutes, Loon will be doing the same.

"Dennis, you coming at ten o'clock throws my whole schedule off. I think I should be having lunch now."

"Sorry, Outcast, but I came to see Stella, not you."

Joy said, "I've known some of these guys for twenty years. I've known Chester for a long time too. It really hurts when he treats me and talks to me the way he does. Do you see the scar above Loon's right eye? I gave that to him. One time he grabbed me by the crotch and I decked him. His forehead split open like a tomato. He's never tried that again, the piece of shit. I'm really surprised that I haven't got into a fight yet today. There's still time."

André was sitting quietly. He said to me, "Sometimes it's safer to not open your mouth."

I asked Jacques, "Do you know if Serge has any family?"

"I don't know. I've known him for a long time. He's never mentioned any family to me."

I said, "I wonder if his friend William knows about his family. Serge stayed with him for a while."

"No, I asked him that. He said, 'I think, maybe, he came from Vancouver or Montreal. I can't remember which. I think he has a sister in Montreal.' Vancouver, Toronto, Montreal — that's a lot of people there, and Robert is a common name.

William has been kicked out of his place. When Serge stayed there, a neighbor complained. He said that Serge was dealing drugs. Can you imagine Serge dealing drugs? I've never even seen him smoke a joint. He just sits quietly. I like that. I talked to Serge about maybe sharing a two bedroom apartment, but now he's nearly dead. I also thought about sharing a place with William, but he was given notice the first night he was at his new place because he was making too much noise. If you're given notice three times, you're out. That's what happened. I don't want to be in the middle of a situation like that, not me. I'll just get me a bachelor apartment, it doesn't matter how small, just someplace quiet. That's what I want.

"Yesterday I found a tent in the garbage. It looks brand new. I set it up in my living room. I've never seen a tent so small. It would only fit one person. There is no way that two people could get in there. If I don't find a place by the end of the month, maybe I'll be sleeping outside. I don't think for too long. Who knows?"

Jake sat next to me. He said, "I've blown my $350 start-up allowance. Now, they're asking for receipts. DOES ANYBODY HAVE ANY RECEIPTS? I NEED SOME RECEIPTS."

Joy asked, "Did you punch Weasel?"

"No, but I spit on him.

"I went to my HIV doctor and he wouldn't give me my needles."

I asked, "Why?"

"I don't know."

Two workers with the Salvation Army came to talk to Shakes. "How are you coming along with my housing arrangements?" he asked.

"We're looking at a few places, the problem is they become available December first, so we'll have to find someplace temporary for you from the 1st to the end of November. Don't worry, we're working on it."

Weasel and Stella were getting ready to leave. Stella showed me the card she had made. It had pictures of Bear as a pup, with his original owner Henri.

Joy said, "I remember when Henri first got Bear. There were two puppies in the back seat of a car. Henri was to choose which one he wanted. Bear jumped out the door and came straight to him. The other dog just sat there. That decided it. They were together until he died."

Bear wandered over to me. I held my hand out — he bit it.

Cutting

25 October 2012

This morning I met with Joy and André. Janine, one of Joy's regulars, dropped two dollars and squatted down to chat. Joy asked her, "How did it go with your dentist appointment?"

"They took x-rays and found all sorts of cavities. In the old days, you'd have a cavity, it would be painful, then you went to the dentist. Now, it seems, they're always filling something. I don't know what they're doing in there."

Joy waved at Magdalene and Alphonse across the street. They came over. Very excitedly, Alphonse said, "Magdalene is pregnant again. She went to see about an apartment yesterday. She's been put on first priority. We find out today if she'll be accepted."

I asked, "When is the baby due?"

Magdalene said, "We're not sure. I took a home pregnancy test and it showed two pink crosses. I'm not taking any drugs or alcohol now."

Alphonse said, "Same with me." He looked longingly at a gram of pot Joy had in her cigarette case. "That looks so good," he said. They walked off together to have breakfast.

Joy handed André a cigarette paper and the pot. He said, "You want me to roll it?"

Joy said, "Well, how is it going to look if I'm panning and rolling a joint?"

André went into a nearby alcove for a few minutes, then came back with a joint that Joy put in her cigarette case.

I asked Joy, "Where did you sleep last night?"

"At Wolf's. I'd been at Outcast's until Debbie came home, then all hell broke loose, so I left. I was walking past Wolf's place and saw Shaggy on the balcony. I called to him and Wolf came out. He asked, 'Where are you going?' I said, 'I'm going downtown to sleep behind the coffee shop.' He said, 'Come on up.' He threw me the keys. 'You can stay here.' His place is in more of a mess than I've ever seen it. He said, 'I know Joy, I'm going to get around to that sometime.' Also, he has cockroaches. At least they don't bite."

I asked, "Were you able to talk to Stella about menopause?"

"Yes, she said she could talk to me until my ears bled, but it wouldn't do any good because every woman is different. My being bi-polar and schizophrenic just makes it all the worse.

"I go to see, Annie, my probation officer, today at 10:00. Hopefully, I'll find out how many more visits she wants me to have. November twelfth is the day my probation is supposed to end, but I may have to see her after that. I don't know if it will be once every two weeks, once a month…

"I've had three sessions with Christienne. It's probably more time than I would've had if I'd been with a group. She's going to be away for a couple of weeks. They said, 'It's no problem, we're all trained, others here are familiar with your case. We can arrange an appointment with someone.' I said, 'I signed a confidentiality agreement with Christienne, nobody else. I don't want to start from the beginning again with a new person.'

"I don't want anybody to know that I've started cutting myself again either. Annie asked, 'Why do cut yourself?' I said it's hard to explain, but when my mind is going a hundred miles an hour, in a ten-mile per hour zone, I don't know where I'm going to stop. I need something to distract myself. Cutting does that for me.' Mind you, the second time I cut myself I was thinking, 'Hey, this hurts, I don't want to be doing this.' Chester nearly freaked when he saw me coming out of the bathroom with a towel wrapped around my arm. It was a deep cut too. It was gaping open. I didn't want to go to the hospital this time. I used band-aids to pull the skin together."

I asked, "Where will you sleep tonight?"

"I have to go home to get the rest of my clothes. Chester doesn't want me to leave. I don't know what I'm going to do."

I arrived at work and phoned Craig from the Salvation Army. He has been in telephone contact with the hospital concerning Serge. I said to him, "I understand that you're trying to contact Serge's family. I've talked to everyone I know and even his closest friend, William, said, 'He's either from Vancouver or Montreal, I can't remember, and he may have a sister in Montreal.' I didn't learn anything more definite than that. Craig said, 'I've heard the same stories, probably from the same people.'

"The latest news from the hospital is that they've taken the breathing tube out. He's still in ICU, but seems to be doing fine. Later tests will determine if he'll have any lasting effects from his fall."

I hope to visit Serge in the hospital this evening.

At noon I met the gang at the park. They were all in their usual places.

I asked André, "How was the rest of your morning?"

"It was okay. I had to fill out another form for my ODSP *(Ontario Disability Support Program)*. They lost the last one. This is four times I've filled out the same form. Joy and I have the same worker, Jenna. She's been busy lately, so we're going to be switched to Susan. I've known her from before. She guaranteed that Joy and I would have our own apartments before December 1st. I hope so, because once it gets close to Christmas, it'll be hard to get things delivered. I'll be getting an $800 start-up allowance to buy furniture. I'll be able to get a new double bed from Sears. I don't want to spend Christmas sleeping on a bare floor. I'll also get a $100 for groceries."

I asked, "Do you know when your court date is?"

"November 2nd. It'll probably be in Courtroom 5, but to find out for sure, all I have to do is check the dockets. I think I'll have it remanded until I'm able to contact my lawyer. He's sometimes hard to get a hold of."

Wolf called me over. "I appreciate you helping me out the other day. I drank too much, I couldn't make it home, so I slept outside. I wasn't here yesterday because I was too hung over. At my age I can only drink for two days, then have to take a day off. I don't know how these guys like Weasel do it. He came to my panning spot at seven in the morning and he was drunk already. I had to tell him to get lost. My regulars know that I'm an alcoholic, but they don't want some stumbling, incoherent drunk hanging around. He was pissed off when I told him to go, but we're okay now. I'm going to his place this afternoon. Shaggy can play with Bear and I'll cook supper. It'll be chicken or some kind of fowl, that's what I like.

"I got a surprise the other night. At 9:00 at night someone is banging on my door. They'd managed to get through the lobby door. Usually I don't let anybody in. If any of these guys came over, I'd tell them to fuck off. If I was expecting somebody, they'd yell and I'd throw the keys down. I looked through the peephole, and it was Joy.

"I guess you heard how Chester was trying to paw her. I can't understand these guys. You don't touch a woman without her permission. They can't seem to get that through their heads.

"I asked her, 'Tell me the truth now. Outcast invited you over to his place, then when Debbie came home, he threw you out. What's that all about? That's no way to treat a friend.' I've got no use for him anyway. He's living with one woman and invites another woman over when he's alone. That doesn't seem right.

"Anyway, I invited Joy to stay the night. I gave her the sofa and I slept in my room with the door locked, but first I told her, 'I wanted to watch Law and Order, C.S.I. and Criminal Minds. Those are my favorite programs and I'm not going to miss them.' I've only got one channel, and with rabbit ears, sometimes the signal doesn't come in too clear, but that night the reception was good. Some people need HBO and all the movie channels, but I get a hockey game Saturday night, a NFL game on Sunday and all my favorite shoot-em-up shows. It's all I want, besides, I can't afford the hundred dollars a month. If I wanted them badly enough I could afford them — like if I quit drinking.

"I spend a lot of my time reading. If you saw my place, you'd see books laying all over the floor. I always have a few going at a time. Every so often, I like to come down here, have a drink with my friends. I take Shaggy for walks. She's getting old so she needs to go out five or six times a day.

"Joy asked me, 'Does anybody else have a key to this apartment?' Now, what do I look like? Would I let other people come and go as they please in my place? You know me better than that. I like my privacy, but Joy was paranoid. I said to her, 'No, there is nobody that has a key to my apartment.' She relaxed after that. She was up at 5:30 in the morning, off to her panning spot."

I mentioned that I would be away in San Diego on vacation.

Wolf said, "I've never been to San Diego. I've been to Florida, Philly, Detroit. I haven't been to Chicago or New York. If I was to go there, I'd turn right, right again, right again, another right and I'd be back where I started. I wouldn't want to find myself in some dangerous neighborhood and not know my way out.

"I have a brother in Virginia. There are a lot of red necks down there. The confederate flag is flying everywhere. If you get caught with a doobie, you get tossed in prison and they throw away the key, but — and this is a big but — you can carry two loaded guns. It's in the constitution, and you can buy your beer and ammunition at a gas station. (*I've since been informed that gas stations don't sell ammunition; Walmart does.*) I don't know how I feel about that. On the one hand, you know everybody is armed, so you don't cause them any unnecessary aggravation. You know what I mean? On the other hand, having a psycho on the loose, carrying a loaded gun, is a scary thought.

"I'm on a pension. After I pay my rent, I've got $300 for everything else. It's not much. I'm an alcoholic, my drug of choice is beer. I may have an occasional blast, but I'm not on Percocet, Percodan, Perco-this, Perco-that. I pan to get extra money. I live a quiet life with Shaggy, enjoy my books, my TV and my beer… that's it."

I asked Jacques if he had found an apartment yet. "No," he said, "I was talking to Shark's landlord. He had a bachelor for $560. I could have managed that, but he rented it to somebody else. If I can't find a place by the end of the month, I'll store my stuff in a locker and rent a room for a while — not too long.

I asked, "How much does a room cost?"

"About $500 a month. A bachelor is $600 and up, a one bedroom, $700 and up, a two bedroom, $800 and up. I thought of getting a two bedroom and sharing with someone, but who would I share with?

Tonight I visited Serge again. They've moved him from bed 29 to bed 1. His breathing tube was out. He didn't seem to recognize me, spoke only French and didn't respond to names of his friends that I mentioned, except William. He scowled and said, "William!" and his blood pressure shot up from 130 to 180. He seemed agitated and pulled out his intravenous tube. The nurse said his confusion is probably temporary, due to his concussion. His blood pressure eventually returned to normal. He sipped from a can of Labatt Blue, then hid it under his hospital gown.

Barfly

26 October 2012

As I approached Joy, she started getting up. "Go ahead," I said, "I'll watch your stuff." She headed to the library. When she returned I said, "I visited Serge, yesterday. He didn't recognize me or the names of his friends, except William. He scowled and his blood pressure went from 130 to 180. He was clenching his fists and pulled out his intravenous needle. What do you think that was about? Do you think William pushed or punched Serge?"

Joy said, "I've never liked that guy. I'd rather punch him in the face than talk to him. I told Serge that his bruises looked more like they had been caused by a fist, and not a fall. I've had a lot of experience in that area. I'm going to have a talk with William."

"Did you sleep at home last night?"

"Yeah, I was tired. I walked in, took one look at the kitchen, and lay on my air mattress. I slept until about 3:00. Chester came home, I said, 'Look at this mess. Didn't you tidy up at all while I was away. I looked in the cupboard and said, 'You've eaten my last can of soup. What am I supposed to eat?' He said, 'Well, I don't have anything to eat either.' I said, 'Take some of the change you've got on the table and buy yourself something.' His check comes tomorrow, maybe he'll buy some groceries, but I'm not counting on it. I've even thought of going back to the women's shelter, just until they find me a place."

A woman stopped and handed Joy a huge lollipop. "What flavor is this?" asked Joy.

"I don't know, all the other ones have been really good."

"Through the wrapper it smells like strawberry. Thanks!"

To me she whispered, "This is the last thing I need. Look at all the food I got: chocolate bars, a club sandwich with chicken, lettuce, bacon and tomato, some kind of bagel, an apple, a banana. Here, you take the banana, it hasn't even touched the sidewalk. After my stomach operation, my doctor told me not to eat bananas, too much potassium, it could kill me. In the winter when I'd get a banana, I'd put it on the sidewalk and when I'd pick it up, half of the peel would be stuck to the concrete. The apple I'll give to Jacques. What I really want is a drink."

"How was the meeting with your probation officer?"

"I'm so happy. I asked her, 'So, when do I come back next? Do I have to report twice a week, once a month?' She said, 'You're done. No more visits, although I would like you to meet with Doris from the Elizabeth Fry Society. You seem to have made some progress with her.' I agreed, I said, 'She's away for a week or so, but when she's back I'd like to see her, but nobody else.' I didn't like the way that other woman talked to me on the phone, let alone sitting in a room with her and spilling my guts. Doris even lets me drink there. I told her, 'If I'm sober, I'm not going to say a word. If I can drink, I'll relax a bit and will feel more comfortable. Some of the shit I went through is still upsetting.'

"I got letters from two of my sons. The youngest calls me Aunt Joy, but he was really close to my mother — I don't mind that. They're both doing well. I'm going to write back to them. Finally, I have contact with two of my sons again."

At noon I said to Joy, "You must be happy, with no probation to worry about."

"I'm happy alright. I'm also drunk. As long as I don't get arrested before November 11th, I'm free and clear. This afternoon I just want to go home and sleep. I have to switch keys with Chester because he's staying out. When I have his keys, with the electronic card for the outside door, I feel like I've got the keys to Fort Knox. I can do anything I want, eat whatever I want, watch whatever I want on TV.

"Chester, when I get home, do I have dishes to do?"

"No," said Chester, "I did them."

To me Joy whispered, "I'm going to have to do them again. He's lousy." She counted her change and gave Chester enough to buy a couple of beer.'

"Sometimes I wish I looked more like a woman. A guy asked me why I wear a do rag. I took it off and asked him,

191

'Would you give me money if I looked like this?' He said, 'No, I guess not.' I said, 'Well, there you go.' Some people think I look like a dyke. I like men, it's just that I don't want to be somebody's property. I like my independence and privacy.

"Hey Barfly, do you know you've got a cigarette burn in the crotch of your sweat pants?"

"Yes, I know. These are my court clothes. I was in court this morning."

I asked Jacques, "Have you found an apartment, yet?"

"No, I'm going to be homeless at the end of the month."

"Are you going to get a locker, and take a room for a while?"

"I checked on the lockers this morning, first thing at 9:00. They want you to keep it a minimum of two months, and it costs seventy dollars a month. I can't afford that. I'm going to talk to Shark, maybe he has a little place in a corner where I can store my stuff. I don't have much, me: my fridge, my microwave, my George Foreman grill and my cooking pot. That's all. If I need anything else I might find it in the garbage. Every week people throw stuff out. I found a toaster, I took it home, plugged it in and it worked great. Did you see my new bike?" He pointed to a new looking bicycle with front shock absorbers. "I bought that for five dollars. It's no good to me. Can you see me riding something like that. Imagine Shakes trying to ride that. He can't stagger straight, let alone ride a bike, same with Jake. He might start off sober in the morning, but in the evening he's all over the place. I sell it for what I paid for it.

"In the place that I'm in now I pay five hundred and ten. That's with everything. That's a good price. I don't need anything big. I threw out my old mattress because of the bed bugs. Every time I move I throw away about 70% of my stuff. I don't like to pay for movers, so I just take what I can carry on my back and what will fit in my cart.

"I spoke to Shark's landlord. He had a place that I really liked but it was eight hundred a month. I can't afford that. There was another that I liked — he rented it. There may be something coming up soon. I like where Hippo is living. He could only get a single bed, the place is so small, but that would be okay for me."

I mentioned to Jacques, "I visited Serge yesterday."

"Yeah, you went? I hear he's sitting up in bed, looking much better. Willliam is going to visit him later today. They are good friends, they both speak French."

I said, "When I mentioned William's name, Serge scowled and his blood pressure went from 130 to 180. He was clenching his fists and pulled out his intravenous needle."

"That's strange," said Jacques.

November 2012

Staying at the Sally

9 November 2012

Joy and André were sitting together, sharing the cold. Joy borrowed a cell phone from one of her regulars and requested that her appointment with the Salvation Army worker be moved up to 9:30.

"Chester had better be home when I go there to get my stuff. He's been a real asshole lately. He's drinking beer and mixing it with sherry. It's making him act really crazy. Last night he was opening and slamming doors all night long. I got even. When I got up four this morning I made sure that I opened and slammed every door at least twice. He asked me, 'You washed your dishes and left mine in the sink?' I said to him, 'Chester, you're just a hair away from having your face punched in, so watch what you say.' I'll be so glad to get away from that place. He's even started stealing my sherry. He snuck into my room and I saw him drink out of my bottle. I bought a carton of cigarettes, I haven't even opened the bag, but I can see there's a handful missing.

"Did you hear that Bear bit André this morning."

I asked, "Were you sleeping outside last night, André?"

"No." Andre said, "Weasel lets that dog lick his sores. Bear could have HIV. He could have infected me."

Joy said, "I told him, 'Weasel, if it weren't for Bear, nobody would have anything to do with you, not even Stella.' He said, 'That's not true.' I said, 'You don't look after her, you're always passing her off to someone else. You take advantage of people. Nobody likes you.'

André said, "When I see him later, I'm going to ask him, 'Do you know what a dog bite feels like?' Then I'll pop him. It was the same when my stepfather would keep bugging me at the table. My mother could see that I was starting to shake, so she told my step dad, 'Keep that up and Andre's going to hit you.' He kept it up, I stood up and knocked him right out of his chair. He was laying on the floor and my mother bent over him and said, 'I told you.'

Joy said, "We have some good news about Serge. Some of the guys and I have been visiting him in hospital. He's looking a lot better. He looks strange with his head and beard shaved. They had to do that because of the lice. He had them bad. Apparently he's lost a lot of weight. They're giving him some beer and sherry, trying to get him off the Listerine. He asked me, 'Joy, could you get me a bottle?' I said, 'No way, I can still smell that stuff on you.'

André said, "It's just like when I was in hospital last, with my heart attack. I lost a lot of weight."

I said, "I remember that André, you were pale, weak, your face was gaunt."

A police car had pulled up, in front of the park, and two officers were talking to the guys sitting on the curb. Jacques waved at me. I waved back.

André came over and whispered to me to me, "I told them I'm just waiting for my worker. This is where she told me to wait for her.

"Dennis, could you do me a big favor. They made me pour out all my liquor. I need a bottle.

"I'm on my way to an appointment, so I can't go on a liquor run."

"I don't have any money," I said."I don't carry any cash, but I'll see what I can do." I stopped in at the Transit Office to pick up my bus pass, then went looking for a liquor store. I found a vintage wine store, but they laughed when I asked for Imperial Sherry. I walked a few blocks to another store and was able to find what André wanted. I brought it back, but he had already left with his worker.

I said to Jake, "André asked me to pick this up for him, could you see he gets it? I know he'd want to share so, could you also see that Shakes gets a drink?"

Some people would think that what I did was enabling, but an alcoholic needs some alcohol in their system or they can't function. Without a drink they also feel very sick.

Casino

12 November 2012

The regulars were gathered in a circle near the Park. Joy said, "I moved to my apartment on Friday. My back is sore, because I don't have any furniture, just an empty room. I sat in the middle of the floor all weekend. Yesterday, Mariah brought me down two folding canvas chairs. She also brought me some kind of a quilt or comforter. I opened the bag and it stunk. I said to her, 'You brought me dirty laundry?' I took it to the laundromat nearby, they have only one double washer and no double dryers. They ate quarters like you wouldn't believe.

"Wednesday we go to Chester's place to pick up the rest of my stuff, mostly shoes.

"When they cut a tree down in my back yard, some of the bark got tracked downstairs. There were these little wood worms that curl up when you touch them. All morning I was flicking these with my thumb. It was just like playing marbles with my son."

I said, "It must feel good to have a place to go to where you can lock the door, it's quiet and you can do whatever you want."

"It will take a bit of getting used to, but I have lots of security. There are three doors that have to be unlocked in order to get to my place."

I asked, "How about your health card, will you be getting that soon?"

"Yeah, I really need to be on my meds."

I said, "That should make a big difference in how you feel."

"My fibromyalgia is really acting up in my legs and my arms."

Luther came over, "I'm sorry to hear about the son you lost (my son isn't lost). You have my condolences. I was telling you last week about my daughter that was lost, actually it wasn't my daughter it was my god-daughter. Her father is doing time in prison — twenty years for murder. So, while he's in jail I'm responsible for her."

He showed me his birth certificate from Prince Albert, Saskatchewan. He said, "See, my last name is actually Italian."

"I'm in trouble with my partner. I have addictions. I went to the casino — I can count cards — I made some money. The dealer said, 'I can see you're a card player.' I said, 'Take me to the Blackjack table.' I won ten thousand dollars, but the cops were standing at the door waiting for their cut. I walked up to them. I asked? 'Do any of you have a smoke?' One handed me a cigarette. I asked, 'Do you have a light?' He pulled out his lighter and lit my cigarette. I don't smoke. They asked, 'Did you have a good night?' I said, 'No, I lost.' Then I walked out the door with my case full of money. I spent it on my brothers. It all went on booze."

A squad car pulled up with two police officers inside. One of them said to Outcast. "We saw you throw a can into the bushes. We're going to have to charge you." He pulled out his pad and wrote a ticket.

The other officer was writing a ticket for Weasel.

He asked André, "Are you keeping out of trouble?"

"Yes officer, I'm sober. I have been for three days."

"How about you Luther? Why are you standing so close to me? Is this some kind of a confrontation?"

Joy said, "I wouldn't stand too close to those dreadlocks. If you look close you can see little white things. It isn't dandruff."

Two more police cars pulled up. Female officers got out of each car. One said, "How's everybody doing?"

Joy said, "I've just moved into a place of my own, so I dropped by to visit some of the guys."

"That sounds good, Joy. You should be at home having a house-warming, not down here."

"Most of these guys I wouldn't invite over. If I had a party, would you come?"

"I think I'd pass on that, but thanks anyway."

One of the female officers came over to André. She reached down and picked up his leather gloves. "Where did you get these?"

"I bought them at the Sally Ann."

"They look a lot like a pair I lost." She examined them inside and out. There was a call on her radio, a group of twenty people were leaning against the wall at the Mission. They got back in their cars and left. The other two left shortly after."

André said to me, "The reason she was looking at my gloves is because when she stopped me a few days ago I stole her SWAT gloves. She stopped me yesterday and I stole another pair."

Joy said, "I'm so glad they left, I'm on the last day of my probation and I've got pot in my backpack and a bottle under my sweatshirt. Those female officers could have searched me and my bag."

Baghdad

13 November 2012

I joined the group standing near the park.

Darren asked me, "We've met before, haven't we?"

"Yes," I said, "I saw you yesterday and I also met you two years ago down the street, where the benches used to be. You told me that you'd lived in Boston and that you'd been in the army."

"It was the Marines. I was in Baghdad and Afghanistan. When we'd walk along the streets, there would be bodies just lying there on the sidewalks – dead bodies. We'd smell the rotting flesh.

"I've been getting these migraine headaches. It feels like someone hit me with a baseball bat at the back of my skull."

I asked, "Was that because of your car accident?"

Alphonse said, "He's had a tumor."

"Yeah, where this missing patch of hair is. The surgery wasn't so bad; it was the chemo that I really hated. I'd keep throwing up and wouldn't be able to stop. It was every morning. I went to the doctor recently about the headaches.

He ran some tests. I don't want to go on morphine; I've already got one addiction, I don't need another. I have to go back October 31st. Halloween – I think it's this Thursday — to get the results."

"Darren," said Alphonse, "it's November thirteenth, Halloween was two weeks ago."

"Do you mean I missed my appointment?"

I said, "It's no problem, Darren, phone them, they can make another appointment for you."

"I've been staying in shelters, but I hate it. To wake you up in the morning they kick you in the foot."

I said, "I've heard that there are a lot of crackheads there, getting up every hour, walking around, keeping people awake."

"Not only that, but they smoke crack in the bathrooms. The smell makes me sick. It's like burning tires. My former wife used to be on crack. I'd wonder where all our money was going. We could never seem to get ahead. One day I came home and found two guys on top of her. One of them broke my leg. I took our two kids in the truck and they stayed with my mother. The next time I saw her she patted her backside and said, 'Kiss my ass.' That's the last time I saw her."

Alphonse said, "Magdalene has been going to a women's shelter to have a shower and get cleaned up. She said there are always women smoking crack in the bathrooms."

"Yeah," said Magdalene. This morning I saw a woman with a hypodermic needle to her throat. I don't know what she was shooting. I couldn't believe it."

Alphonse said, "We have some good news. We've applied for assisted housing and I think they've found us a place. They still have some other applications to go through, but I think we're going to get it. We'll a get a 'street allowance' because we're living on the street. We've also made application for

O.D.S.P. *(Ontario Disability Support Program)*. We'll be getting a health card and a bus pass."

Darren said, "Congratulations! Lately, I've been sleeping outside. I really admire you guys — sleeping outside for two and a half years.

"I was in court this morning for a pre-sentence hearing. Do you know Old Alphonse?"

"No," I said.

"Anyway, Old Alphonse gave these two kids money to buy a bottle. It was a girl and a guy. They never came back. Later on I saw them. I grabbed the guy in a headlock and took him back to Old Alphonse. He didn't have the money, he'd spent it on crack, so I laid into him. I felt a hand on my shoulder and without thinking, I threw a punch. It was a cop. He didn't identify himself. How was I to know? A couple of them jumped me, had me in hand cuffs face down on the ground. One had his knee on the back of my neck. The others put the boots to me. It was the fat blond woman who split my ear. I think they have metal plates on the toes of their boots.

"One lawyer told me I should sue. Another told me to let it go. I've got until January 1st to prepare my statement."

Alphonse said, "Something similar happened to me and Magdalene. We were panning down the block. A guy came along and lay down beside us. Magdalene told him to move along. He got up to swing at her and I clocked him right at the back of the jaw. He fell into the street. The police and ambulance came. I told them what happened; that I was just defending my woman. There was a woman nearby who also witnessed it. The cop said, 'Alphonse, you shouldn't have done that, but I understand why. Just move along and we'll forget about it.'

"So, Dennis," said Darren, "you seem to know what it's like for us. Have you ever slept on the streets?"

"No, but my brother did. He slept on the streets of Calgary. After not eating for three days, he was ready to jump off a bridge, when someone suggested that he join the Army. He had to lie on his application, because he had been dishonorably discharged from the Navy. When they found out that he'd given false information, he was already in Korea. Later, he became Eastern Canadian Boxing Champ. He was alcoholic and got into lots of fights. He's dead now — asphyxiated on his own vomit, sleeping in a Toronto hotel. He'd also been robbed and beaten."

"I'm sorry to hear that," said Darren.

"We sure got wet last night," said Alphonse. "I gave Magdalene my inside pants because hers were soaked."

I walked over to talk to André and Shakes. "Hi, André, how have you been?"

"So, now you decide to come over and talk to us. I thought we were being ignored."

"No, André, it's just that I haven't seen Darren for a long time. How has it been going with your worker?"

"Thursday, I signed the papers for my health card. I filled out the application for housing. Now I'm just waiting. I see my worker again on Wednesday.

"Shakes and I slept outside last night. We were picked up by the cops. They phoned the shelter, They said they had room for us. When we got there they said they were full, so they took us to the Sally. They said they were full – at 9:00 they're full. I think they were pulling something. I can't believe that in buildings with four floors, that they couldn't have found a space for us. I would have been happy to sleep on the basement floor. It would have been better than being in the rain, but they wouldn't let us in."

I asked, "Did Jake give you the bottle I brought you?"

"No, I saw him last night. He didn't say anything about a bottle."

"Friday, the afternoon you had the meeting with your worker, the police were writing tickets. You asked me if I could do you a favor and buy you a bottle. I said, 'I'll see what I could do.' I knew that you guys would have had to pour out all your booze, so I brought back a bottle of Imperial sherry from the liquor store. You weren't there so I gave the bottle to Jake. I said to him that you'd probably want to share it, and to make sure Shakes got a drink."

"I didn't know that. Thanks!" Actually I didn't pour out my booze. I didn't have any to pour out. I was sober Friday, Saturday and Sunday. I spent the weekend at my cousin's."

Shakes had his head down. With his hat on I could barely see his face. I bent down and looked into his eyes. "Hi, Shakes, how are you doing. Are you getting there?"

"Hi, Dennis, I'm getting there, slowly but surely."

"Shakes, I heard that you were robbed twice last week."

"Yeah, twice."

André said, "What happens is — it doesn't matter if you have a pad lock on your locker or not — guys will come, in the middle of the night, with bolt cutters and cut your lock.

Everyone knows that Shakes will have a bottle, some pot and some change. I think it's the staff, they've got access to bolt cutters."

Milk Boxes

14 November 2012

As I approached the group in the park Shaggy started barking. Wolf said, "She's okay, she just wants you to scratch her. She leaned against my leg and I scratched behind her ears and along her side.

It took me a few minutes to recognize Serge. He had new pants, shoes and winter jacket. His hair and beard was just starting to grow out since they shaved him. He still had a bump on his forehead and the left side of his face has some yellow bruising. I said to him, "It's good to see you Serge. Do you remember me visiting you in hospital?"

"Yes, I remember."

"William said he was going to visit you. Did you see him?"

"No I haven't seen him since before I went to hospital. I have to go there every day. They put a needle in my arm."

I walked across the street to another group that included Donny in his motorized wheelchair. Eventually, Serge walked slowly across the street to join us.

It took a while for Jacques and the others to recognize him.

Jacques said, "I saw that guy over there and I wondered to myself, who is that guy, he looks familiar. I wonder what he's doing there." Jacques and Chester both spoke to Serge in French.

I said to Joy, "It must be nice having your own place to go home to."

"Yeah, except for the fact that I've got no heat. The bathroom faucet sprays all over me when I try to brush my teeth, so I use the kitchen sink. My air mattress leaks. They brought over some furniture: a wooden chair that looks like it's been used for painting, a three shelf bookcase with a hole kicked through the middle shelf and a lamp. The only thing I like is the lamp. I phoned my worker. I told her that my fibromyalgia is really bothering me, so I need a decent place to sleep and a comfortable chair."

Jacques said, "What you need is one of those folding garden chairs, the lazy boy recliners with a thick mattress on it."

"Do you have any extra?" asked Joy.

"No I only have the one. I had some other garden chairs, but they got all wobbly from people sitting in them crooked. I threw them out. What I'm looking for is bunk beds — the metal kind. I'll sleep on the bottom and on the top I'll have plastic milk boxes. I won't need a dresser, I'll just put all my clothes and stuff in the boxes. It'll make it easier for moving."

André asked Joy, "So, when are you going to invite me over to your new place?"

"Never. Can't you take the hint, André. I don't like you. We aren't friends. The only thing I'd like to do is take a gun to your head."

"Joy, I can just see you in army fatigues, holding a gun. You'd look so hot."

"How about I take a machete to you?"

"That image is even sexier."

"André, I'd rather do myself than have you anywhere near me. You're drunk. You think you're being entertaining, but you're not. You're just babbling and nobody's listening."

André said, "I guess I got told."

I said to Joy, "Your place must be quiet."

"Yeah, the only thing I hear is The Bear."

"What do you mean?" I asked.

"Mariah brought me down a radio. I've been listening to The Bear FM. They've got some good music."

I said, "You should try Dawg FM."

"Yeah, I have. They play some cool blues."

Alphonse said to me, "At 3:00 today we go to sign the papers for direct deposit. Housing Outreach will pay a third of our rent, directly to the landlord. We've already signed the application for the apartment, so we're one step closer.

"Thank you my friend, for helping us. We won't forget it."

Shakes said, "I'll be getting a place on December 1st. It'll probably be near Jake's place. I'll have to take a few days off from coming down here. I'll be refurnishing and I'll need to get a bus pass."

Sarah walked across the street. Joy said to Danny, "She's got the hots for you."

"Yeah, I know, but she spells trouble with a capital T, make that three T's. I've been out with Inuit women before and when they drink they want to fight."

Joy said, "I don't know what it is with you white guys and these muk-muks. The last time I saw that one she was an inch away from my face and she spit when she talked. I put my hand on her head and pushed her away. She went to take a swing at me, but Inuk clocked her. She said, "You don't touch my Joy."

Jake came from across the street. He had been talking to Wolf.

I shook hands with Shakes, he was smiling. He held on to my hand and nodded toward Jake. " Jake," he said, "Did you give that bottle to André?"

Jake asked, "What bottle?"

"The one Dennis gave you, to give to André?"

"When?"

Shakes asked me, "What day was it, Dennis?"

"Friday."

"I don't know anything about a bottle.

"Oh, I remember. I waited until nearly six. André didn't show up. None of us had anything left, so we drank it."

Cockroaches

15 November 2012

"Good morning, Metro" I said, "I'll take a paper today." He smiled because he knew I would be using it, not for reading, but for insulation between my backside and the sidewalk — not that it made any difference to him. When he's handed out his daily allotment of papers he goes home.

At noon Wolf and Shaggy were sitting at the curb, at the park, while the rest of the group was across the street.

"Hi Wolf," I said, "You're all alone here."

"Yeah, well, I don't like to take Shaggy over there, because the traffic is so heavy — more chance of her getting killed. She's already been hit by a car, I don't want that to happen again. She's all I got. Even if someone calls Shakes she's ready to run across the street. She's crazy that way, just like the dog in the cartoon — you know the one — her head is all over the place.

"It's cool today, isn't it. I don't know why those guys think it's warmer over there. They have to come across to my side of the street to piss, then Shaggy wants to follow them back. I should charge them a toll. What do you think?

"Look what I got this morning. A lady gave them to me, red, Olympic mittens, with the crest on the back and 2012 on the palm. I've already got gloves but I was really happy to get these.

"Tomorrow, Stella's bringing me some between season shoes. These sneakers have mesh on the top and sides that lets the cold in. I've got winter boots for forty below zero, but they're heavy and awkward. I don't want to wear them in this weather.

"It's time for me to take a leak. I'll probably see you tomorrow, since I'm coming to see Stella, anyway. I have to get my fresh air and I like to have a couple of beer outside. I'll see you then."

I walked across the street to where the group was congregated. I sat on the curb. Jacques handed me a copy of the Metro to sit on.

"It's not much," he said, "but it helps."

"Thanks Jacques, I had my own, but forgot it at work."

Joy said to Shakes, "I'll trade you seven for one... okay eight for one. Come on Shakes, my last offer nine for one. I can't believe he's saying no to me. Okay ten native cigarettes for one Pall Mall.

"No," said Shakes, "I'd have to walk all the way to the corner store to get some more."

"Shakes, "said Joy, "you're going there anyway.

Donny, in a wheelchair, reached into his coat pocket and handed Joy a tailor-made cigarette. She gave him ten native ones.

"Donny, can you ask your brother to do me a big favor? Can you ask him if he'll go to the liquor store and pick me up a bottle of Imperial sherry?"

Donny said, "He says he'd go, but he has some errands to run first." Donny's brother left on his bicycle.

Debbie asked Joy, "Why can't you go there?"

"I'm barred, ever since I punched Drew Carey in the head."

"You mean, Drew Carey the actor?"

"No the short, fat fuck with the glasses. We call him Drew Carey. One time a few years back when Digger and Old André were still here we went in. I was standing behind Digger. The guy behind the counter said, "You stink, why don't you take a shower?"

"I said to him, 'Hey man, just because these guys sleep outside doesn't mean they don't wash. What about you? You live with your mother, sleep in her basement. She makes your lunch every day.' After that I just lost it. I jumped over the counter and started pounding on his head. They have a picture of me in the back. All the staff have been told not to serve me.

"If you think you can get in, you can get yourself a beer on me. I'd really appreciate it."

"No problem." Said Debbie, "I could use a beer, then I have to go to work panning.

"So, how's your new place?"

"It's good. At least I don't have to listen to Chester coughing and complaining all the time. I've got some wood bugs, from when they cut the tree down in back. They threw all the wood down the stairs to where my apartment is. They took the wood out, but the bugs stayed. They're those kind that roll up into a ball when you touch them. I thought I'd swept them all up yesterday and could go out my back door with just my socks on, but there they were again. On the weekend, when I was drunk and stoned, I was playing marbles with them, flicking them against the wall. They would have been better off if they'd stayed with their brothers outside."

Shakes said, "I haven't played marbles in forty years."

Debbie said, "I know all about those bugs. When my kids were young, I used to go into the forest, find a rotten log and take the bark off. Some of the pieces were almost six feet long.

I'd wrap them in a sheet — that's the only way I could carry them — bring them home and put them under my kids beds. Whenever they'd see me with one of those sheets over my shoulder they'd say, 'No, Mom, not the bugs again.' I'd brush off the bark, let it dry then hang them on my walls. They looked really nice.

"Now, I've got cockroaches. I didn't have them before, but the exterminators came to my door and said they were spraying the whole building. I said, 'You can't spray here. It would kill all my plants.' They said they could use a gel that wouldn't be harmful to plants. That sounded good, but this gel, I found out, attracts roaches. The exterminators brought roaches in on their clothes, now I have a problem."

Joy said, "Wolf has roaches, so did Jake in his old place, Weasel had them, but his place was so bad they had it condemned. He'd pulled all the plasterboard off the walls, the windows were broken and snow piled up inside. Rodent's place was nearly as bad."

Debbie said, "I like Rodent."

"Rodney the Rodent, he's the one sponsoring Big Jake, for a place to live, after he gets out of prison. He gives me the creeps. He came to Chester's place in the summer when me and Outcast were there. We were all in the back yard. Chester was wearing shorts and had his shirt off. Rodney sat right next to him. He was rubbing Chester's back, pinching his titties and touching his thigh. It nearly made me and Outcast sick. Chester went inside and put on long pants and a shirt. He told me that Rodent made him feel uncomfortable. Chester only had one beer and was working on his second. All of a sudden he's acting really drunk. I think Rodney dropped some pills into his beer. I can only imagine what happened when Chester went to Rodney's place alone."

Debbie asked, "Where is Big Jake now?"

"Collins Bay — it was right around this time of year that he went into prison, so it's been fifteen months since I've been with a man. You remember my Jake don't you? Sometimes they used to call him Sasquatch."

Debbie said, "I went seventeen years when my kids were growing up.

" Timmy's just leaving. What do you think of him?"

"I wish he'd wear tighter pants, it looks like he's got a good bod."

Respect Your Elders

16 November 2012

There was a large yellow garbage truck parked in front of Joy, who was talking with the driver. I walked up to him and said, "Hi, I'm Dennis. I always say hello to you, but I don't know your name."

"It's Delmar, I don't give my name out to too many people. It's a habit from my past."

Joy said, "That's a nice name. I'm the same. When someone asks my name I ask, 'What do you think it is?'

I said, "Or you say, 'What name did I give last time?' "

Joy replied, "I generally don't carry a wallet, or identification. I just don't trust people."

Delmar said, "It's time to get back to work." I held out my hand to shake his. He said, "You probably don't want to shake this hand, because of where it's been."

Joy and I sat down. I asked, "So, how was your night? Are you getting used to the place?"

"Now, that my workers have me in an apartment, it seems they want to forget about me. Hippo got a brand new bed from Sears when he moved in, so did Jake. I want a new futon, so I can fold it up during the day. My worker offered me a hundred-dollar gift certificate for their store. She said, 'Maybe you can get a futon there.' I don't want someone's used bed that they've cleaned up a bit. I've had enough trouble with bugs.

"I've never liked the Salvation Army. They've never helped me before, so I never donated money to them, or the Mission either.

"They fixed my bathroom sink. They checked the heating and said that the pressure was low. He adjusted it, but I've still got no heat. I'll call my worker again. I turn on the oven to low. That keeps the apartment warm, but at night, because of menopause, I get night sweats and have to open the door from my apartment to the hallway, to get some cool air in. That works fine."

I asked, "Aren't you worried about security, leaving your apartment door open?"

"No, there's another door to the outside. Only me and my landlord have a key to that door.

"I haven't been sleeping too well. I've been sick, throwing up every morning. I asked André to get me a bottle of sherry this morning to settle my stomach. I'm feeling a bit better now. I'm pissed off with him though. I've never led him on. I've told him I'm not interested and never will be; not if he were the last man on earth, but he keeps picking, picking. This morning he bent down to kiss me. I said, 'Go away, man.' He said, 'It was worth a try, anyway.' I said, 'I talked to Debbie and she told me how you treated her.' 'Yeah, well I got a cut on my cheek.' I said, 'You deserved it.' Here's a woman who has opened her door to this guy, she feeds him. After he gets out of the shower, he comes out stark naked, with a hard-on, and says to her, 'Take your clothes off and lie down on the bed.' She said, 'No fuckin' way, man! Now, get out of here!' He punched her in the chest, then backhanded her. If it was me I would have knocked him out, dropped him in the hall and threw his clothes on top of him."

I said, "Apparently, he doesn't believe in romance or foreplay."

Joy said, "I asked her, 'Did he at least have the decency to put on a condom?' 'No,' she said. That was the day of the Dr. McGillicuddy's fiasco."

"What does that mean?"

"André and the boys were drinking Dr. McGillicuddy's Peach Schnaps. That stuff'll kill you. Chester was drunk too. He asked me why I was leaving, I said, 'It's cold. I want to go home and lie down. My legs are sore.' He said, 'Well, fuck you then. Maybe, I won't let you have the rest of your stuff back.' He staggered half way across the bridge and did a face plant. Somebody phoned the police and he was taken by the paramedics to the Shep'. If he did hold onto my stuff I'd feed his dentures to him piece by piece.

"I was always told to respect my elders. It doesn't seem like Chester and I are that far apart in age now, but he's nearly twenty years older than me. I take care of these guys, and they treat me like shit.

"I remember when my son called my mom a crusty old bitch. I sat him down at the table and said, 'Don't you ever talk to your grandmother like that again.' He said, 'She pissed me off.' I said, 'Don't talk like that, and if she pissed you off, it must have been something you did to cause it.' He said, 'So, you can talk that way and I can't.' 'That's right, because I'm your mother.' He said, 'You lay a hand on me and I'll call 911.' I leaned over towards him and gave him a head butt —

knocked him out cold. My mother came in and said, 'What did you do?' I said, 'I just knocked him out. He's not dead or anything.' When he came to he asked, 'What did you do to me. That's not right.' I said, 'I didn't lay a hand on you. Now, I want you to apologize to your grandmother.' He went over to her and said, 'I'm sorry grandma, I won't talk to you like that again.' He never did either."

At noon, Darren said, "I see you nearly every noon hour. What brings you up here?"

I said, "The conversations here are more interesting, than what I hear at work."

"Yeah, I guess that's true, eh? We all have a story. I went to my worker to try to get my rent money, but she wouldn't give it to me. She's going to hold onto it until the first of December, then give it directly to my landlord. I didn't fight it. She said to me, 'If I give you this money you're going to spend it on booze. Am I right?' I wasn't going to lie to her, I'm an alcoholic, the first thing alcoholics think about is booze. For me it's beer and the occasional joint."

"I can understand that," I said.

Joy saw Alphonse and Magdalene approach. She said, "Alphonse, the Salvation Army Outreach workers were looking for you this morning. You should call them." Alphonse borrowed Jacques's phone and arranged to have the workers meet him and Magdalene at the corner.

André passed Joy a joint, he said, "Don't give it to Jake, because he's been told he has a spot on his lung. It could be TB. He was honest about it, you've got to give him credit for that."

Outcast said, "TB is the most contagious disease there is. You don't want to share a joint with a person who is even suspected of having TB. It's rough for Jake, but that's the way it is."

I sat next to Jake on the sidewalk. "How is it going in your new apartment? Do you have any more furniture?"

"I've got a bed and an air conditioner, still in the box. That's all. Chris has a TV for me. I just have to find a way to get it to my place and get the cable hooked up."

"It must be nice to have a place you can come home to, where you can lock the door, where you're warm. It was only a few months ago that you were sleeping behind the dumpsters in back of the coffee shop."

"Yeah, it's good. I just wish I was feeling better. I've had a chest x-ray and a spot showed up on my lung. I don't know what that's all about. I'm throwing up every morning. I've got no appetite."

I asked, "Have you been eating?"

"No, just the thought of food makes me sick. I'm on two thousand milligrams of some kind of penicillin. When the pharmacist saw the prescription he said, 'That's a very high dose.' "

"Hippo," I said, "How is your new apartment?"

"I got a leak coming from the water main. It's dripping down my wall. They're going to have to replace the gyprock. Apart from that everything's fine. Tomorrow they're having the Santa Claus Day parade."

"Are you going to come down and see it?"

"No, I'll just watch it on TV. Jacques, do you know when the Santa Claus Day parade starts?"

"I think it's ten o'clock, I'll have to check."

Shakes asked, "Dennis "Could you help me walk? I've been sitting too long and my knees are wobbly."

"Okay, Shakes, no problem. Do you have problems with arthritis in your knees?"

"Yes, they get stiff." As we passed the hotel Shakes said, "I'm going to stop in here. I've got to go for a whiz."

Self-Sufficient

19 November 2012

This morning I noticed that Joy was wearing the army parka that Stella had given her last week. She also had two garbage bags with her, filled to overflowing.

"Someone dropped these blankets off for me, but how am I going to carry them? My backpack is already full with my blanket and other stuff."

I said, "Perhaps, André will come by."

"He's already been here, I told him to move along. He said, 'People are used to seeing me here. I'm not going to scare off any of your traffic.' I said, 'Yes you are, Mondays are slow enough without you hanging around.' Anyway, he has his court appearance today."

"How about Jacques?" I asked.

"I'm going to give some of these to him anyway, but I don't know if he'll be coming by."

"I can take a bag to work and bring it to you at lunch, if that will help."

"That would be great. I didn't get a lot of sleep last night, so I'm not in a very good mood. The guy in the apartment above me was stomping around, up the stairs, down the stairs. I think he gets up to eat about once an hour. I can hear him get up from the couch, walk to the fridge. There will be silence for about a minute, then he walks back to the couch."

I asked, "Have you tried ear plugs?"

"No, but I don't think I should have to. I left a note on his car windshield. I'll see what happens after he reads that."

I knew that Joy wasn't much in the mood for company, so I said, "I'll let you get back to work and I'll bring this bag to Jacques at noon."

"Thanks, I'll see you at noon."

At noon I gave the bag to Jacques. He thanked me then headed across the street.

Wolf said, "Can you help me up. I was lying around all weekend reading my two books. I took Shaggy for her walks, but I guess I need more activity, or calisthenics. When I woke up this morning, my back was so stiff I could hardly get out of bed.

"Right now, I have to go for a pee, so I'll see you a bit later."

I walked across the street to where the other group had congregated . Shakes was dozing.

"How has your day been, Joy?"

"I made enough for a bottle, that's about all."

Joy said to Mariah, "I was kept awake last night by the guy upstairs stomping around."

"Yeah, I heard him too. He's been told about it. I don't know how somebody can eat as much as he does. I know I couldn't."

Joy said, "I'd think he'd be fatter than he is. It must go right through him."

"I've caught him with his clothes off, he has a round belly, but you're right, he must have a fast metabolism. That's probably why he can't seem to stay still. I wouldn't want to have to pay their bill for toilet paper."

Joy said, "I wouldn't want to pay their grocery bill."

André came across the street, beaming. "I went to court this morning on the charges of stealing meat from the grocery store. My worker gave me a really good character reference, saying that prison time would undo all the progress I've made in the past six months. The judge asked me, 'Why did you steal the meat, André?' I said, 'Well, your honor, I had no money and I was hungry. I know that I could have gone to the Mission, but I was trying to be self-sufficient.

'I'm an alcoholic. If I'm prohibited from drinking I'll be back in court next month. I've tried, but I can't stop drinking.' "

"The judge said, 'One year's probation with no reporting, and stay away from the grocery store.'

"I was just standing there with my head down, shaking. I couldn't believe my good luck."

Hippo said, "I got one year probation with reporting. At first I had to see my probation officer once every two weeks, then they reduced it to once a month. I think I've still got about six months left."

I asked Hippo, "How is your apartment. Have they fixed the leak?"

"No, they sent a Housing Support worker. He said, 'It's dripping alright, but I can't do anything about it. We'll have to send a plumber.' That's what I told them in the first place."

Michelin Man

20 November 2012

Joy was layered with clothing. She pulled up the cuff of her pants to show the pajama bottoms she was wearing for extra warmth. She also wore a tee-shirt, heavy sweater, hoodie, then her army parka.

She said, "I look like the Michelin Man, but that's okay. I like guys to think I'm fat, then they leave me alone. We don't have any 'chubby chasers' around here. The only one I have trouble with is that one (pointing to André), but he's learning. Then there's Weasel. Yesterday, I saw him talking to Wolf across the street. I heard him call me a goof. Wolf said to him, 'Joy heard you say that.' I walked over and said to Weasel, 'Whenever I have anything to say to you, I've got the guts to say it to your face, you goof.' I was hoping to see him today, but he didn't show."

I asked her, "Have they turned on your heat yet?"

"No, I talked to the landlady last night. She's nice, but she doesn't speak very much English. She thought I was complaining that her TV was too loud. I said, 'No, it's your husband walking so heavily on the floor.' She said, 'I told him about that.' Then I heard her yelling at him. I keep the oven on at a hundred and fifty degrees with the door open. It shuts off by itself. The top of the room gets warm, but it's still cold near the floor. My worker said that she's going to bring me a space heater."

From across the street came Jake, wearing a surgical mask. Joy asked, "So, masked man, what did the doctor tell you?"

"It's either a lung infection, pneumonia or TB. They've doubled my antibiotics. I'm wearing this mask so I don't infect any of you guys."

Joy said, "What did I tell you? I said, 'It's either a lung infection, pneumonia or TB.' I was right."

I asked Jake, "How are you feeling? Do you have pain in your lungs?"

"Yeah, it's worse in the morning. You should see what I cough up. It's disgusting."

Timmy said, "I was talking to my worker this morning, she said, 'We might have a place for you soon.' I asked, 'Should I call you back in a couple of days?' She said, 'Call me first thing tomorrow morning.' While I was in her office I saw an email. It had Joy's name on it. There was a list of furniture items: table with two chairs, arm chair...'

Joy said, "I hope they had a futon on that list."

"Yeah, a futon was on the list." I heard her say, 'Now we have Joy taken care of.' "

Joy said, I don't know where I'm going to put a table. I guess I'll use it to put my toaster on. I also need a TV so I can see Coronation Street. I've already missed two episodes. That Tracy sure needs a bullet between the eyes. Chester was saying something about a gay guy and a girl getting together, but I didn't know what he was talking about.

"Does anybody know where I can get a TV? Even one of those small black and white portables would be better than nothing."

André said, "They'll take you to their warehouse. They have hundreds of TVs there."

Joy said, "All they gave me was a coupon for a hundred dollars and it has to be used at either of their Thrift Stores. I don't think I'm going to find anything I want.

"Yesterday, I saw Evan holding hands with Sharon. I asked him, 'When are the wedding bells going to be ringing?' He didn't say anything."

Timmy said, "I really don't like that Sharon. I had a party one time. I bought six cases of twenty-fours. I asked her if I could have a sip from her bottle. She didn't exactly say no, but she put the bottle in her bra, like she does. After that I didn't want a sip.

"One time, early in the morning, I was walking under the bridge. On the hill was a woman with her pants pulled down to her ankles and her shirt up over head. I went closer and saw that it was Sharon. I kicked her in the foot. She woke up. I said,

'Get yourself dressed.' She said, 'I promised myself that I wasn't going to do this anymore.' Later, I saw Gerald. I told him what I'd seen. He said, 'Yeah, that's the way I left her last night.'

"She's so young. She should be in school or something, not getting drunk every day like we do. Does she think that when she's forty-five she's going to be able to get any kind of job? I don't think so."

Joy said, "Yeah, I see so many of these kids. Some of them could be at home, Like Chili, she's only twenty-four and look at the shape she's in. She phoned me from the hospital and asked if I would come visit her. I yelled at her, 'No, I'm not coming over, because if I did I'd probably punch you in the mouth. You were doing so well when you visited your family in P.E.I.. Now, your doctor has you on medication and you're smashing crack into your arm. You're going to kill yourself.' "

Timmy said, "The last time I saw her she was in a wheel chair. I think she has to have a hip replaced, and she's having trouble with her knees.

"Someone that really likes her is Rocky. I was at his place a couple of weeks ago. He has a really nice place."

Joy said, "Rocky really gives me the creeps. A couple of years ago me, Rocky, Jacques, and Shakes were drinking in the park. Jacques and Shakes passed out so it was just Rocky and me. He said to me, 'I'm horny.' I said, 'Dude, that's a personal issue. It's got nothing to do with me.' He said, 'No, I mean I want to have sex with you, right here, right now.' Big Jake was down at the market with Rodent, so I said to Rocky, 'I'll tell you what. You go down to the market and ask Big Jake's permission to have sex with me. If it's okay with him, it's okay with me.' Rocky had this look in his eyes like, I'm going to take what I want now. I just got up and walked away. I've never trusted him since. He's just too creepy."

Blessed

21 November 2012

Joy was in her usual spot this morning, talking to Delmar the garbage man.

"Hi Delmar," I said.

"Hello, Dennis."

Joy said to him, "So handsome, when are you coming over to visit me in my new place, or would your wife object."

"I think she'd object."

I had a newspaper to sit on, but instead I knelt beside Joy, "How are you making out today?"

"So, I came down with seven dollars, I've had drops of three dollars plus some jingle for my cap." I was there for about ten minutes and half a dozen people dropped change into her cap. "You're lucky for me, Sunshine, I was doing lousy before you came along."

"Do you have heat?" I asked.

"No, the landlord came down with a plastic card that looked like a fridge magnet. It was a thermometer. He waved it around, looked at it and said, 'It's a balmy eighty-six degrees in here." I took the card and put it on the heater it registered eighty-two. I kept the card over night and put it in the hall to the outside. There is no heat in there at all, it's the same as the outside temperature. The thermometer read seventy-seven degrees. Last night it went down to freezing. So, I'm done with that. I'll be getting a space heater from my worker and until then I'll leave the oven on."

"How about your neighbor, is he still noisy?"

"I talked to him last night. He was stomping around so I got a shovel and banged on my ceiling. He came down a few steps and kicked on my door. He said, 'What's the idea with all that banging?' I said, 'That's what I hear every time you walk across the floor. So, you can either walk more quietly or you'll get the same in return, your choice.'

He said, 'Maybe we should let the police decide.' I said, 'Sure,' and rhymed off the number for him. 'When you're on the line ask for McQuaid, Curzon, Santorini, Warrington, Harris. Just tell them that you were talking to Joy, they'll know who you mean.' He asked, 'So, you've been in trouble with the police?' I said, No, man, these are family. They're married to my sisters.' That shut him up.

"Here comes trouble."

André was scowling as he approached. "I'm so pissed off. Alphonse and Magdalene sat down beside me. Alphonse asked me for a smoke, then he asked if I had anything to eat. I gave him some pizza, He said, 'I don't like it.' Then he said, 'You're sitting in my spot, would you mind moving on.' Can you believe that? He's lucky I didn't kick him in the head."

At noon I stopped to talk to Wolf and to give Shaggy a scratch. Wolf said, "Hello , Dennis. See the leather coat some lady gave me. This will have to be my Sunday coat, not my going to the store coat. I certainly won't wear it when I'm panning."

He didn't have his dentures in, so he was a bit hard to understand. "Isn't this a beautiful day we're having? 46 degrees, the sun is shining. Tomorrow is supposed to be the same, then we get snow on Saturday. I guess we should appreciate days like this when we have them. Today we're blessed. I'm going to go for a whiz, so I'll see you later."

At the corner the Salvation Army Outreach van was parked. They were handing out socks and purple print underwear.

Outcast brought Shakes a pair of underwear. Shakes said, "These are large, I need a medium. I don't want to have to be hitching them up as I walk down the street."

Jacques said, "They gave me these socks. I think they're nylon. They won't be warm for the winter. See the nice boots that Stella brought for me this morning — real winter boots. I'll put some oil on the leather so they're waterproof and I'll be all set.

"See this paper I got." It was a letter from Jacques' former landlord claiming back rent of $15.00 a day for eight days and a storage fee, for his belongings, of $10:00 a day.

I said, "You're in your new place now, aren't you?"

"Yes he handed this to me when I was picking up the last of my stuff. Some people stay fourteen days and he doesn't charge them. I'm not going to pay this.

"Oh, Oh, here comes Willy. He's staggering. When he's drunk he likes to fight. You know, he served twenty years for murder."

When Willy came across the street Joy started singing:
Oh, where have you been,
Willy Boy, Willy Boy?
Oh, where have you been,
Charming Willy?

Shakes asked, "Have you ever been to sea, Willy?" He was referring to an old Captain Highliner commercial. He said to Willy, "Over at the van they're giving out socks and underwear, if you want some."

"No, I don't want anything to do with those bastards."

Outcast came over, "Dennis, I got an invoice from the city for unpaid liquor violations from December 2010 to now. The total amount is $5,600.00 They're going to be waiting a long time for that."

Joy came back from talking to her worker. Outcast said, "Tell Dennis about the problem you're having with your neighbor, and who you saw today."

"I told my landlady about the problem I was having with my neighbor. I said to her, 'When he walks across the floor my cabinet doors shake.' She doesn't speak very good English and thought that my cabinets had fallen off the wall. When I came up here, snow fences were being put up across the street. Guess who was installing them … My neighbor. I went over to talk to him. He asked me, 'Why did you rat me out to the landlady?' I asked him, 'Why do you think, you stupid fuck?' Then I gave him the finger, smiled and said, 'Your turn will come.' He doesn't know who he's messing with.

The landlady phoned my worker, the one I just spoke to. They both had been in a panic. My worker drove down here to meet me. She was crying. So, we have that straightened out. I asked her, 'So, I'm not being kicked out am I?' That was my big concern. 'No,' she said, 'you're not being kicked out.' I'm going to lay low for a while. I've asked the landlady for more

things in a week, than I've asked other landlords in years. I don't want her to think that I'm a nuisance. I'll just see how it goes."

Jogging Pants

22 November 2012

As soon as I arrived at Joy's spot she said, "Sit on my box. I have to go to the bathroom and I'm not allowed in the pizza place. They say that I'm bad for business. Go figure."

When she came back I asked, "Did I miss anything yesterday, after I left?"

"No, nothing much happened. Weasel showed up."

"Yeah, I saw him on the sidewalk, as I was leaving. Any word about your health card?"

"I think it's all going to happen next week when they bring my furniture."

I said, "I can't believe that it's taking so long."

"I know, I'm not too happy with one of my workers. The young one with all the stuff about love and crap. She's the one that was crying yesterday. I told her, 'I need someone who can keep it together. The other worker has been to sessions at E. Fry with me where I've really spilled my guts. I've told things that I've never told anybody before. If you start crying, I'll start crying.' She said, 'I just want you to know that you're loved and that we care for you.' Anyway, I don't need that shit. The sooner I'm done with them the better."

I said, "Outcast said something strange to me yesterday. It was when André was talking to the worker in the van. Pointing to André he said, 'There's something fishy going on. If I'd been charged like André, I'd be behind bars. Instead, he's free as can be, doesn't even need to report to a probation officer.' "

"I don't trust anyone anymore. Of the original crew, there's only Jacques — Digger's around but he's in a home — there's Shark and Irene, but she's sort of new. Shakes, I've known since I was about twelve years old. He's seen me grow up.

"André has a cousin, five times removed, that's on the police force. Maybe, she's doing something for him. I don't know.

"He was pissed yesterday that I left with Outcast. I got a hammer and nails from Chester and wanted some help hanging a quilt on my wall. Andre's shorter than I am, so he'd be no use."

At noon the weather was unseasonably warm at 52 degrees.

Hippo was reading a grocery flyer. "What are you looking to buy, Hippo?"

"Cat food."

"I didn't know you had a cat."

"I didn't until last night. It was mewing at my door at 1:30 am. I opened the door and in he came. He's awfully scrawny.

He said to Jacques, "Here are the sausages I like. Three bucks for a three pack."

"That's pretty good."

I said to Jacques, "You showed me your winter boots from Stella. Is there anything else you need for winter?"

'No, I think I have everything. Instead of long johns I like to wear jogging pants. They hold more warm air next to your skin."

I said, "I have the kind of tights they use for skiing."

"Yeah, for sports they need something that will stretch when they move. Us here, we don't move so much; just raise our arm to drink a beer, that's all."

I noticed that Shakes was wearing a white watch. I asked, "Is that watch new, Shakes?"

"Yeah, I just got it yesterday. I bought it for two or three dollars from Danny. I stayed at his place last night. I got a new bag, 'cause my old one was stolen. Look what else I got!" He pulled a giant plastic beer bottle, meant for storing change. He put it to his mouth as if he was drinking... ha, ha, ha, ha."

I said, "The cops are sure going to be surprised the next time they stop by."

"Yeah, they sure will."

Mariah's cell phone rang. She checked to see who was calling then said, "I don't want to talk to him. I rather be in the sun and fresh air, not stuck inside somewhere."

I asked Jake, "How are you feeling today?"

"Better than yesterday. I was panning today, made six dollars. I go to my HIV/AIDS doctor tomorrow and my other doctor next week. I have to find out what's going on in my head."

"Are you having headaches?"

"No, seizures. I had one yesterday. I think it's due to all the medication I'm taking. I have to make sure that I eat when I take the antibiotics, otherwise I feel really sick."

Oxymoron

23 November 2012

I approached Joy and she said, "Shakes is here to keep my spirits up. I'm sure glad you guys are here. Do you see the short guy with the orange vest across the street. He keeps staring at me. I see him taking bags of cement into the underground parking garage. I had to go to the bathroom and I asked him if he'd keep an eye on my stuff. When I came back there was a coffee, a cranberry explosion muffin and a breakfast sandwich on my box. I asked the guy where it came from. He just shrugged his shoulders. I gave the coffee and sandwich to Shakes, I'll save the muffin for Jacques."

"Shakes," I said, "Joy tells me that you two have been friends for a long time."

"Yeah, since she was thirteen or fourteen. I used to take care of her. I took care of other people too, ha,ha,ha."

I said, "That would have been when you were in your prime fighting shape."

"Yeah, I was in my prime then."

Joy said, "Remember when we ran through Allan Gardens, chasing all the drug dealers away?"

"Yeah, I remember that… ha, ha, ha.

"Dennis, I slept last night at the Bank of Nova Scotia kiosk, where they have the banking machines. I'd been sleeping when a friend, Pauly came in. He said, 'Hi, Shakes.' He did his business at the automated teller machine, he gave me two dollars then he left. I heard a beeping coming from the machine. He'd forgotten to take out his receipt and bank card. I ran after him but I couldn't find him anywhere. I looked at the receipt, he had seven hundred and thirty-five dollars in his account. I've still got his card, so if I see him, I'll give it back to him."

I said, "You could turn in the card to the bank. They'll make sure it gets back to him."

Joy said, "Shakes' hoping to get a reward."

Shakes said, "Maybe he'll buy me a bottle.

"You know, I may have been a thief sometimes, but I'm an honest thief."

Joy laughed and said, "Shakes, you kill me. That's an oxymoron if I ever heard one."

"What's an oxymoron?" asked Shakes.

229

Joy said, "It's two words used together that have opposite meanings, like jumbo shrimp, alone together or honest thief. If you're a thief you can't be honest. If you're honest you can't be a thief."

I asked Joy, "If you could have three wishes what would they be?"

"I'd like a house in the country, all to myself, close to nature. I'd like just enough money to get by, and I'd like to be healthy."

I asked Shakes the same question. He said, "I'd just like to be me." He gestured with his hands as if to say, 'All this is mine.'

Joy said, "You are YOU, Shakes, or maybe there is a real you and an imaginary you. I don't even want to think about that."

One of Joy's regulars stopped by and said, "How are you, Joy?"

"I'm great. Two weeks ago I got my own place."

"That's great. How do you like it?"

"I'll like it better when I have furniture and heat."

The woman asked, "You don't have heat? Won't they fix that for you?"

Joy said, "I asked twice, I don't want to ask any more. First thing in the morning, I turn the oven to 500 degrees with the oven door open. Once the place warms up I turn it down to 150 degrees. It turns off automatically. I don't pay for electricity. I'm on an air mattress now and the floor is cold, but once I get my bed I'll be up where the heat is. Also, my worker is supposed to bring me a space heater."

The woman said, "Just make sure you don't fall asleep with the oven on. That could be dangerous."

Joy replied, "I always turn it off when I go to bed, or if I'm going out for a while."

It's A Vicious Cycle

27 November 2012

There was a crowd at the traffic island. The first person to greet me was Jacques, "Have you any news?"

"Yes," I replied, "I visited Joy last night at the hospital."

"How is she?" asked André."

I replied, "She's in a lot of pain from her fibromyalgia. The pain was previously just in her legs, but now it has moved into her back and neck. She was first given an injection of Delaudid. She threw up, but felt better later. Then they started giving it to her in pill form and it just made her nauseous. She's hoping to get morphine, but in that case she'll need Gravol."

"She'll get a good buzz from that," said Jacques. "This is the third time in hospital for her this year. That's not good. I don't know how much time she has left."

André said, "That's a wakeup call from the Man upstairs. She has to quit drinking altogether."

I said, "At least she has her own place now."

Jacques said, "Yes, that's good, but you can't stay all by yourself, all the time. I can't. She'll want to come down and talk to her friends sometimes, even when it's cold out."

Timmy said, "I saw my workers this morning. I've been leaving messages. This morning I decided to go to the office and they were there. They're going to look at a place for me. If it looks alright they'll show it to me tomorrow. They have to check it out first, to see if it's livable. I don't care what it's like, I grew up in a place worse than you can imagine. Do you know Lachine?"

I said, "No."

"I've got to get off the street. I'm losing my patience with people, they way they treat us. One day, I'm just going to flip out. I'll need Valium just to pan.

"I have some skills, I'm a specialized gas fitter, but there's not much work in that field. I'm a welder, but I don't have my ticket. They offer a seven month course in welding at Seneca that I might qualify for. It costs about five thousand dollars. The government will cover one time re-training. It's sort of like a student loan.

"It's a vicious cycle living in shelters. In order to get a job they want me to have an address where I can receive mail and phone calls. If I'm living at a shelter it's sometimes difficult to get any sleep, so I'd either miss work, or be so tired that I'd get fired. In order to get an apartment, they want me to have a job. I can't win."

I asked, "How long have you been on the streets, Timmy?"

"For a while, in Montreal, then Vancouver, but I really can't count Vancouver, because I was working there."

I said, "You'll never freeze to death in Vancouver, but it costs a lot to live, doesn't it?"

"It depends on how you live. I had a bachelor apartment with an adjoining bathroom. They call it a Jack and Jill. I didn't mind. I just had to make sure that when I went to the bathroom I locked both doors. It cost me four hundred a month."

I asked André, "How was your day after I saw you at noon."

"It was cold. I tried panning in a few places, but there was nobody out."

Jacques said, "I talked to Mariah, she's coming down here tomorrow. She will bring Joy's keys, or some of her stuff. We'll work it out."

I went to the hospital tonight. All the information desks were closed. I asked two paramedics if they knew where the Acute Recovery Area was. They'd never heard of it. One said, "They keep changing the names around here. "I showed the paper where I'd written the room number — 505. "Take the main elevator in the old section and go to the fifth floor, maybe someone there can direct you."

I went to the fifth floor and asked a nurse (or an orderly — someone in scrubs) where the Acute Recovery Area was. He said, "Go straight down the hall until you see a single door open. Turn left, pick up the telephone receiver and tell them the name of the patient you're here to see."

I managed that. Looked around, couldn't find a bed or room number. A voice behind me asked, "Sir, can I help you?"

I answered, "I'm looking for bed number 105."

"Right here, sir," said a nurse with blond wavy hair in the style of Madonna or Lady Gaga.

Joy said, "I saw you go past my bed. I tried to call to you, but I've lost my voice. I'm susceptible to pneumonia and this is the way it usually starts."

"I could tell right away that Joy was feeling better. The pained look was off her face. She said, "I wasn't expecting you to come tonight."

"I said I'd be back."

"I know, but I thought you meant later in the week. Now they have me on Dilaudid and Morphine. My skin is really itchy, I can't help scratching. It's a good thing I don't have long fingernails or I'd be cut to shreds. I'm also on Heparin so my blood doesn't clot. I talked to my doctor about getting back on Seroquel. He said, 'Why do you think you need Seroquel?' I said, 'My mind feels like its traveling a hundred miles an hour in a ten-mile an hour zone. Can you wrap your head around that?' He said, 'Yes, we'll put you on Seroquel.' I can now look

233

forward to a good night's sleep. They don't give it to me until 10:00 . I don't know why they wait until 10:00. Where I was before they gave out all the meds at 9:00.

I heard a banging sound on the other side of the curtain. Joy said, "Sometimes I think that woman is possessed. She makes the strangest sounds." Soon, I heard a wailing noise, 'Piro, Piro!'

"It wouldn't be so bad if she spoke English, but I have no idea what she's saying. She was at the other end of the ward. I don't know why they put her beside me. Sometimes I feel like strangling her, or holding a pillow over her face. The nurses also lose patience with her, especially the blond one."

I asked, "Do you have ear plugs with you?"

"No, but the dark-haired nurse said she'd get me some. I'm going to need them. Now that they've got me hooked up to all these wires and tubes I can't go anywhere. When I was just on the intravenous, I could get into my wheelchair and pull the intravenous stuff along with me. I was told not to leave the area, but I slipped past them five times already. I needed to have a smoke and I wanted to go to the coffee shop for a decent cup of tea. The last time it was security guards that brought me back. They asked, 'Are you Joy?' I said, 'Who wants to know?' They said, there's a nurse up on the fifth floor who thinks you may have gone AWOL.'

"The nurse made me a cup of tea. It tasted like garbage. I asked her, 'What did you do to destroy this tea?' I couldn't drink it. I left it on the table and asked Al to dump it when he came in. They asked me if I wanted a nicotine patch. I said, 'I had one of those the last time I was in. I was throwing up for three days.' She asked, 'Do you want to try a Nicorette Inhaler?' I said, 'I'll try it.' All it does is give me a sore throat.

"Good news is, I was able to eat a piece of toast, mind you it was after taking Gravol. When they brought in this heart rate and blood pressure monitor I thought I was getting a TV. At least I have something to look at as the numbers go up and down. It's good now, 127 over 113. It had gone as high as 180. They were worried that I might have a stroke."

I asked, "Have you had high blood pressure before?"

"Yeah, when my oldest son was born. I've always known I had high blood pressure, but it didn't bother me."

I said, "I notice that you have a phone now."

"Yeah, I tried phoning Jacques, but all I got is his voice mail. He's probably drunk by now. I'll call him tomorrow."

I said, "André told me that your workers know you're in hospital."

"Yeah, they're going to visit me sometime. My check should be coming tomorrow. I have to find someone to bring it to me, then find a way to get to Money Mart."

I noticed that Joy had difficulty even lifting a paper cup full of tea. She said, "The nurses told me to ask for help going to the commode, but I told them, 'It's only two feet. I can manage that.' I don't like that thing. I'd rather go to the washroom, but I'm too wired up. Earlier, when I snuck away, I just pulled out the intravenous needles, but I got shit for that. The nurse said, 'We have enough trouble getting blood as it is. Every time you pull the needle out we have to flush the vein.'

The blond nurse came in to take a blood sample, but was unsuccessful. She flushed the vein, still no luck. "We'll try to find another vein. It's not going to be easy. She tried three or four times with Joy saying, 'ouch' and 'oh, that hurts' each time.

Joy said, "I'm a real wuss when it comes to needles. I always have been."

I asked, "Is all this due to your fibromyalgia?"

"It's caused by a combination of factors, lack of exercise, poor diet and drinking. I'm guilty on all three counts."

Friends

25 November 2012

It's Sunday. I don't get to see my friends until tomorrow, but I miss them. I wonder where Shakes slept last night. Was it in a bank kiosk? I also wonder where André slept last night. Perhaps it was behind the dumpsters in back of the coffee shop. I wonder if Joy slept last night since the temperature went below freezing. I've slept in a tent in those temperatures and know that it isn't life threatening if one has the proper sleeping bag and warm clothing. I can also remember shivering so much that I couldn't get to sleep. There wasn't anything I could do to improve my situation at the time.

When I read over my previous entries I realize just how important my friends are to me. Despite their addictions, their choices and what life has thrown at them, they are doing the best they can with what they have. Can any of us do any better? They are always entertaining and a joy to be with.

Several colleagues at work have seen me sitting with Joy before I go to work in the mornings. They ask about her story. I give them a condensed version of the facts as I know them. They ask, 'Do you believe that what she says is the truth?' I have known Joy for two years now. When she tells her stories there are variations, perhaps due to memory, perhaps due to the amount she's had to drink, the amount she wishes to reveal, but in essence, what she has told me is consistent and I don't believe her to be a great actress who can pull tears out of nowhere.

I've been asked, 'Are these people dangerous?' I know that several have committed murder. Two have served sentences of

twenty and twenty-five years in prison. Another wasn't
charged, but has lived with the guilt, even attended the dead
man's funeral and met his family. These people, my friends,
are capable of murder. I'm capable of murder. Most people, in
certain situations, especially under the influence of drugs or
alcohol, are capable of murder.

I know that if I was in a desperate situation any of my
friends would do their best to protect me, or help me, with
whatever resources they had. They've offered food, drink and
protection on many occasions.

I don't really know why I am drawn to the park at noon. I
tell people that the conversations there are more interesting
than what I hear at work. That is certainly true. More than
that, I see raw life without a safety net. Like Silver, who died
September 29th at the age of 52, most of my friends are only too
aware that they won't see sixty. Many are surprised, and
sometimes disappointed, that they made it through the night. I
enjoy sharing the time they have left. I am honored to have
made their acquaintance.

Joy in Hospital

26 November 2012

Monday morning and Joy isn't in her usual place. I wasn't
surprised, Mondays are noted as being bad days for
panhandling. People tend to be grumpy because of having to
come back to work after a weekend.

At noon I met Jacques and André at the corner. Jacques
said, "Did you hear about Joy? She's in hospital. They took her
there by ambulance yesterday. She phoned me this morning.

It's about her kidneys, she says that they were so sore she couldn't get up. She didn't have a room yet. They had her all night in the corridor."

I said that I'd phone the hospital and see if I could get any information. André said, "Me, I don't go to hospitals, but because it's Joy, I'll see if I can visit her sometime."

Jacques said, "It's bad for her. This is the third time in a year that she's been hospitalized for the same thing. The doctors told her she should move somewhere else and stop drinking; but it's hard to leave your friends, go to someplace where you don't know anybody. But it's her body telling her that she can't drink anymore. It doesn't matter if she waters it down; she has to stop completely."

I said, "She's been waiting so long for her health card. She drinks to forget her past. She drinks because of the pain in her legs and she drinks to get to sleep at night."

I asked André, "Where have you been staying?"

"At the Sally. It hasn't been too bad. I'm in a room with just one other guy. When he starts snoring, it's not just sawing wood; it's like a Husqvarna chain saw. He's a big guy and makes a lot of noise just rolling over on those plastic covered mattresses.

"Yesterday I was at the library. I knew I couldn't get back in time to sign for my bed, so I phoned them. They said, 'No problem, André, we'll put you down for another night.' When I got there, they had cut my lock and were hauling my stuff out of the room. They told me, 'You can't sign in until seven o'clock, so I had to sit in the lobby with all of my stuff until then. Meanwhile, there's another guy sitting across the room. They ask him if he'd like a bed. I said, 'Hey, I'm waiting for a bed, now you're giving my bed away to someone else.' The guy said, 'I was here first.' I said, 'What do you mean, you were here first? I've been here for six years. I've grown roots in the cracks of the floor here.' Anyway, they gave him a bed in the basement and where do you think they put me? In the same bed they just kicked me out of.

"I'm thinking that I should talk to my workers about getting me a room, until an apartment becomes available. I've got to get something started because they're cutting off the start-up allowance in the new year. It's one of the government cutbacks."

"Hey, hey," said Jacques, "The last start-up check is going to be issued December 15, so you have to apply before that. If you apply later, there is a good chance you'll be rejected."

I asked Jacques, "You're in a bachelor apartment, aren't you?"

"No, I'm in a room for now, but I'd prefer to be in a bachelor. We share a kitchen with two sinks. One side is always full of dirty dishes. I don't like that. I like to have my own place, so I can keep it tidy, or not – whatever I want.

"They didn't want to give me a start-up allowance because I was coming from a bachelor to a room. They thought that I should have everything I needed. I told them that I had to throw away most of my things because of the bed bug. They said, 'There's no report of you having the bed bug.' They sprayed three times, but my landlord didn't give me a paper saying that. I could have gotten two hundred dollars, if I had that paper."

Timmy stopped by on his bicycle. I asked him, "How was your weekend, Timmy?"

"It was okay, quiet. The chicken man was by yesterday morning."

I asked, "Was he handing out five dollar bills?"

André answered, "No, just fried chicken. He only hands out five dollar bills on special occasions, like Christmas, Easter — on Mother's Day he'll give one to the ladies; on Father's

Day the men get one. Last year the owner of the pizza place came by with four large pizzas. I was the only one there. He said, 'Make sure you share these.' Did he think I was going to eat four large pizzas? I said, 'Don't worry, I'll share them.' If I didn't, I'd probably get my head kicked in.

"I haven't seen Jake today. I wonder how he's doing."

I said, "He seemed to be feeling a little better on Friday."

André said, "He's taking a powerful dose of antibiotics, but he's still drinking. I said to him, 'Jake, if you drink, you're cancelling out the benefit of the antibiotics.' He's taking other daily medication every day as well. He sees his doctor every day."

I asked, "How are you feeling, André?"

"I'm feeling okay now. When I had the walking pneumonia, I had a pain in my chest like a red-hot iron rod going through my lung. I was in real pain. I could only take shallow breaths. I still don't have full use of my lungs. Jake may have something different from what I had. I don't know."

I phoned the hospital. I was informed that Joy was doing okay. She is still in the Emergency Department, Medicine Service. They are still waiting for a bed for her. I will try to visit her tonight.

It's about 6:30 pm. I took the bus to the hospital. I went to the Emergency desk, was given a pass and told to follow the green dots on the floor. The receptionist at the Medicine Department desk directed me to bed 116. The curtains were closed, so I asked a nurse what I should do. She said, 'Just call her name, she's resting.' I called and heard a faint, 'Dennis?'

I stuck my head behind the curtain. Joy said, "I thought I heard your voice, but I thought, 'That can't be.' I wasn't expecting you to visit."

"I said I would, if you were ever in hospital again, and here I am."

"Have a seat over there. Just move my stuff to the other chair. I'm in so much pain. These doctors — there have been five of them so far — they keep asking me the same questions. I asked one of them, 'Don't you guys talk to each other?' The guy said, 'We do, but we have to hear it firsthand.' They keep asking, 'When did you have your last drink?' I said, 'Friday.' They asked, 'How often a day do you drink?' I said, 'Once.' They asked, 'How much do you drink each day?' I said, 'A bottle, a bottle and a half, two bottles, it depends on how I'm feeling.'

"I was feeling sick on Sunday. I went upstairs to Mariah's place. It must have taken me forty-five minutes to climb the stairs. She said, 'You look like you're in pain!' She gave me two Tylenol 3. They didn't do anything. She said, 'Go back downstairs and try to get some rest.'

"Then Buck and Dillinger came over." Joy rolled her eyes. "He brought me some Ensure and some pears. We smoked a joint together and he left me half a gram. I've still got it in my bag.

"I just kept feeling worse and worse. Finally I couldn't stand it anymore. My cell phone didn't have any time on it, but the emergency numbers still worked. They asked me my phone number. I couldn't remember it.

"When I first came in, they gave me a shot of Delaudid. I threw my guts up, but felt better after that. Then they gave it to me in pill form. That didn't do anything for the pain, but made me feel nauseous, caused my mouth to dry up. I need morphine, but I told them I'd also need some Gravol. I tried to eat some of the meatloaf they served for supper. I took two bites, that's all I could handle.

"I can't sleep. I'm not even in a proper hospital bed. This mattress is thin and hard. I ache all over, my legs, my back, it's even into my neck now. They had me out in the corridor for a long time before bringing me in here. The guy beside me coughs all the time. They have me in some kind of quarantine, because of a virus I picked up the last time I was here. It's contagious for people with a low immune system."

Al, a male nurse, came in to take Joy's blood pressure. It was 188/113. He said it's coming down. It was 244/113. He said, "They have a bed for you now. You'll be moved soon. I'll try to get them to hurry with your meds. It's medical students who are working on it. They can be slow."

Joy said, "Thanks, Al."

To me she said, "He's cool. He lets me know what's really going on.

"I want to go out for a smoke. Is it cold outside?"

"It's been snowing."

"I don't care. Can you bring my wheelchair over and help me to the front entrance. While I'm outside could you do me a big favor? I'd really love a steeped tea, with one milk and two sugar. The stuff they serve at the other coffee shop is garbage. I'll meet you back here at my bed."

After the cigarette and tea, another nurse came in to check Joy's heart rate. I felt that she needed some privacy, so I said that I'd come back tomorrow.

"I need some stuff from home, especially a toothbrush. I don't know how to get them."

I said, "If Mariah can pack some things and bring a bag downtown, I'll bring it to you here at the hospital."

"We'll work something out. Thanks for bringing me the tea. I'm going to try to get some sleep now."

Lazy Bones

30 November 2012

It was cold at noon, -4 degrees and windy. The only person at the corner was Shakes. Beside him was a sports bag, a purple plastic shopping bag with a globe sitting on top — all his worldly possessions.

"Dennis," said Shakes. "I've got a favor to ask you."

"What is it, Shakes?"

"I need a bottle."

"Sorry, Shakes, I don't have any cash on me."

"That's not what I asked."

He pulled an envelope out of his pocket and handed me a twenty. "Would you please go to the liquor store for me? Get a coffee for yourself."

"Sure I'll go, Shakes, but I don't need a coffee. We get it free at work."

"Don't say I didn't offer."

It's only about a five-minute walk to the liquor store. I didn't mind making a run, and Shakes is barred for life. "Okay, Shakes, I'll be back in a few minutes."

When I came back, Shakes was talking to Fred. I looked at the globe and asked, "Shakes, are you planning to do some world travelling?" He laughed.

"How about Australia?" I asked. "Would you like to go there?"

Fred said, "I have a friend who came from New Zealand."

I said, "I've seen pictures of New Zealand. It's really beautiful."

"Yeah," he said, "they also have seventeen women to every man. I asked my friend if it was true and why he left. He said, 'They have lots of women alright, but they're all ugly.' I don't think any women are ugly. Every one of them has something beautiful about her."

I asked Shakes, "Have you heard anything about Joy? Did she phone Jacques?"

"First things first. I lost my glove."

His yellow glove was just a few feet back, near where we were standing previously. Every time the sun moved farther behind one of the tall buildings, Shakes moved out of the shadow and into the sunlight.

"Where have the others gone?"

"They had places they had to go. Jacques, André and Travis were here. Do you guys know Travis?"

I said, "I know Travis. He talks a lot."

'Yeah, he not only talks a lot, but it's what he says. Sometimes I just have to say, 'Travis, go away. I don't want to listen to you.'

"I'm waiting here until 2:00. My workers are coming by in the van, to pick up me and my stuff. They're going to be giving me the keys to my apartment."

Little Chester and Donny in his motorized wheelchair came over to where we were standing. Chester picked up the globe and looked at it. I pointed to Iceland, where my grandparents came from.

He pointed at Newfoundland. "This is where I came from. They're the same color."

I said, I've always wanted to go to Newfoundland. It's really beautiful."

"No, it's not. I lived there for twenty-four years. I couldn't wait to get away."

"I hear the economy has really picked up since the oil discovery."

"I've been hearing about that for forty years. I don't think anything has happened yet."

I asked, "Were you a fisherman?"

"My mother said I had lazy bones. I've always had lazy bones. I snared rabbits. Once, me and some friends were out in the bush. We had a cable and made a lasso out of it. We hung it between two trees. A moose came running along, right into the snare. My friends hauled it up in a tree. We had meat to last us all winter. Lots of people have heard of snaring rabbits, not too many have heard of snaring moose."

I said, "I've eaten moose. It's really good."

Shakes said to Chester, "Get the fuck out of my sun!"

"I don't understand you, Shakes. What did you say?"

I said, "I think he means you're making a shadow on him. You're standing in his sun."

"Oh, I didn't know what he wanted. Sure, Shakes, I'll move down."

December 2012

Sky's Newswire

3 December 2012

"How do like your new place, Shakes?" I asked

"It's fine. I got robbed there Saturday night."

"Shakes, how did you get robbed in your own place?"

"I was drinking with a guy who lives downstairs, in the same building I'm in. I gave him money to go out and buy me two bottles. I left my door open so he could get back in. He didn't show and when I woke up, my other bottle was gone. I'll make sure I get those bottles next time I see him."

Loretta said, "Do you see the boots that guy walking by is wearing? My boyfriend, Vance wears that kind of boots. He has to, he's a roofer. He's working his last day today. The season is over. He can't roof in the snow. This hat I'm wearing is from where he works."

Jake said, "What does he do when he's not roofing?"

"He goes on unemployment insurance, so I'll have him all to myself."

Jake said, "He doesn't come around here very much. Doesn't he like us?"

"It's not you he doesn't like. He doesn't like me drinking with you guys because that's when I get into trouble."

Jake said to me, "These antibiotics I'm taking make my face itch and my ankles swell. I have to keep taking them until the end of December. I see my doctor this afternoon. He's putting me on a special diet. I took the menu to my worker. She says that I'll qualify for an extra $200 a month.

"Did you hear that Debbie was hit by a bus last week? She had bags of groceries in both arms and was running to catch the bus. She was banging on the side, trying to get the driver to stop. She slipped, groceries went flying and the bus ran over her arm. I told her to go to the hospital, but she didn't want to. Her upper arm is all purple now.

"I should bring my mountain bike down and sell it. Right now I'm using it to hang my clothes on."

I asked him, "How is your new apartment working out?"

"I won't be getting my furniture until January — it'll be better then.

"It's nice here, in the sun. I don't want to get up at all. How about you, Shakes?"

"I just want to sit here."

A security guard wearing a reflective vest walked by. He looked at us, but didn't say anything."

Jake said, "That's the nice one. He doesn't care if we're here. It's the old guy who tells us to move along. Shakes got a ticket the other day for trespassing."

I asked, "Did he get the ticket here?"

"Yeah, right here. He wasn't charged for alcohol, just trespassing."

Jake asked Loretta, "Are you going to the liquor store today?"

"No."

Jake asked, "Are you barred from there?"

"No, just from the other one."

"I can't find anyone to go for a run. I guess it doesn't matter. I've got no money anyway. Shakes, have you got any money?"

"I've got five dollars and five cents."

"Loretta, have you got any money?"

"I don't even have enough to buy a pack of smokes, but I'll buy a cigarette off you for a dollar."

"I'll buy one too, Jake," said Amigo. Amigo paid Jake, took the cigarette, and left.

Jake said, "Well, we've got enough for a bottle, we just don't have anyone to go for a run."

I said, "You could have asked Amigo."

"I don't know him well enough, at least not well enough to trust him with seven bucks. He might not come back."

After leaving work I met Sky.

He said, "Did you hear that I was kicked out of a city council meeting? Not only that, two goons, that's what I call them, escorted me out of the building. The police arrested me for trespassing. How can I be trespassing at our city hall? Tell me that! The police roughed me up in the car and again when we got to the jail.

"I appeared before the judge the next morning. I told him how I was treated and mentioned that our mayor is in a conflict of interest situation. He also sits on the board of Ontario Hydro. I was at the council meeting expressing my concerns about the city not adopting my idea for a solar-powered mono-rail, similar to ones they have in Europe. Of course the mayor was against the idea because it's going against what Ontario Hydro wants.

"Montreal's former mayor quit amid multiple corruption allegations last month. Did you hear what his severance package is worth? It's more than two hundred and sixteen thousand.

"Have you seen my website?"

"Yes I have, Sky. It's very impressive."

"Did you see my presentation to city hall? What did you think of that?"

"I thought you put your ideas forward very effectively. Are you still sleeping outside?"

"Oh, yes, I always do. I don't mind it. There was a lady who offered to let me leave some of my stuff in her backyard. Now, she says I can't. Do you know of any place I could store my grocery cart? Someone mentioned a place near the bus depot. Maybe I'll try there."

"That sounds like a convenient location for you. It's within walking distance."

"Did I tell you that I'm building a solar-powered ship? A friend of mine from Newfoundland, an engineer, is working on it with me. It will have condos aboard, the world's largest dance floor, swimming pools. We're looking for investors. Are you interested?"

"Not now, Sky, but let me know how it is progressing."

Joy Still In Hospital

11 December 2012

On the bus I met Trudy, she asked, "Have you heard about Joy?"

"I heard that she was in the hospital. I visited her a couple of times."

"Yesterday she was transferred; that's what Jacques told me. She's able to move around a bit now, in her wheel chair."

I said, "That sounds like good news. How have you been? I haven't seen you for a while."

"I'm okay, Mary, my mom has been sick. She hasn't been out lately. Nick and I have been staying in. It's just been too cold to do anything. My brother, Larry has gone back to Iqualuit." Trudy got off the bus.

I moved closer to the front and met Jake and André. They were going to Jake's new apartment.

"Hi André, Jake, it's good to see you."

"Have you heard about Joy?"

"I heard that she'd been moved to another hospital, but I don't know why."

André said, "I think it's because there are tests that they can do there that they aren't able to do at the other one. I also think that she's been moved out of intensive care and they needed her bed. When I was there, they gave me an intravenous drip because I'm alcoholic. Towards the end they were just bringing me glasses of brandy once an hour. I'd save them, so I could drink them all at once and get a bit of a buzz.

"A bunch of us are going to get a taxi and visit her. I hope that she lets me in her room. I'd hate to pay that money and have her say I couldn't come in."

Jake said, "I'm sure she'll let you in."

André said, "Guess what? I'm getting my own apartment by the first of January. They took me to see it. It's really nice."

Something Different For Everybody

12 December 2012

At the park Jacques said, "Joy phoned me this morning. She was a bit weepy because she thinks they're going to keep her in hospital until after Christmas. I think they want to keep her so she doesn't start drinking again. If they let her out, she's going to visit her friends and they'll all be drinking, so she'll start again. She drinks that wine, eh? That's bad. Me, I just drink a few beer, so far it hasn't caused me any problems, except for a big belly."

Mariah said, "I'm a reformed alcoholic. I went right down hill. I was a falling down drunk. Now I can buy a small bottle of cognac and it will last me a week. I just have a few sips a day. I cut out smoking and drinking when I was pregnant."

Jacques said, "People tell me that maybe I'm pregnant. I hope not.

"I like to have a bit to drink, just beer, with maybe some pot every once in a while. With some people it's beer, with some wine, with some pot, with some crack — something different for everybody.

"I'm still looking for my bunk beds. I'm going to have to get out of the place I'm staying. Jake said I should talk to his worker, but she's been sick. When I talked to her last she said she could get me an apartment, a start-up allowance and arrange for me to get ODSP (Ontario Disability Support Program). I don't have any of that now. Maybe she could even get me into one of those over 60 places. I'm only 56, but if I could get into a place like that, I'd avoid a lot of the crackheads.

"You should see where I am now. It's just a room. I share a kitchen with two native guys across the hall. There is a double sink, both sides are filled with dirty dishes. There is a table that is filled with clean dishes. I have no place to sit to eat my food, no place to wash my dishes. I went to turn on the stove, but first I had to move the cockroaches. I don't have them in my room, just the kitchen. Me, I shut up about that. That's how I lost my other place. My neighbor said there were mites. When the inspector came, I let him in. He took pictures over here, over there. When he came back, he had a notice saying the place was condemned. I don't want that to happen again.

"I don't need a big place. I live alone. My last place was a bachelor. There was just room enough for my fridge and a table, with about this much space in between. I think that the bathroom was bigger than the rest of the apartment, but I didn't mind."

Two police cars stopped at the curb. I decided to move over to talk to Wolf, so there would only be two groups of four. We've been told before that they don't like to see groups larger than four people. Nobody was blocking the sidewalk, there was no alcohol visible and nobody was drunk.

"Hi, Wolf," I said, "what are you reading now?"

"It's a book about Hollywood in the 1950's. It's called *Suicide Hill*. I forget who wrote it (*James Elroy*). It's like that book *The Choirboys* by Joseph Wambaugh. If these guys think they have it bad now, it's nothing like it was in the 1950's. This detective, Lloyd Hopkins, goes after bad guys and what he does to them isn't exactly legal. The cops would do 'wino runs' where they'd pick up winos and addicts.

"I'm an alcoholic and I smoke a bit of crack. Maybe it's the German in me, but I respect authority. I respect what the police do. I'm polite to them, not like some of these guys. Daimon has beaten up Shark; he beat me up. If it weren't for the cops, who would protect us?

"In the book they wouldn't give out tickets to the winos, like they do here. If they wanted information, they'd beat them, and believe me they'd talk. Sometimes, either before or after they talked, they'd kill them, for no reason. Suicide Hill was a place in Hollywood where the police would dump the bodies.

"I guess you've heard about Joy. Jacques was talking to her on the phone this morning. He asked her if she wanted to talk to me, she said, 'No.' What am I going to do? I've never been her boyfriend, or anything like that, but I let her stay at my place when she was beaten by Big Jake. I don't get involved with women very much anymore. I live alone, pay for the odd hooker once in a while. There was a woman who stayed at my apartment last night. I sent her out to buy me a case of beer. She said that when she got back she had a surprise for me. I like surprises, but she didn't come back, so I put her bag and clothes out in the hall.

"Joy has to quit drinking. We've all told her that, but she won't listen. Maybe she'd listen to you."

I said, "I don't think so. When I saw her last, the doctors had told her to stop drinking or she'd die. She said, 'You told me that the last time, and I had another ten months on the street.' "

"I know," said Wolf. "I've been in hospital, for injuries. I was in that car accident. I've had my cheek bone smashed when I was beaten up. I've broken my arm when I fell, but nothing internal. When your kidneys or your liver starts going, you have to quit drinking There's no way around it. Look what happened to Silver just a few months ago. Anyway, if you can talk sense to Joy it might save her life."

Two outreach workers came by. One of them was carrying a backpack. He said to Wolf, I've got some dog biscuits. Would you like some for your dog?"

"I wouldn't mind some for me."

The worker said, "I've also got a sleeping bag in here. Would you be interested?"

"Sure, I'd like it."

"Can you use the backpack as well?"

"Thank you very much. I really appreciate this."

I Don't Do Hospitals

13 December 2012

"I'm always happy," said Jacques, "especially when the sun is shining. I come down here to the park – Where else am I going to go? I was looking in the Loblaw's flyer today, they got the big lasagna and the big cabbage roll, the five pound one for $7.00. I love that, but living alone, I can't eat that much. Even Hippo, he can't eat that much. At the market I buy camembert and brie, the round ones. At Loblaw's it costs $4.75. Me, I can't afford that, but at the market they sell the ones near the expiry date that they can't sell in stores, two for five dollars. I leave it at room temperature for two days and and spread it on crackers."

Wolf said, "I don't like cheese that much. The only kind I buy is mozzarella, and on a hamburger, I'll have cheddar."

"You like mozzarella, that stuff they shave? It tastes like puke."

"I like it, okay? I know, I'm German, they make lots of cheese, but I just like Mozzarella. You don't have to like it, but it's what I like!

"Jacques is supposed to be watching his cholesterol. I've heard of beef stew, chicken stew even rabbit stew, but have you ever heard of someone making bacon stew? If his doctor knew that, he'd flip."

"I eat bacon every day," said Jacques. "I like to fry it and then cook my eggs in the grease. That's what gives them the good taste.

"In my place, you're not supposed to cook after 10 pm; but at 1:30 in the morning, I woke up and smelled grease. The young guy was frying something. He's not a very good cook, but the smell of that grease frying sure smelled good. He left his frying pan and dishes in the sink for another day."

I asked, "Has anybody heard anything from Joy lately?"

Jacques said, "I went to the hospital to see her this morning. She was looking okay. She's moving around a bit."

I asked, "She isn't walking yet, is she?"

"She uses a walker. She seems weak on her left side. Her left foot, she kind of drags. They told her that she can't drink any more, but already she told me that she has two bottles of sherry in her fridge at home. They want to keep her over Christmas. She says she wants to be out to spend it with friends and have a few drinks. The drinks might kill her."

Wolf said, "Sometimes they'll do that, let patients out for Christmas, but in her case it isn't such a good idea.

"People are different, what hurts one, may not hurt another. It's the same with animals. Weasel really gave me shit for giving Shaggy a little piece of chocolate. I can't see the problem of giving her just one little chunk. It's not like I'm giving her a whole chocolate bar."

Jacques said, "I saw on TV a doctor was saying that for some dogs, the sweetness of the chocolate turns into a poison inside the dog, but it's not all dogs."

"Well, Shaggy's had chocolate before and it didn't kill her, so I guess she's not one of those dogs."

This Is All We Have

14 December 2012

Although warm and sunny, there were still patches of ice on the sidewalk, but for the most part walking was easy. Little Jake was hopping about weaving in and out of the group. I asked, "What are you pretending to be, Jake, a Christmas Elf or a Christmas Grinch?"

"I'm a Christmas Mouse. I'm a sneaky little muthufukka."

Jake was putting a cigarette in his mouth backwards. Mariah yelled at him, "Turn it around the other way!"

I said, "You're picking up bad habits from André. He stayed at your place the other night, didn't he?"

"Yeah, the night we saw you on the bus. It was the night he hit the old lady up for four hundred bucks. She left her card in the cash machine and he was able to get into her account.

"I really don't like André much. He owes me cigarettes, he owes me a bottle, he owes me pot. I spent money on groceries. Wait until he gets his place, we'll all come over and sponge off him."

Mariah said, "I guess I can kiss goodbye the twenty that he owes me. I'm never going to see that again."

Jacques said, "Jake, you're standing too close to me."

I said, "What's the matter Jacques? Are you afraid of a Christmas Mouse?"

Chester said, "I haven't been to see Joy yet, but I hope to before Christmas. I've been invited to a party at the Church-Community Center. There's going to be singing, dancing and they'll be serving a Christmas meal."

Someone asked Chester for a cigarette. He held up a clear plastic bag full of cigarette butts. "This is all I have." To me he said, "I go for a butt run every morning. I just pay for rolling papers. It costs me hardly anything. I smoke all I want to."

Jake said, "I can't wait until January when I get my furniture."

Debbie said, "Jake, you shouldn't always be thinking about the future. Appreciate what you have here and now. The sun is shining, it's warm, you're with friends. I try to think of the present, not the past where the pain is." She crossed herself and blew a kiss into the air. "This is all we have." Debbie is an attractive woman, but the scar across her nose indicates a violent background.

Mariah said, "I won't be going to see Joy. I've nothing against her, but I just don't do hospitals anymore. Remember, Jacques, when Willy was in the hospital at the same time as my old man? I was at the hospital all the time. Willy could be moved around, so he was always wanting me to push him in his wheelchair outside to have a smoke. My old man, the one I dumped ten months ago, was hooked up to all kinds of tubes and wires, so he couldn't get out of bed. It was back and forth, back and forth all day. I'm just not going to do that anymore. I need to take care of myself."

At that point two bicycle police pulled up.

"What are you people doing here?"

Jacques said, "We're just enjoying the warm weather, the sun, the fresh air."

Debbie said, "Don't worry, we don't have any booze or drugs."

One officer pointed to a clear drinking bottle, filled with an amber liquid. "What's that? Is it beer? Shake it for me."

A patrol car pulled up at the curb. A familiar officer was driving. The two bicycle patrol officers said, "Your friends are here, we'll leave you to them."

The patrol car left and a police van with another patrol car pulled up. Two male and two female officers got out. One of the men walked over to Jacques and started writing a ticket.

One of the female officers said, "We've got a zero tolerance policy for alcohol now."

The other female officer said, "Would someone please pick up that newspaper and the other junk on the ground?"

Chester picked up the newspaper; I picked up a chip bag. The officer said, "There's a garbage container at the next corner. You can dispose of it there."

Debbie asked, "Are the rest of us being charged?"

"No," said one of the female officers, just this gentleman here. The rest of you are free to go."

Prison Shoes

15 December 2012

It's Saturday. I visited Joy in the hospital. I went to her room and an elderly woman said, "She may be in the sun room down the hall to your right, or she may have gone to the cafeteria, or outside to have a smoke; she may be anywhere."

I thanked her and headed to the sunroom. I hardly recognized Joy. She looked so small. She was crying. I sat next to her.

"I'm glad you came. I wasn't expecting you. Why did you come?"

"I just came to see how you are. Why wouldn't I come? Jacques told me about visiting you yesterday. He said you were upset about the possibility of not getting out before Christmas. He also said that sometimes they let patients out for Christmas day."

"I don't know what's going on. I hate it here, especially on weekends. It's like a morgue, and I can tell that the nurses don't like being here on weekends either. I guess you met Emily. She moved in yesterday. She's okay, but sometimes I want to smother her. She didn't know how to flush the toilet. I don't mean just after she peed. I'd come into the bathroom and there would be poo floating in the toilet. I asked her about it. She said, 'I pushed all the buttons, but nothing made the toilet flush.' I showed her which handle to press. She must have gotten up five times last night to use the bathroom. I guess she didn't close the door before she flushed because it woke me every time. After the injection they give me at night, I'm usually gone to the world.

"She thinks she's getting out Monday. She needs help from the nurses for everything, even to put a pillow between her knees. There's no way she's getting out soon. I've even talked to her daughter. They live about a mile and a half apart, but the daughter has a family of her own. She doesn't have time to look after Emily.

"So how's everybody? Jacques just sort of came, dropped off some stuff for me, took me down for a cigarette, then left."

I said, "Tuesday, I saw Trudy on the bus. On Wednesday I saw André and Jake. He's pissed with André, said he owes him money, owes him a bottle and Jake has paid for all the food."

"The Monday before I went to hospital," said Joy, "it was raining, so we were all down by the river under the bridge. I told you that André had punched red-haired Debbie. Trudy walked up to him and punched him in the face. Then she punched him again. He had blood trickling from his mouth and he sat down on the grass away from the group and started crying. Trudy said, 'You think you're such a big man, but now you're crying like a bitch.' He said, 'I'm crying because I can't hit you back.' Trudy said, 'You can't hit me back because there are other people around. If we were alone, you wouldn't have a problem, just like you didn't have a problem with Debbie.' André is on the outs with everyone. He owes Little Jake, he owes Jacques, he owes Buck. You can't keep taking from people and not giving back."

"I guess you heard that Shakes has his own place now."

"Yeah, not only that, but it's completely furnished. Jake has been waiting for two months and still doesn't have any furniture, except for a bed."

"He also has an air conditioner, still in the box."

"Yeah, that he sits on. They promised me furniture on the Tuesday after I was brought in here. I hope Chester still has my other stuff. My workers were in to see me when I was at the the other hospital. They checked my place, said that the heat was on now. They asked me what I wanted for Christmas. I said, 'Having an apartment full of furniture would be nice.' I've been telling my physiotherapist about how difficult it is for me to get down on my air mattress, and it leaks so I wake up on the hard floor.

"I'm practicing going up and down stairs. There are four of them. I can go up alright, but my right leg is too weak for going down, that's why I have to use this walker and a wheelchair. I seem to have to drag my right leg and can't use my right arm very well."

I asked, "How would you feel if you had a walker when you left here?"

"I don't know. I haven't got my head around that yet.

"I just don't want to be in here. I had planned to get a turkey, cook a Christmas meal, have my friends around. It would have been nice. The doctor said I might be able to get out just for Christmas day, but what good is that to me? I have no family, no place to go, no furniture. My friends have their own things to do."

I said, "Chester was saying that you were fine during the five months that you lived with him. It's just since you moved out on your own that you've had problems."

"Chester's had Raven over for most of the time that I've been gone. He owes Jacques money, he owes everybody.

"I hear that Outcast has been talking trash about me. Telling people not to feel sorry for me, that I brought this all on myself."

I said, "Outcast talks trash about everybody. When Stella was by last, she said to him, 'Outcast, it's not always about you.' He said, 'Of course it is. It's always about me.' "

Joy said, "He's pissed with me because whenever he's come over, he's tried it on. I said to him, 'Outcast, you're living with another woman. You sneak over here and expect that something's going to happen. It doesn't work that way.'

I said, "Did you hear that Debbie had her arm run over by a bus?"

"No, how did that happen?"

"She was drunk, holding two bags of groceries, running beside the bus, pounding on the side to get the driver to stop. She slipped. The groceries went flying and she fell with her arm under the bus. The rear wheels ran over it. Jake said her upper arm is purple and misshapen, but she won't go to the hospital or to a doctor."

Joy said, "She's stubborn like that. I've been in pain for a long time, but as soon as I saw that my pee was brown, I knew that my kidneys weren't working properly. It's lucky that the emergency numbers on my cell phone still worked. The paramedics had to chair lift me out of my apartment. It turns out that my problems are mostly due to epilepsy, not drinking. Now, I'm getting medication for that. One of the reasons they won't let me out is because I get a pain injection morning, night and when I need it, during the day. I wouldn't have access to that if I left. I get ten pills in the morning, twelve with lunch and another fourteen before bed."

I asked, "Couldn't they arrange for you to have injections at a clinic, close to where you live?"

"My doctor doesn't seem to want to go along with that. I said to him, 'Couldn't I just have the injections in pill form?' He said, 'Because they're narcotics, I don't recommend that.' I guess he thinks I'd sell them.

"Another thing, Emily is in because of cervical cancer. I haven't had a pap smear for decades. I asked the nurses about it. They said that, if I wanted one, it would be my doctor here that would be doing it. There's no way I want that slime ball down there.

"I've even got hemorrhoids now. I've had five children. I've spent most of the past ten years sitting on the cold sidewalk. So, why now do I have hemorrhoids? The nurse said it's probably because I've been constipated. They've given me fiber, laxatives, suppositories. I was doubled over in pain, so finally they had to give me an enema. It was worse than giving birth. I think I'm still constipated, but I haven't been able to eat for nearly a week. I keep throwing up. They keep telling me to have some toast. I don't want toast. The food here really sucks."

I asked, "What about intravenous?"

"They took the tube out a few days ago. See the marks all over my arm? I don't want to get any more needles than I have to.

"I want to go for a smoke, I'll bring this walker back to my room and grab a wheelchair. Do you want to drive?"

"Sure, I'll push, you give directions."

Before we left, Joy called for the nurse. She said, "Sweetie, can you give me an injection for my arm? The pain is really bad."

When we got outside Joy said hello to a couple who were also having a cigarette. She said to me after they passed, "It's sad, she had a baby a week ago. It's left lung isn't fully developed. They don't know when the baby will be released. They have other kids at home."

I asked, "Was the baby premature?"

"No, it was a full term. They don't know what went wrong."

We went back into the hospital. An Inuit couple stopped to talk to Joy. After they left Joy said, "Could you smell the sherry? I could smell it as soon as they came into view. I know all the muk-muks from downtown. They hang out on the same street."

Another woman said hello as we passed. Joy said, "She looks familiar, but I don't know where I've seen her before. Did you notice? She's still wearing prison shoes."

Ian

17 December 2012

Ian is now clean-shaven with short hair. We haven't seen each other since summer.

"How've you been, Ian?"

"Okay, I've been in alcohol recovery for the past few months. I've been trying to get in there for five years. Finally my name got to the top of the list. I'm in a no smoking building now. I'm trying to transfer to a building where they allow you to smoke in your room.

"They've got me on a program where I get an ounce of wine every hour. I'm not allowed to drink anyplace else.

"I went to court and the best my lawyer could do for me was six months probation and sixty hours community service. Also I'm not allowed to be anywhere near where they serve or sell alcohol. Right now I'm heading to a meeting with my probation officer."

Christmas Dinner

19 December 2012

Temperature was slightly above freezing, no wind. Streets were slushy, but most of the snow had either been cleared, or had melted – an ideal opportunity to visit my friends at the park.

I said to Wolf, "I downloaded the James Ellroy trilogy, the one that ends with *Suicide Hill*."

"You say you downloaded it? How did you do that?"

I said, "I have an electronic reader, a Kindle, and I downloaded the book from the Internet."

"I didn't know you could do that. It's a great series. It really gives you a feel of what life was like in Hollywood in the 1950's. They didn't have cameras everywhere like they do now. No cameras in the holding cells. The cops could do anything they wanted. Don't tell anybody I said this, because some of these guys, criminals, gangsters, think they're tough by spitting on the cops and calling them names. Not me, it's, 'Yes officer, no officer.' If I'm drunk and they take me to jail, which they've done a few times, I'm polite. I say, 'I don't want to cause any trouble.' We have it good now. I'm glad you got those books, you'll enjoy them.

"Does anyone want a chocolate covered muffin?" Wolf passed the plastic container to Jacques who took one. He broke off a piece and asked Wolf's permission to give it to Shaggy.

"Sure, Jacques, Shaggy likes chocolate." To me Outcast said, "Now if it was Weasel, he'd have a fit if anyone offered chocolate to Bear. He'd kill them. But, I figure, a little piece of chocolate, just a little one, mind you. I wouldn't give her a whole chocolate bar, but one square of a Cadbury's Caramilk, or something like that, isn't going to hurt her. I know I shouldn't smoke or drink beer. I shouldn't use pot or the other stuff — that we don't talk about — but I'm healthy. I don't have stomach problems. I enjoy a drink and a smoke with my friends every once in a while. It's a treat for me. Shaggy needs a treat sometimes too."

Bearded Bruce walked over and shook my hand. He said, "I haven't been around here for the past four months, but I was hoping I'd see you. I have my own apartment now. I've been there about three weeks. I still can't believe the words coming out of my mouth, but I have my own place, my own brand new oven and fridge, a new floor. I still sleep on the floor in my sleeping bag, but gradually I'm getting some furniture. I've got a couple of chairs to relax in.

"Jenny from the Shepherd approached me a couple of times. She said, 'We have spots for ninety people in our housing program and we want to choose you to be a part of it.' I said I wasn't interested, then she visited me in jail, when I did the five months. I was in there with thirty guys. When she came we were allowed to go to a big empty room to talk. Just being in a room with so much space got me thinking about how much I was missing. Anyway, when I got out, I started on this program, she found me the apartment, got me on ODSP (*Ontario Disability Support Program*). They cover part of my apartment rent, the rest comes directly out of my monthly check. I haven't even cashed my last Welfare check. Jenny asked me about it. I said, 'I've still got some of my start-up allowance.'

"I'm cooking Christmas dinner. It'll be Weasel, and some of the homeless people. If you don't have any plans, you're welcome to come. I got a fourteen pound Lilydale grain fed turkey. I'll be cooking that on Christmas day. I'll be getting a ham Friday. I'll cook that Christmas Eve, because my oven isn't big enough for them both. We'll have mashed potatoes, stuffing and all the trimmings. I'm a certified chef you know. I'm qualified to work at the the elite restaurants.

"I have a good resume, good qualifications, it's just the five-year gap when I was into drugs and alcohol. I've been to a few interviews, and I'm straight forward about my time in jail. I just have to find an employer who's been there, who knows where I'm coming from."

"It'll come, Bruce. Just give it time."

"I've also joined A.A., but I don't like it. I may find another group I like, but at this one there's too much talk about God. I'm not a God person. I was when I was little, and I may be later on, but not now; so that puts me in conflict with a lot of the steps in the twelve step program. I've cut my drinking to about eighteen beer a week. I smoke more pot, but no crack, no other drugs. I won't even allow them in my house.

"Have you seen Hippo?"

I said, "Not for the last week or so."

"Tell him that I want to see him. He owes me money, but he doesn't have to worry. I'm not going to beat him up. I wouldn't beat up that lovable, fat bastard. I forgive him the debt and I want to forgive him in person. It's a Scottish tradition that on New Year's Eve I put on new clothes, new socks, new underwear, and forgive all those people who have wronged me, or who I have wronged."

"That's a good tradition. Have you seen Joy? She's in hospital."

"I mean to go see her. She may not want to see me. We had kind of a falling out a while ago. I said some bad things to her. I want to apologize and set things right."

Wolf had been to the food bank. Bruce asked him, "Wolf, will you sell me those eggs for two dollars?"

"Sure, I'll even throw a loaf of bread in for free. Sorry, I don't have any cheese, you could have made an omelet."

Bruce said to me, "See, Wolf knows I cook, and Inuk's tasted my cooking. Inuk, tell Dennis what a good cook I am." She nodded.

"Inuk, you're welcome to come over to my new place. I won't sleep with you, but you're welcome to visit."

J.D.

20 December 2012

"Dennis," Wolf said, "I was at my usual place panning this morning. From 7:00 to 10:30. I made more money than I usually make in a week. I made $340 in just those three and a half hours. It only happens at Christmas, that's the only time people feel generous."

Jacques said, "That was the same with me when I first came to town. I was panning with my dog near Christmas time. I made $700. It's never happened since."

"Jacques," I asked, "do you have any plans for Christmas?"

"No, I'll be here. For me it's a day like any other."

"Will you be going to any of the special Christmas dinners at the shelters?"

"I always hear about them a day too late. I may go to the Mission for breakfast on Christmas, that's all. When Pikpik was around we used to celebrate, but he's not around anymore. Maybe we'll go to Shakes' new place. It's big. I only have a room and I don't like cigarette smoke. All these guys smoke. I don't even have a window that I can open. There's plywood where the window used to be. Shakes has a big patio door that he can open. The smoke has a way out then."

"Jacques," Shakes asked, "If you smoke pot, why is it that smoke doesn't bother you?"

"It's just different. I don't know why. Maybe it's because I smoke it from a pipe."

Shakes said, "When I was fourteen, I was in a juvenile home. The guy who ran it had a collection of mary-jane pipes, really nice ones. I stole one of them one time. He knew exactly who took it. He came knocking on my door. 'Shakes,' he said, 'I know you stole my pipe. Now give it back.' I never gave the pipe back to him, ha, ha,ha."

Jacques said, "I used to have about twelve pipes, but with all the moving around I lost most of them. I make them out of river rock. I find the nice smooth ones, then I drill them until they break. All I have is a drill. To make the sides smooth I rub it against a concrete wall. It acts just like sandpaper.

"You see here, a pot pipe has a larger hole in the stem. Resin collects there, even after the last of the pot has been smoked. Holding a flame to the bowl will light the resin. You can get a buzz just from that. This pipe has been broken, see the crack, so I fixed it with glue. It works fine."

"Dennis," said Shakes, "Will you do me a big favor? When you're ready to leave, will you walk with me to the liquor store and buy a forty of J.D. for me. I'll give you the money. I'm barred, otherwise I'd buy it myself."

Shakes is barely able to walk at the best of times. His knees give out on him, so I agreed. When it was about twenty minutes before I had to be back at work, I said to him, "Are you ready to go now, Shakes?"

"Dennis, would you mind going by yourself and bringing the bottle back to me?"

"I guess I have time. Sure, Shakes."

Wolf asked, "Are you going to the liquor store? Would you mind bringing me back six cans of Old Milwaukee?"

I hadn't thought about the Christmas line ups I'd have to face.

2013

January 2013

A Glass Of Wine Every Hour

2 January, 2013

"Hi Dennis," said Magdalene, "Alphonse is in hospital."

"I'm sorry to hear that. Which hospital is he in?"

"He's at the General. He's been there for a couple of days. He has pneumonia. Also, he's had paranoia. He thought he saw people standing around his bed, but there was nobody there. He thought they were trying to kill him. He ran outside. The police brought him back in. They said that if he stayed outside, he would die.

"When he got back to his hospital bed the nurse gave him a glass of whiskey because he's an alcoholic."

I said, "Ian is on a program at the Shepherd. They give him a glass of wine every hour. Gradually he'll be able to stop drinking. He wants to get back to work. He does furniture moving, but it's hard for him while he's an alcoholic."

Magdalene said, "We've been sleeping outside lately. We're on a list to get an apartment, but nothing has happened."

"Where exactly have you been sleeping?" I asked.

"Down this side street. If you go to the end, there is a little boutique there, turn left into the alley. There's a place with a heater that blows down. We have a covering that goes around us.

270

"For a couple of days he wasn't able to eat. His face was getting very thin. That's when he decided that he should go to the hospital.

"Have you thought of staying at one of the shelters?"

"After Alphonse gets out of hospital, we may have to. I don't like those places. They're rough, noisy, crowded and stuff gets stolen there."

I said, "Shakes told me that every time he sleeps there, his things are stolen: his backpack, money, bottles, pot even his clothes."

"I'm going to see Alphonse at the hospital this afternoon, but first I have to go to Welfare to see if I can get my bus pass. Alphonse has a check waiting there but only he can sign for it. I'm going to talk to them and see if they can release it to me. I'm listed on all his forms. I don't even have his phone number at the hospital."

I asked, "When you visit your worker at Welfare, can she help you to get an apartment?"

"Maybe, I don't know, they were looking for us, but we haven't been back there for two weeks. Maybe they found someplace.

"Alphonse has an appointment with his probation officer, tomorrow morning at 8:30. He's going to have to cancel. I don't know the phone number. I hope he's awake, so I can get the number from him.

"This morning I ate at McDonald's. I didn't think I had any money, but I found $4.25. I was so hungry.

"Next week I start a program for individuals who have been abusive to their partners. They're going to help me."

271

Lean on Me

18 January 2013

Friday night, as I was on the bus heading home. I heard a commotion at the front. There were people standing in front of me so I couldn't see what was happening. I heard, "Jesus Christ, can't you give a guy a break? He's been hit by a car and just wants to get home. He doesn't have any money."

Things settled down, gradually people exited the bus and, to my surprise, sitting across from me were Little Jake and Shakes. We greeted each other, then Shakes said, "Dennis, did you hear what happened to me? Last Wednesday night I was hit by a car. The woman driving said she didn't see me. The piggies drove past and didn't even stop."

Jake said, "Shakes, you were dressed all in black with your hood pulled up. That's probably the reason she didn't see you."

I asked Shakes, "Did you go to the hospital, or see a doctor?"

Jake said, "No, he doesn't like hospitals or doctors, but you should see his knee, it's swollen like a grapefruit."

I said, "Maybe he needs a brace for his knee or crutches."

"He doesn't want that, he'd rather lean on me. By the way have you heard from Joy?"

"I went to see her in hospital before Christmas. She seemed okay. I pushed her in her wheelchair so she could go outside for a smoke. I know she has issues about staying alone, especially without furniture."

Jake said, "I have issues about staying alone. I trashed my apartment last week. I went to see Debbie, my worker, and she's going to send a cleaning team Monday morning. She's really great. They're going to bring mops and buckets and cleaning supplies. I told her she didn't have to do that. I'll have the place cleaned by Sunday, but she wouldn't listen. She's arranged for me to see a doctor as well. I'm going to the hospital where Joy is. I know she doesn't like people to just drop by on her, but if I have a reason to be there, it should be okay."

"Jake, do you have your furniture yet?"

"No, I was supposed to contact Debbie the first week of January, but I just wasn't up to it. I don't have a phone, so she wasn't able to contact me. I've just got the bed and the air conditioner, still in its box. I don't have any money, except for a few coffee shop cards. I go there, have a coffee and watch TV. I pick up butts, that's all I have to smoke."

Shakes had his head on his knees and his eyes closed. I asked Jake, "Is he asleep?"

Shakes opened his eyes. He said, "I'm not asleep, it's just that I'm in pain because of my knee."

I said, "I've been to the park a few times, but nobody's been there except for Magdalene. I talked to her one day. I've had a cold, so I haven't been going out much at noon. I heard that André has an apartment now."

Jake said, "I haven't seen anybody since before Christmas. The last time I saw André, he was bumming off us. We didn't part on very good terms."

Their bus stop was coming up, so Jake said, "Come on Shakes, let me help you up. We have to get off soon." Shakes put his arm around Jake and they hobbled off the bus. I was surprised at how much I had missed them.

Work Would Be Good

23 January 2013

This morning on the bus I met Ian. I hadn't seen him for a long time. He said, "I have to go to see my probation officer. I told you, I got six months probation with community service. I'm in a 'Managed Alcohol Program.' I'm doing really well."

"I can see that. You look good. You must be anxious to get back to work moving furniture?"

"Yeah, going to work would be good."

Business As Usual

24 January 2013

When I got off the bus this morning I was greeted, as usual, by Metro and Two-four. Metro said, "Hey, Joy was here yesterday. She's using a cane now. She only lasted about ten minutes because of the cold."

"It's great to hear that she's out of hospital."

"Yeah, she's looking good."

Two-four was wearing a balaclava. I asked him, "Are you going to rob any banks after your shift?"

"Yes, as a matter of fact, five of them: the Royal, the Canadian Imperial, BMO, TD and another one. I can't remember the name."

"Well, Two-four, you don't need to know the name of a bank to rob it. Good luck with that and stay warm."

2013 March

Too Many Gone

Weasel and Bear were panning on the sidewalk. He asked me, "Have you heard anything about Joy?"

"No, I haven't, but I phoned the hospital today. They don't have a listing for her as a patient. She has her own place now. Friends are nearby if she has any problems."

"She has to stop drinking. For the past year she's been watering her wine down to almost nothing, but she still gets sick. Her kidneys are ready to shut down. She may have been on dialysis again. I don't know. Do you have her phone number?"

'No, I've never had her phone number."

Weasel said, "I have a phone, but I don't have any numbers on it. I barely know how to use it.

"It's hard to quit drinking, I just got out of the hospital myself. I was dehydrated. The doctor said, 'I don't want to state the obvious, you should quit drinking, but if you have a glass of juice or water between drinks of alcohol, that will help.'

"The people at the restaurant here, kind of mother me. Mia will come out on her break and bring me a bottle of vitamin water or Gatorade. She'll say, 'Now, Weasel, I want you to drink this to keep up your electrolytes. I'm going to stand here until you drink it.' Another waitress will bring me a bottle of something when her shift ends.

275

"Wolf and I were talking a while back and we counted fourteen of us who have gone this past year. That's really sad. I'm not going to last much longer."

I asked, "Have you seen anything of Serge, lately?"

"No, I haven't seen him for three or four months. I don't know what's happened to him."

I said, "I visited him in hospital when he had his last fall..."

"Yeah, he said it was a fall, but nobody falls that much. He was beaten, probably by some of those young punks. He was a nice guy, always quiet, minded his own business, kept to himself."

Joy Still Missing

7 March 2013

There was a stranger sitting in Joy's spot. I introduced myself. He said, "They call me Clark the Cadaver." (*he does look a bit like a cadaver, with hollow cheeks, deep circles beneath his eyes*) "You're a friend of Joy's aren't you?"

"Yes!" I said, "Have you heard anything about her?"

"I don't know her very well, but what I know as a panhandler is, if you're not out panning over Christmas, there must be something terribly wrong. I heard that she was down here for a few hours in January, but that's it."

I said, "I visited her three times in the hospital. She was released, then went back in. I'll try phoning the hospital again."

I phoned and they don't presently have her on record, so, looking on the positive side, I guess she's been released

Dodging Bullets

10 March 2013

This morning, to my surprise, Joy was sitting in her usual spot. She said, "I was wondering if you still came by this way. I've been out of hospital for thirteen days, but it was just too cold to come down here. I'm using a cane now, so I have to be careful walking on icy sidewalks. They gave me a walker to use at home, but I can't carry it up the stairs. I've been put on a list for subsidized housing. They're going to try to find me a place with no stairs."

I said, "Weasel was worried about you, I talked to him last week."

"Weasel should be worrying about himself. Did you hear what happened to him?"

"He mentioned that he had been in hospital."

"He went really crazy. They had him in the Psych Ward. He thought that people were shooting at him. He was sitting there dodging bullets. I guess they have him on meds now."

"Do you have your health card?"

"No, they seemed to have lost it at the hospital. I don't have my prescriptions either. I thought they would be in the envelope they gave me, but they weren't there. I was just anxious to get out.

"Before I went into the hospital I had portions of food in baggies. I forgot to put them in the freezer. When I got home, there was a horrible smell and a real mess in the fridge."

A small group was huddled in the rain near the park benches. Wolf said to me, "You missed Joy, she just left."

277

"I didn't think she'd stay out in the rain."

"How are you, Jake? Do you have your furniture yet?"

"No, I fucked up again. I was supposed to have seventy dollars for the delivery. You don't get anything for free. I'd spent the money, so they put me on the list again. Maybe next month."

I said, "I heard that Weasel was in hospital."

Wolf said, "He was out with me. We were both over at Shark's place doing some mushrooms. It was about 1:30 in the morning. I guess Shark wanted to go to bed, he asked us to leave. That's why I don't like to have people at my place, you can never get them to leave. Anyway, Weasel and I staggered back to my place. He was in rough shape. We'd both been into the Cosmo thing — if you know what I mean. I think he'd been snorting some dummy dust. I put him in the bedroom, then I heard crashing noises. I went in, and he'd torn my metal table in half and was hiding in the closet saying that people were shooting at him. I was pissed off, so I told him to leave. Half an hour later he came back with three cops. I told them that I had to put the two dogs in a room, so I had plenty of time to stash my pot and anything else I had.

"I opened the door, invited the cops in. They asked me about shooting. I told them, 'There's been no shooting here. It's all in Weasel's head.' I showed them the mess he made. Showed them some photos of him and me together with the dogs, so that they knew we were buds. I asked them to take him somewhere. They said, 'We don't operate a taxi service.' I said, 'Do what you like then, but he's not coming back in here.' He was in the hospital about five days. When he came back to get Bear, he apologized, but he didn't offer to pay for any of the damage. If he'd offered me a hundred bucks, I wouldn't have turned him down."

Don't Think About the Future

11 March 2013

Wolf said, "Hello, Dennis, I hope you're going to help me beat up Jacques today. He really pissed me off. The number of years I've been around, I don't need anybody telling me where to sit. I've been downtown since 6:00 this morning. I was at my spot until 9:00 then came here. I'm soaked, Shaggy is soaked and our caboose is soaked. I got something here, but don't tell anyone." He pulled out a bottle of sherry from under Shaggy's blanket and took a drink. Then he took out a can of Old Milwaukee poured some it in his drinking bottle, some down his leg.

I said, "Sit down, Chester. Oh, I forgot, we had this conversation yesterday, you prefer standing."

"Yeah, I like to stand. I'm short enough anyway. The only way I get to look down on people is if they're sitting and I'm standing."

I asked, "So, how's it going, Chester?"

"About five feet, one and a half inches. Standing on the curb makes me a bit taller."

"No, I meant how are things going for you?"

"I'm doing okay, I only think about what's going on right now. I don't think about the future."

"That's a good attitude. We don't know what's going to happen tomorrow. We don't even know what's going to happen in the next hour."

Been There, Done That

21 March 2013

I saw Joy huddled in her blanket, hood pulled up, with another blanket wrapped around her legs. Under the blanket she was wearing white and pink striped socks over her summer shoes.

After we greeted she said, "Where were you yesterday? I was worried about you. I even asked Metro if he had seen you. I guessed that you drove to work."

I said, "Yesterday I was running late and took a different bus route. Because it was snowing, I didn't think you'd be here."

"Yeah, I was here. I'm freezing now. This cold weather is really hard on my fibromyalgia. My legs are stiff. At least at home I have the heater that a friend gave me. I even take it into the bathroom with me. What I'm looking forward to now is a nice hot soak in my bathtub. At home I'm fine. I wouldn't be here if I wasn't running short of money.

"I see these chicks wearing miniskirts up to here, nylons and pointy heeled come-fuck-me-boots. I want to say to them, 'Put a pair of pants on. When you get to work you can peel off in the washroom and come out looking fly. Who are you trying to impress out here on the street… me?'"

"Do you have your health card and your prescriptions, yet."

"No, I'm still trying to get in contact with my worker. I've left all kinds of phone messages. I told her, 'Either I'll be here, panning, or I'll be at home.' How complicated is that?

"There is an apartment opening up on the main floor. I'd be between the guys that stomp around — there's a third one now — and the crazy lady that screams all the time, but I could take care of that.

At the traffic island were Shakes, Buck, his dog Dillinger, and Weasel with Bear. The two dogs didn't get along, so Weasel tied Bear to a fence on the far side and Buck kept Dillinger on his leash. There was still some barking, growling and howling. Weasel said, "Bear thinks he's the boss, Dillinger thinks he's the boss. It's better just to keep them separated. Dillinger is just a pup."

Weasel asked Shakes, "How's it going? Everything okay at your place?"

"No, I haven't had a drink."

Weasel said, "I can help you with that." To the rest of us he said, "Shakes and me are the only ones of us who can't function at all before we've had a couple of drinks. I can't even make it from my couch to the fridge, and I live in a small bachelor apartment."

Shakes said, "Besides that, they've cut off my hydro. I phoned my worker about it. They're supposed to take care of that. She said, 'Just take your last bill to the bank. They'll look after it for you.' I said, 'What's the point of me taking it to the bank? I don't have any friggin money. I didn't even have money for the bus yesterday. I got on with Jake, he showed them his pass and I just sat down. The driver said to me, 'This bus isn't leaving until you get off.' "

I asked, "Did you get off?"

"No, I just sat there. Other people were getting off. They were asking, 'How long do we have to wait here?' The driver said, 'Until this guy gets off, or the police come, whichever happens first.' Eventually the transit security guys came. They took me off, then gave me a day pass so I could catch the next bus to get home."

Weasel said, "So security didn't mind you bothering another bus driver. They just didn't want you bothering that one."

"I guess so. Another problem I'm having is my phone doesn't work. It exploded."

Weasel said, "Don't give me that, Shakes! You threw it against the wall. We've all been there, done that."

Buck asked, "Did you hear that Donny in the electric wheel chair died? It happened just last Friday. They amputated both his legs, but the gangrene went higher. He died in hospital.

"His brother came down from Montreal. Donny had already died by then. The first thing the brother did was to contact Donny's worker, then he had the locks changed. That's strange, isn't it? Donny had a roommate. Now the roommate can't get in, get his stuff out or anything. The brother went back to Montreal."

Jacques said, "I saw Joy earlier. She and Chester went over to his place. They asked if I wanted to come, but they both smoke. I don't want to breathe that stuff. I'd rather stay out in the fresh air. I'd go home, but my window is boarded up and it's dark in there."

I asked, "Has anybody heard anything more about Luther?"

Jacques said, "You mean guitar player Luther? Last I heard, from somebody here, was that Luther had been beaten up and was taken to hospital. He wasn't expected to live through the weekend."

I asked, "Does anybody know his last name? Maybe I could look him up on the computer."

Weasel said, "John Jakes. His real name is John Jakes."

I said, "His real name is John, but they call him Luther for short?"

"Something like that."

If Only I Had Hydro

22 March 2013

I greeted the group standing on the traffic island and was about to sit on the concrete. Jake said, "Be careful, Dennis, don't sit on that metal plate. You'll freeze your ass off."

Jacques handed me a folded hoodie, I sat on that. When I was settled, Shakes said, "Thanks Dennis for giving me those bus tickets yesterday. I paid my fare and they took me home in handcuffs.

"I wasn't even drunk, I was just tired. I fell asleep and when I woke up I was in the bus garage at the end of the line. The driver called security. They drove me home in hand cuffs.

"I still don't have my hydro. I phoned my worker this morning. She said, 'I don't think we'll have time to see you today, Shakes.' I said, 'You mean I'm going to have to go all weekend without hydro? How would you like to go all weekend without hydro?' Then she said, 'We'll try to make room for you sometime this afternoon.' "

"Where is their office? Where do you have to go to meet them?"

"Their office is about a fifteen minute walk from here, but they know where I'll be. Where I am every day? At my office."

Jake asked, "Is everything turned off? When I had problems with hydro, a guy took me to the basement. He flipped a breaker switch and everything was okay after that."

Shakes said, "My heat isn't on, my stove doesn't work, my fridge doesn't work, my radio doesn't work, my lamp doesn't work, my microwave doesn't work, my dish washer doesn't work…"

"Shakes, you don't have a dishwasher!" said Jake, "but you've got a hell of a lot more than I have."

Jacques was paging through a flyer from the grocery store. He said, "I have to buy some margarine. They have Beycel here for $3.79, but that's too expensive. Here they have the meat pies I like. They're so good. Three meat pies, they call them, for $3.50 each. If someone had hydro, he could buy some of these. They're frozen, you just heat them up in your oven or microwave."

Jake asked, "When you're finished with that, Jacques can I have a look at it?

"When do we get our check this month?"

"This month we get it on the Thursday, because the next day is Good Friday."

"My birthday is on Wednesday. You mean I get my check the day after my birthday? For four days my younger brother and I are the same age. I get that extra $200.00 for my special (HIV/AIDS) diet. I'm spending it all on food this time. I'm going to stock my freezer full."

Jacques said, "Don't forget your bus pass. It's only $35. I always buy mine on check day. That way I don't forget."

Jake said, "Okay, Jacques you remind me and we'll both get them at the same time."

"I don't mind buying yours if you promise to pay me back."

"Thanks, Jacques. I'll pay you back. I'll be able to pay everybody back, as long as I don't celebrate too much on my birthday.

"Look over there, Uncle Wolf is really drunk. Shaggy is rolling in the snow."

Jacques said, "She wants to go home. She's been out all morning. Look who else is there, Jerry and Gnome, the biggest leeches in town. I bet they rob him blind. They know Wolf always makes lots of money on Friday because people know he won't be panning on the weekend. If Wolf sends Gnome on a run, he probably won't come back."

Pacing in Circles

25 March 2013

"It's my birthday." Jake said to me, "I turn 42 again, ha ha ha! I'm half in the bag now, thanks to Wolf, and I got some pot from Andre."

"Happy birthday, Jake!"

I walked over to Hippo, who I hadn't seen for about six months. "Hi Hippo, it's been a long time. How is everything going?"

"Fine, same old, same old. I got a picture on my phone here that I want to show you. It's a D-11 'dozer, the kind I drove in B.C."

"That looks like an expensive phone."

"Yes, it is, very expensive."

"Do you have any plans to go back there?"

"No, they're getting me set up on disability allowance. I'll wait to see how that works out."

Wolf called me over, "Dennis, I'm a bit wasted, but I wanted to tell you about a book I'm reading. It's written by a guy..."

Little Chester interrupted, "Hi Wolf!"

"Chester, will you give us a few minutes? I'll lose my train of thought. Now, where was I? If I get distracted, the little mice running around in their wheel in my brain get confused and go in every which direction, then I never know what will come to mind. Anyway, the book was written by somebody Sandford. I can't remember his first name (*John*). The title has 'Prey' in it, there is a whole series of them (*Eyes of Prey, Winter Prey, Naked Prey, Silent Prey, Night Prey*). The main character is Lucas Davenport, a so-called detective from Wisconsin. One of my ladies gave the book to me. I was surprised — it's a bit raw for their tastes. Anyway, you'd like it — a real shoot-em-up. You know the type. It's about this ninety-one year old man with dementia who thinks the Cold War is still going on. He believes he's in some kind of a sleeper cell working for the CIA. He engages his grandson to do his dirty work. He gets him to shoot an envoy from the Russian Embassy; of course, the grandson screws it all up. You get the idea."

Shaggy was getting restless and started barking. Wolf said, "Shaggy, stop pacing in circles. Pick someone, anyone, and bite them. How about Andre over there? No, it's just Andre's shoes you like to bite. How about Jake, or Chester? Okay then, just lie down on your blanket and be quiet. Here's a doggy biscuit. Dennis, you give her a biscuit. She'll love you for life."

I asked Jake, "Do you have your furniture yet?"

"No, not yet. I'm hoping to get some things soon."

Jake asked Gaston, "Do you guys ever come across used or discarded furniture?"

"Sometimes we do. What is it you need?"

"I really need a microwave."

"We'll see what we can do."

"Thanks, man, I'd appreciate that."

Could I Have a Cigarette?

26 March 2013

"Dennis, did I see you here yesterday?" asked Wolf.

"Yes, Wolf, I was here."

"I thought you might have been, but I couldn't be sure. I'm a bit foggy about yesterday, it being Jake's birthday and all. It was my job to take care of him, so to speak. All I remember is being woken up at the heater at 11:00 by the police saying I couldn't sleep there. It took me another two and a half hours to walk home. I stopped at the coffee shop on the way. I left Shaggy's blanket behind. I left her water dish behind."

"It's a good thing you didn't forget Shaggy."

"No, I'd never do that. She'd remind me. We've been through a lot together."

"So, Dennis, do you have a cigarette for me?"

"No, Wolf, I haven't had cigarettes for thirty years."

"You're no help!" To a passing woman he said, "Excuse me, ma'am, could I buy a cigarette from you?"

"Sorry, I only have a few left."

"Weasel, I hate to ask you since you just sat down, but could I have a cigarette?"

"Yes, Wolf, here you go. Jacques, will you pass this down?"

"Thanks, Weasel. I hate asking. I don't mind panning. I can get ten bucks that way, but asking for a cigarette? Some of my regulars won't even give me money if they see me smoking."

Jake asked , "Weasel, do we get our checks today?"

"I got mine, Joy got hers. Yours should be in the mail today."

Roommates

27 March 2013

The Salvation Army van was parked beside the traffic island. About a half-dozen people were milling around.

Buck said to me, "Joy's over there."

Shortly after, Joy came limping across the street. "I'm sorry I haven't been around much. My legs are really giving me trouble."

I asked, "Have you talked to your worker about getting your health card and your prescriptions?"

"I was just asking these ladies to pass a message along to her. I better go back, there's still some stuff I have to discuss with them."

"I'll come with you."

"André!" I said, "I haven't seen you for months, and you shaved this morning."

"I not only shaved, I've been sober for three months now. I've just been staying around home. I haven't been down here for ages."

"How is your stomach feeling?"

"A lot better now. I've still got problems, but not nearly as bad as before."

Chester said, "Dennis, remember those bus tickets you gave me a while back? I think I gave them to Joy or somebody. Do you have any more?"

"Sure, Chester, I've got extra."

"Thanks, Dennis, I'm going to be leaving now."

Mariah said, "He's just going to the Mission for his lunch. Joy and I were over at his place yesterday. Joy brought some steaks. Raven was there. Joy was really polite to her. She said to me, 'This is Chester's place, he can have anyone over that he wants to. I just wish he'd stay away from the people who are just after his money.'

"I don't know why he invites her over. She probably lets him play with her a bit, I don't know how far it goes.

"Anyway, Joy was cooking the vegetables and had the steaks in the frying pan. Raven comes over and starts fussing with the meat and flicking her hair. Both Joy and I got pissed off. Joy said, 'Just why are you here? Were you invited, or did you just decide to drop by? I'm trying to cook dinner for my friends.' Raven got the hint and left. Chester didn't say anything.

"I don't go out very often. I like to be alone and I have a certain reputation, being that I've lived in the building for four years. Whenever there is a vacancy, the landlady always asks me if I know them, and what kind of a person are they. There was a real problem with the guy who used to be in the basement. He was a real nut job. I probably had something to do with getting him to leave. He destroyed that apartment. The landlady sued him, but he must have had a really good lawyer because he didn't have to pay for any damage."

"What kind of damage did he do?"

"The kind of flooring that he had came in a roll, but it had lines on it. Do you know the type I mean?"

"Linoleum?"

"Something like that, anyway, when it's flat it looks like tiles. He used duct tape over every one of the lines, every place he thought a draft might come through. He took a hammer to the counter, left that in pieces, ripped the cupboards down. For some reason, he threw a bucket of water at the door. Like I said, he destroyed the place.

"I like to smoke every once in a while, when I lived at the back, I could never see the landlady coming. I'd hear her in the hall yelling, 'I know somebody's smoking here.' I'd get out the Febreze and some other things I use to clear the smell from the air. Now, I live in the front, so I can see her car pull up. She told me once, 'I know you smoke, but I've never seen you.'

"Yesterday, I invited Joy to come up. Outcast came over and they went back to her place for a while. He didn't stay long. She came back up and we listened to music, danced a bit, smoked, had a few beer.

"Every once in a while I have my concerts in the evening, the Eagles, another night it might be Santana, whatever I'm in the mood for. Around 10:30 I lower the volume. I don't want to get in trouble with my neighbors, but they all know me."

As I was leaving Wolf said, "Dennis, if you're coming by tomorrow, could you bring me a book? You know what I like, a spy story, espionage, that sort of thing. I've got the whole Easter weekend and no book to read."

Exotic Cheese

28 March 2013

As I approached the park I could see Wolf rummaging around in Shaggy's caboose. I handed him a Ken Follett book.

"What's this about?" asked Wolf.

"Espionage, the kind of stuff you like."

"Yeah, Ken Follett, I've read some of his stuff. He's good. Thanks, Dennis.

"Can I get you to fill Shaggy's water dish? I'd do it myself, but she wants it right now. There, see, she's trying to drink it before it even comes out of the bottle.

"I didn't even go to work this morning. Do you know what time Shaggy and I got up? 8:00, imagine that. Usually, I get up at 4:30 to get ready for 5:30, but not today, no siree. I had to come down here because I owed Jake forty bucks, otherwise I would have stayed home. Now, I'm drunk.

"Did you see the game last night? Boston against Montreal. At one point Montreal was behind four to two, then in the last thirty seconds they tied it up and won in overtime. That's why I have my Montreal sweater on. See what I'm wearing under this, another Montreal sweater. I got my Montreal cap and I'm sitting on a Montreal cushion. Just wait until some Boston fan comes by. I've got everything covered. It was really a fans game. I'm just waiting for Weasel to come by, he's a Boston fan. He's probably hiding from me."

Jacques was feeding Shaggy some pieces of his sandwich. Wolf said, "At least give her a piece with meat. She smells the cheese in your pack."

"Dennis," said Jacques, "you like cheese? Look what I got this morning at the store." He showed me a plastic container of garlic spiced, creamed cheese. "Two of these for five dollars, that's about half price. When they're near the expiry date they put them on sale. Smell this! You like Limburger? I love it, me. Again, two for five dollars. I had some brie, but already I ate all of it. It's better warmed up a bit. It was cold this morning so it didn't have much taste."

Wolf said, "Jacques and his exotic cheese. Yesterday I boiled some big chicken drumsticks with carrots, onion and celery. Just like my mother used to cook. She'd say, 'Now you boil it for an hour and a half, so it absorbs all the flavor from the carrots and celery.' It was delicious. Of course, Shaggy got some of it."

Jake said, "Jacques, do you want to come over to my place for some surf and turf? I'm really a good cook. I've got steaks, a bag of shrimp. I spent fifty bucks. My arm is sore from carrying two plastic bags of groceries all the way home. I really pigged out yesterday."

Jacques said, "I can't go to your place, I still have to get my pills."

"Shit, that's something I forgot to do, get my pills!"

Chester got up to leave. "I'll be back," he said, "I just have to pay my TV bill."

"Dammit!" said Jake, "I got a TV bill at home that I haven't paid. I forgot all about that. I hope they don't cut off my service."

2013 April

Book Club

This morning was finger numbing cold. Joy was wrapped in her blankets, sitting on a plastic box.

I asked, "Is this the first time you've been here this week?"

"Yeah, I've had a cold and have been staying inside lately. I'm really glad that you came along; I really have to pee. I'll have to go to the library this time. Can you watch my stuff?"

"Sure."

When Joy returned she said, "My legs are really bothering me today."

I asked, "Do you have your health card and your prescriptions yet?"

"No, I haven't seen my worker for a while. The one day she came by my apartment, I wasn't home. I'm entitled to go visit my friends, sometimes, especially since I still don't have any furniture. I didn't know she was coming. She said that I should get a phone, I said, 'Okay, you pay for it.' I'm damned if I'm going to pay for the expense of having a phone, or paying fifty cents to use the pay phone.

"I was over at Andre's place yesterday. Boy, you should see it. It's fully furnished. He's got a land line *and* a cell phone. Shakes, Weasel and Jacques were there. I didn't stay long. He said I could sleep on the couch, but I didn't want to, not with my own bed at home. I even forgot my groceries in the fridge."

"I hope you got them back."

"Yeah, I cooked them a nice dinner of spare ribs, potatoes and corn. They really appreciated it."

I asked, "Have you seen Serge lately? The last time I saw him was when he had his head and beard shaved."

"That's when he escaped from hospital. All he was wearing was a hospital gown. The guys brought him some clothes. He went back to hospital after that. Two of the workers from the Sally told me that they didn't expect him to come out of hospital alive.

"I get a kick out of the clothes some of these people wear. I wonder who dresses them. It couldn't be their mothers. Yesterday I saw this guy with his pant legs rolled up wearing nylons. I've heard of men wearing support hose, but these were nylons."

Shaggy started barking as I approached. Jacques handed me a folded yellow towel to sit on. Wolf handed me Shaggy's folded blanket. "I'm lending this to you on one condition," said Wolf, "you have to feed Shaggy." He handed me a tinfoil package of Lamb and Lavender dog treats.

I asked, "Do I give her one at a time, or all at once?"

"It's your choice."

I put a handful of treats in front of the dog.

"Wolf?" asked Joy, "what's the lavender for? Does it make her breath sweet?"

I sniffed the opened bag, but couldn't smell lavender.

Joy said, "That's the first time I've seen anybody smelling dog food."

Wolf said, "I didn't know there was lavender in this. I just saw lamb. What is lavender, anyway?"

"It's a flower," said Joy.

He read from the bag, "It says *the ingredients are all natural, no fillers*, so it's all good stuff."

Joy said, "I'm reading this book by Justin Cronin, it's from *The Passage Trilogy*. I'm just about finished it, the second book is *The Twelve*. It takes place in the future. They talk about 2013 as being about a hundred years from now. What would that make it? Anyway, the government injects these inmates with something that turns them into vampire like creatures. They got into a maximum security prison and started biting the inmates. Anyone bitten becomes a vampire. Their fingernails glow yellow and they sleep hanging upside down. They escape and wipe out most of the world. I can't wait to see what happens next."

Wolf said, "Speaking of books, have you read any of the Ed McBain books? Here it is, *Killer's Wedge*. There are about fifty of them in a series with Steve Carella and his fellow detectives of the 87th Precinct. Some of the cops are dirty, some are drunks, you know the type. I don't have to tell you. Anyway, they're an easy read. That's all I have to say about that."

Shaggy started barking at a woman passing by. Wolf said to Joy, "You're friend sure jumped this morning when Shag started barking."

"She's not my friend, she's my worker. I told her she didn't have to worry, but she said Shaggy bit a guy in the van. I said, 'She's bitten lots of people, me included.' "

Wolf said, "I've got a really good way of getting Shaggy home. I let Joy walk in front and Shag starts to chase her, but I have her on her leash. We're home in no time; no in and out of the cart, she just follows and chases Joy."

I said, "So you saw your worker this morning? Did she arrange for your health card and your prescriptions?"

"I've got a new validation number. I think I can take that to a doctor to get my prescriptions. The problem is, I switched to Little Jake's doctor, and now he's got about sixty custys (customers or patients) so I can never get an appointment.

Maybe I can take it to my old doctor. He kind of gave me the creeps, he's one of those turban heads. I've got some female stuff that needs checking and I'm not sure I want him down there. I wish I could find a woman doctor."

I said, "I know of a female doctor, but she's quite a distance from where you live."

"I don't want that. My old doctor was just down the street and I hardly ever went to him.

"They've got me set up to get furniture next Tuesday. I hope that works out. I fucked it up last time.

"Uncle Wolf, can I trade you eight brown (*native*) cigarettes for four white ones? Here's nine."

"That's not nine!" said Wolf.

"Well, that's not four," said Joy.

I said, "I'm glad you guys aren't getting into higher math, or you'd have a problem."

I'm Not Good at Accents

5 April 2013

It snowed last night, so the sidewalks were damp. Joy was sitting on her plastic crate, I sat on my backpack.

"I'm really cold," said Joy. "Under this blanket and coat I'm wearing a wind breaker, but I tell you, it's not breaking any fuckin' wind. Every time I lean over, a breeze whips up my back. When I woke up this morning, I noticed that I had a starter of $14. I didn't think I had that much left from yesterday. I was going to stay home, but I figured, I'm up, there's nothing else to do, so I might as well go to work.

"André was over last night. I cooked supper for him. At 10:30 I was getting tired, I told him, 'Look, you've got to go. I have to be up at 4:30.' He asked, 'Can't I just sleep on the floor?' I said, 'I wouldn't feel comfortable.' He said, 'You look comfortable, sitting there in your long johns and sweater.' I said, 'If you weren't here I'd be in my boxers and tee shirt.' I don't have to worry about André, apart from his usual groping, but I don't like men staying over. I like my privacy.

"I have to piss like a race horse. Can you watch my stuff? I'm going to have to go to the library. I went into the pizza place this morning and he was waiting for me at the bathroom door when I came out. He said, 'You can't just come in and use the washroom. It's for customers only.' I said to him, 'A lot of your customers are buying coffee and breakfast for me.'

"André and I ate breakfast there last week. They serve too much food. I had to stuff the sausages in my pocket to eat later. It must have cost us about thirty bucks, but it was sure good. I love sausages.

"I'm really feeling cold. I'm waiting for one of my regulars, the Australian guy. He comes every Friday if he's in town. I'm going for forty dollars this morning, so far I've got thirty-four. If he doesn't show, I'm going to leave."

I said, "Last time I was at the point (the traffic island), I had a long talk with Mariah. She seems really nice."

"Yeah, she is. André told me that she was a nympho, so I asked her about it. She said, 'Yeah, I am.' I said, 'But, you don't have a man around.' She went to one of her drawers and pulled out a bunch of toys and told me how she used them. That was too much information. She's not into women though, neither am I.

"Hi sweetie," Joy said to a man I recognized. "I was just telling Dennis here that I was waiting for my Australian friend."

"Actually, I'm not Australian, I'm Dutch."

"I'm sorry, I'm not good at accents." He handed Joy a folded bill.

"Thanks, that just made my day. You've been traveling, haven't you?"

"Yes, I've been away."

To me she said, "That's it, I'm out of here!"

Furniture Day

8 April 2013

Joy was in good spirits this morning. She has an appointment at 2:00 with her workers to get furniture for her apartment.

"I just hope they show up this time. Twice in the past I waited around all day for nothing. I hope I can get a DVD player, then I'll be able to return the one I borrowed from Mariah. I'm going over to Chester's later to borrow some DVDs. I'm tired of watching Transformers, the Godfather and Bladerunner over and over and over. I thought I'd never get tired of Bladerunner, but now I have the entire dialog memorized.

"André has a new couch for me. He's got it in storage along with a big table. It'll have room on it for my TV and some of my nick-nacks. He invited me over for supper, but why should I go there when I have plenty of food at home?"

I said, "I was talking to André last week. He said he'd been sober for three months."

"Well, he got drunk this past weekend.

"This morning I'm going back to tidy up, not that there's much to tidy, just my air mattress and some laundry."

Just Friends

15 April 2013

This morning was cold. Joy was wearing two hoodies, a jacket and a heavy sweater over top. Her legs were wrapped in a blanket.

"Hi Sweetie," she said, "I'm glad you're here. I have to take a major piss and I can't go into the pizza place. Will you watch my stuff and do your magic?"

I sat on her crate and guarded her cap with the change (*the jingle*). I smiled and tried to look needy, but nobody was buying it. I noticed the averted eyes. Some of my friends passed without saying hello.

Joy returned. I said, "I didn't have any luck."

"Mondays are always bad. I didn't want to come out today, but I missed Friday and Thursday because of the weather, so I figured I better get out."

"How did Tuesday go?" I asked," Do you have your furniture?"

"No, and I'm really pissed off that they cancelled again. I phoned my workers at about 1:00 Tuesday. As I was crossing the bridge. I heard one of them in the background say, 'If that's Joy, tell her we'll have to reschedule.' She couldn't even tell me herself. I said, 'I've been waiting five fuckin' months, this is insane! All my other friends have been taken to the warehouse to get furniture. Why is it that I have to wait so long?' I don't know what that woman has against me. If I gave her a shot in the head, they'd phone the police. I guess that wouldn't be a good move."

"I'm not like some of these other people. I have no family to turn to. Mind you, I'd have plenty of places to crash if I lost my apartment."

I asked, "How was your weekend?"

"It was cool. I went over to Andre's. Snuffleupagus was there, that's what I call Hippo. He was whining the whole time. 'I don't have any money in my bank account.' I told him that his GST *(Goods and Services Tax)* refund would be coming soon. His income tax refund would take a little longer. He'll just have to wait, like all of us. You can't hurry the government; but he wants it now!

"Weasel is pissed with me because he invited me over and I haven't been there yet. He had Jake over and split his eyebrow. I told Jake that when he mixes sherry and beer, like he does with his Jakeonator, he flips out and becomes a real asshole. That's what happened, so Weasel smacked him upside the head, chased him out the door and across the parking lot.

"Weasel said to me, 'You know I'd never hit you, Joy!' I said, 'Why not? It's not like I've never been hit before. Is it because I'm a woman? Well, I don't punch like a woman, so don't worry on that score.'

"I passed out on the couch. Weasel was asleep in a chair and André slept on the floor. Andre's sister was over. I like her. She's moving into a beautiful place. It's great if you can afford it. He'd been telling her that he wants to get together with me, but that's not going to happen. She'd look over at me with those questioning eyes, 'Why don't you like my brother?'

"It's not that I don't like André, I feel about him like he is my brother. Nothing's going to happen between us. I've been telling him that for two years now. Even when he and Weasel walked me home, he had this pouty face and said, 'Can I at least have a hug?' When I did hug him, he tried to kiss me on the mouth, but I turned my head and he got my cheek." I said to him, 'That's the reason there'll never be anything between us. The more you try to get closer, the more I'm going to push away.' Then he said, 'So, you want me to just leave you alone?' I said, 'Yes!' Maybe he'll eventually catch on.

"I'm still short four bucks. You don't have four bucks do you?"

"No," I said, "I only use plastic — to get the Air Miles."

"It's okay, I see my Dutch guy coming. This could be good."

The man said, "Hello" and dropped two quarters.

"Thanks, honey," said Joy. To me she said, "That's not good."

Protecting Sacred Ground

16 April 2013

It was raining this morning, so I wasn't expecting to see Joy, but there she was in her usual place. I said, "I'm surprised to see you here. I thought you'd stay home."

"I was up early and didn't have anything else to do, so I came here. It rained three times and it stopped three times. Who knows what the rest of the day will be like.

"Boy, I'm really glad you came, I'm near to busting with having to go to the bathroom. Can you watch my stuff?"

"Sure, you go ahead."

When she returned I asked, "So, did you talk to your workers? Is there any news about getting you furniture?"

"Yeah, that's set up for 1:00. The only thing I haven't done is the dishes. I'll do them before they arrive.

"I saw the guys yesterday. Jake threw Shakes out of his apartment. Shakes has lived outside all his life, he doesn't know how to act inside. Jake doesn't have furniture, just an air conditioner, still in its box, but just the same, he likes his place kept tidy. Shakes was flicking his cigarette ashes everywhere, grinding his butts out on the hardwood floor. It's not his fault. It's just the way he's lived all these years.

"Chester came with Raven, but as soon as she saw that Jacques had money she went with him. Chester wasn't too happy about that. Before they left Jacques said, 'Maybe, me, I get to play with a little pussy this afternoon.' I'm just glad that I'm single and celibate, no cooties for me. Some of the women these guys go out with — they're not pretty — most you'd have to double bag, and I mean Hefty bags.

"Can you mail a letter for me? It's to my youngest son, he lives with his older brother. I'm trying to get some communication going between us. The others I haven't heard from in a while. One's up in the Northwest Territories, working in a gold mine. He was raised by my sister and sent her a huge nugget. She had it appraised at twenty thousand dollars. I said, 'Hold on to that, he's going to need that for college.'

"I saw André yesterday, while he was still sober I said to him, 'You know there is never going to be anything between us. You're like a brother to me. Do you understand that?' He said, 'Yeah, I guess so.' "

"So, do you think he got the message this time?"

"I hope so."

At noon it was still misty, as I passed a bus shelter I saw Danny and Shakes. "Hey, it's been a long time, man!" said Danny.

"Yes it has, Dan.

"Shakes, do you have your hydro turned on yet?"

"Yes I do. That Friday that it went off, I phoned my worker and said, 'I want my fuckin' hydro turned on. It's a long weekend coming up. How would you like your fuckin' hydro off for that long? I'm going to be out this afternoon, but when I get home for supper the fuckin' hydro had better be on.'

"You told her, Shakes!"

"Yeah, I sure did, ha ha ha."

"So, Danny, have you been panning near the mall?"

"No," he said, "Did you hear what happened to me there a couple of years ago? I wanted a Happy Meal from McDonalds, but I was a bit drunk and I knew they wouldn't serve me. I didn't have any money, but I had just been to the pharmacy and had my prescription for Percocet refilled. I asked a guy going into McDonalds if he used Percocet. He said, 'Yeah!' I asked, 'For three Percs would you buy me a Happy Meal?' He said, 'Sure!' What he did was go straight to this big security guard and told him I stole some Percs from him.

"The security guard came out and tried to put his hands in my pockets. I wouldn't let him and pushed him away. Another security guard came along and grabbed my arm. The other one kicked my leg from behind and broke it. It was sticking way out to the side. They put me in cuffs and phoned the police. I managed to squirm my way, with the broken leg, to a pay phone. With the handcuffs behind my back, I was still able to pull myself up, knock the receiver off the hook and dial 911. I said to the operator, "I've been beaten by security guards and they broke my leg. I need an ambulance. The operator said they had already received a call and an ambulance was on its way.

"By that time the police had arrived. They wouldn't listen to anything I said. One put his knee on my head, breaking my glasses. The other one took the pills out of my pocket and handed them to someone.

I said, "I have a prescription for those pills, just ask at the pharmacy. They didn't even check. The cop said to me, 'You're nothing but a homeless, drunken Indian. If you don't shut up we're going to take you out of town and bury you.'

"I yelled to people in front of the mall, 'My name is Daniel Marois. The police have just told me they are going to kill me, take me out of town and bury me.'

"The ambulance came and took me to the hospital. They set my leg, put it in a cast and a brace. I was supposed to go for physio therapy, but I'm an alcoholic. There's no way I could sit in a room for three hours without a drink. Besides, it was on the other side of the city. I didn't even have money for bus tickets -- I hadn't been panning, so I had no money coming in.

"I wore that leg brace for a year and a half. In the end, it did help me. People are more likely to give money to a guy in a brace than one without.

"Ever since then I've been afraid for my life. I'm supposed to be part of a native group protesting the wind turbines scheduled to be installed on Thunder Mountain. They want to put them on sacred land. If the police see me, I'm afraid that one of them will push me in front of a car.

"I was talking to the Anishinaabe Clan Mothers at Maniwaki and in Cornwall. I explained to them that this protest could end up like the one at Oka. The young people wouldn't remember, but I was there. Some of them wouldn't feel comfortable carrying guns, but there would be guns behind them, protecting them.

"It was our Chief that signed over the land to the wind turbine company. I said to him, 'It won't be you standing in the front lines blocking the equipment. It'll be me.' I've served over fifteen years in correctional institutions and mental institutions. I don't mind going to jail. In fact I would be proud to give my life to protect our sacred ground. It's all we have."

Interesting Times

This morning was interesting, as in the Chinese curse, "May you live in interesting times." Joy was on her crate as usual, standing behind her was a powerful looking man and a small woman. I recognized them, but hadn't seen them for about a year.

Joy said, "Dennis, you remember Daimon and Lucy in the Sky?"

"Yes," I said, "I haven't seen you two for a long time."

Joy whispered to me, "This is scary."

Daimon pulled out a bottle of sherry, took a swig and passed it to Joy. She hesitated, but he insisted.

Joy said, "I really appreciate you guys coming by, but I don't want any of my regulars to see me drinking. I've been out here since 6:00 and I've only made about $2.00. Have a look in my cap."

Daimon said, "No problem, Joy, I'll help you."

A man walked past and Daimon said, "Hey, don't forget about the hat!"

Lucy laughed and said, "That's what he does when we're panning."

Joy asked Daimon, "Have you been in any fights lately?"

"No, not for about a year."

"Of course, you had your leg in a cast for most of that time."

"No, it wasn't that. I didn't have the need to fight anybody."

Joy asked, "How about you, Lucy?"

"No, I haven't been fighting. I robbed a guy yesterday. It was his stupidness. He didn't see Daimon standing in the background. He asked if he could have anal sex with me. I said, 'Sure, let's go into the alley.' Daimon followed us in there. He said to the guy, 'Give this woman all your cash, then fuck off.' The guy ran. What was he going to do? Call the cops?"

Joy said, "Something similar happened to me last week. A guy propositioned me. I said to him, 'It'll cost you eighty bucks and cab fare to my place. Cash up front, now.' We hailed a cab, and when we got to my building, the guy was busy paying the driver, I hopped out the door — I can be pretty nimble when I have to. I ran across the parking lot into my apartment and locked the door. The guy didn't know where I went. Served him right."

Daimon and Lucy moved down the street. Joy said, "They told me they were feeling drug sick. He said he has a check coming, so they didn't hassle me. When Big Jake was around, I got in a fight with Lucy. Daimon punched me in the side of the head. Jake picked him up by the front of his coat and threw him right on his ass. He said 'This is girl stuff. Let them fight it out themselves. If it's man stuff you want, you can take me on.' Daimon just sat there in the middle of the street."

Joy asked me, "Do you know what time it is?"

"No," I said, "I don't have my watch."

"You hid it when you saw Daimon and Lucy. Am I right?"

"No, I just forgot it at home. I'll let you get back to work.

10:00 am, at the point. I sat between Joy and Chester. Chester said, "The buses are free for seniors today, but do you have any spare bus tickets for tomorrow?"

"Sure, Chester. How are your legs feeling?"

"They're okay. They hurt a bit. I've been sober for the last three days. I can do that. It gives my body a chance to recover."

Joy asked Chester, "Can I borrow your phone? I want to call Buck to see if he can bring me some weed and some cigarettes."

On the phone Joy said, "Hi Sweetie, where are you? In bed? I'm sorry, did I wake you? I was going to ask, were you whacking off? but, you beat me to the punch. So, are you coming down? Okay, we'll see you then."

To me she said, "Poor guy, he walks all the time and he wonders why he gets tired."

I asked, "How did the meeting with your worker go? Do you have furniture yet?"

"It was a joke. They took me to the Thrift store and gave me a voucher for sixty dollars. I was supposed to get a hundred. Anyway, I bought a comfy office chair and a foot stool that opens up at the top for storage. I also got two black fluffy mats. One I'm going to put under my air mattress. The other I'll put in the hall. What I really wanted was a love seat they had, but the price was a hundred dollars, so I'll have to make do with what I got. They'll be scheduling a visit to the giant warehouse, that'll be in about two weeks or so. I guess they'll bump me to the top of the list. I'm not quite sure how that works.

"When this furniture deal gets settled, I'm going to have a showdown with my worker. I want to find out why she treats me the way she does. I know she's a dyke and I've got no problem with that. What people do in their private lives is up to them. What they do when they're working for me is what I'm concerned about. I'm not the only one having trouble with her.

"By the way, when I went back to the library again, to use the washroom, I saw Daimon and Lucy. They were sitting on one of the top benches. Daimon said, 'We're up here looking down on everyone.' When I came back they were both asleep."

Drug Sick

19 April 2013

When I squatted down to talk to Joy she said, "Daimon and Lucy have been creeping about this morning. They're both drug sick. Daimon went somewhere to get some sleep. Lucy said she'd stop to talk with me, but she had to get fixed. You won't believe it but she asked me, 'Do you have a rig with you?' I said 'I'm not a user, and even if I was, I wouldn't keep that stuff on me.' It would be just my luck to have a cop check my bag and get pricked with a needle. That would be an attempted murder charge against me.

"Anyway, Lucy slunk off to the coffee shop to use their bathroom. They won't let her into the pizza place. She'll be smashing in there. It's been a while since she left. Maybe she's nodded off. I guess I'll find out when I go there later.

"She was looking really rough, wearing baggy winter pants. It looked like she hadn't bathed for a while.

"I've got a sore neck from that office chair I got. It has a high back and the only way I can rest my head is to stretch out. I have to hunch my back to watch my DVDs. Hippo brought me a bunch. The ones I enjoy the most I've been watching over and over, there's The Godfather, Serpico, Bladerunner. I have the dialog memorized from that one.

Pirates of the Caribbean. He also brought me Charlie's Angels. I can't see myself watching that."

I said, "I like movies with Johnny Depp."

"They're weird, man."

"Do you mean weird as in Edward Scissorhands?"

"Yeah that and Willie Wonka, and there's the one where he plays the Mad Hatter and Finding Neverland. I heard that in real life he wears women's underwear under his clothes."

I said, "He played in the movie Ed Wood. His character was a producer of B movies, who is also a cross dresser."

"That wouldn't be much of a stretch for him. I can't imagine any guy wanting to wear women's underwear. Even I don't like to wear women's underwear. I wear men's boxers, because they're more comfortable.

"When I was with Big Jake, he wanted me wearing these panties cut way up on the sides. He thought they looked sexy. He even had me wearing a thong. Can you imagine walking around with a string up your ass? If you sat or squatted wrong, they'd cut you."

I asked, "Have you been taking your medication?"

"I've been taking it, but not the way I'm supposed to. I'm trying to make the pills last until I get my health card. It pisses me off that my worker hasn't got me one after five months. Everybody else has theirs."

A well dressed woman stopped to talk to Joy and dropped $5:00. She asked, "How have you been, I haven't seen you around for a while?"

"I was in hospital from December to the end of January. It was because of the fibromyalgia I've got in my legs. I was in a wheelchair for a while, then a walker, then a cane. I couldn't get out much."

"How are you feeling now?"

"I gimp around a bit. I won't be running anytime soon. If I get chased by a ferocious dog, I'll just lay down and get eaten. I won't have any choice."

"All the best to you," said the woman as she walked away.

I said, "She seems nice."

"Yeah, she doesn't usually drop me money. She's a big shot with the government. When she's alone, and only when she's alone, she'll stop to talk with me. When she's with people from work, she doesn't even look at me. I guess she's embarrassed."

I met the rest of the group at 11:00 at the point. I asked Joy, "Did Daimon and Lucy come back after I left?"

"No, and I checked the washroom. I just can't understand people smashing that stuff in their arms. It just makes you nod off."

Two women, Sophia and Becky approached. Sophia said, "We just graduated on Tuesday, so we're free now."

"Congratulations!" said Joy. "Hey, you've put on some weight. The other day I saw you from across the street. I was going to say, 'Sophia, your ass is bigger.' I decided not to."

After they left I asked, "What did they graduate from?"

"I don't know, probably rehab. I think that was part of Sophia's parole, that she'd have to attend rehab. They're confined to a house. They have to do chores. They're monitored all the time."

"When I was released from Kingston, I was sent to rehab in Hamilton. It was all paid for. I was using crack then.

"They gave us these little, blue Twelve Step books from AA. I said to the woman, 'I'm not here for alcoholism; I'm here for drug addiction.' She said, "Just replace the word alcohol with the word drug. It's the same program.

"I got kicked out of there. You couldn't buy crack in Hamilton, so my friend and I went out and got drunk. They made a mistake in refunding me the unused portion of the money paid for the program. I got really wasted after that.

"My mom wouldn't speak to me while I was taking drugs. I quit, but I'd lost weight, so she thought I was still using. She wouldn't let me see my kids. I had lots of money then. She liked that."

"Earlier, I tried taking a pee behind that brick wall. Bruce yelled over at me, 'Joy, I can see your bum.' I tried to turn around a bit, but the shrubs don't give much cover. I couldn't pee after that. I'm going to go back there and try again."

Joy walked across the street and I talked to Bruce, who I hadn't seen since he'd invited me over for Christmas dinner. "How are things going in your new place, Bruce?"

"Great, sometimes I don't even want to leave. I pan in my usual spot from 6:00 to around 9:00. I make about twenty bucks, enough to buy my smokes and a few groceries. I go grocery shopping twice a week. My freezer is full. I'm eating well. I only drink once a week — today.

"My place is small, just a bachelor with a big double bed. My girlfriend had been staying with me, but she had to go to hospital for gall stones. They did what they call non-invasive surgery. They put a tube through her nose and vacuumed the stones out that way.

"It was awful when I went in to see her. She had the tube in her nose, the oxygen tube, she had to have a blood transfusion. There were machines with wires hooked to her arms. Her blood pressure was going up and down. I thought I was going to lose her.

"Then she developed pancreatitis. I'm sure she picked that up in the hospital, because it was antibiotic resistant. She'd never taken antibiotics before so she wasn't immune. It wasn't an allergy. Anyway, they had to use two of the strongest antibiotics they had. She's fine now.

"She's gone to stay with her folks for a while. I hope she doesn't start drinking again. When she was here, I could keep an eye on her."

My Friends

21 April 2013

Today is Sunday, which means that I won't be seeing my friends until tomorrow. Following are some word portraits, so you can get to know them:

Joy

Love is amazing –
when we give it freely
it doesn't diminish,
it enriches our souls.
Joy, is a panhandler
(incapable of anything else),
she is also my friend.
Each morning
(on my way to work)
I eagerly anticipate
her greeting and warm smile.
I sit with her
on the sidewalk,
as witness
to her blackened eyes.
I listen to her stories

of beatings and abuse,
give comfort
when she cries.
"Tears are a sign of weakness"
her father used to say.
I bring her tea
(cream and three sugars),
a bagel with cream cheese,
on mornings when frost
is on the ground,
and on the hearts,
of most passers by.
She gives to me
her hand to hold,
an attentive ear
to my daily problems,
and a hug
(when a hug is needed).
With her kindness,
Joy has enriched my soul
and filled my heart with tenderness.
She has given me so much
that I didn't know existed –
I am deeply in her debt.

Antonio

My friend, Antonio,
greets me
with a salute and a bow
(it's his way).
I am very glad to see him

and very honored.
I don't see him very often,
he has his own schedule,
not necessarily
corresponding with mine.
He's a free spirit.
Through dark glasses
he sees the world
(so not to offend).
He is very conscious
that his appearance
may cause concern.
He wears a beard,
his clothes are ragged,
all his belongings
follow him
in a shopping cart.
He feels uncomfortable
in enclosed spaces,
so he sleeps outdoors,
summer and winter,
on a park bench
(with his friends
the squirrels),
when temperatures
are well below freezing.
He is not immune
from assault,
beatings
(having his teeth kicked out),
not because of what he does,
but what he is,
how he appears.

I usually see him
in front of the library,
one of his favorite places.
He likes to look at books
and see pictures
of kings and other people
he has studied
in school.
Occasionally,
he joins me for coffee.
He tells me
the most wondrous stories.
Sometimes,
I think he makes them up
for my benefit.
In any case
I am honored.

Through Shaded Eyes

A breathless beauty,
enchanting and fanciful,
where castles of ice abound –
if we didn't know just where to look
they never would be found.
A wonderland of mystery
in a public park downtown.
The squirrels know what life's about –
in Antonio's sleeping bag
they tunnel in and out.
They scamper
over drifts of snow,

no boots upon their feet.
When he awakes, he'll feed them
the little he has to eat.
Through shaded eyes
he views, the world passing by.
With gentleness and thoughts of kings
he tells me of his precious dreams.
A shopping cart, holds all his worldly things.

André

So, I'm panning
in my usual spot.
This suit walks by –
in passing he says,
"Get a job!"
"Hire me!" I say.
"Take a shower!" he says.
"I may sleep outside,
that doesn't mean
I don't wash –
I wash all over!"
"Hey," I say,
"if you're so successful,
why do you look
so unhappy?
"I've made the price
of my bottle.
I've got some smokes,
a little pot.
"Me, I'm the happiest guy alive."

Shakes

it's nice
waking up
in the morning.
If I don't,
I know
something's
wrong.
I don't know
where I am,
or how I got here,
but, I'm here.
I got some wine,
some cigarettes
and some 'mary jane' –
I start walking,
ain't looking
for trouble, but
it finds me.
how am I?
I'll be doing fine
soon as I get
this drunk on.

Alphonse

I look into your eyes,
grey with tears and sorrow
from the Arctic Ocean.
I feel your hurt deep inside,
hear your thunder,

see your rain.
With your fist at your chest
you open your heart,
tell me of hardship,
betrayal and pain.
I listen
with my heart
as one who has been there.
With my arm around your shoulder,
as a brother,
I urge you, to act with patience
and with love –
to be LOVE.

A Lost Brave

a lost brave
leans against a building
(tho he is unwelcome)
beside a busy walk.
everything he owns
fills a pack
upon his back
he is far
from his fishing boat,
an ocean teeming with fish,
from the majestic forest,
from his children,
his clan
his eyes reveal
a story of hurt and pain -
the uncertainty of the city.

a sidewalk for a bed,
charity of strangers
his only grace
a challenge
every day -
a new beginning.
beyond the fire
that tames his demons
the only plan that matters
is to survive
far from home
he can scarce remember.
a lost brave, fighting back tears,
pride in the knowledge
of his ancestry,
his place -
his blood

Venting

23 April 2013

"Hi, Sweetie," said Joy, "I listened to Buddy the weather man this morning. He said it was supposed to be warm, so I didn't wear my long johns. As soon as I got outside I thought, *That was a mistake, but it's too late to go back now.* I'm sitting here shivering. I'm glad I've got my blanket. I'm also glad I have this crate to sit on. When I was down on the sidewalk, I could see way too much. Now, at least I'm above ass level.

"Some of these women wear skirts that are way too short for the size of their waistlines. I don't need that view before breakfast."

"How was your weekend?" I asked.

"I wasn't here yesterday because I was feeling sick. I was at Andre's on the weekend. I cooked spare ribs. We got barbecue sauce from this Chinese place where we got the ribs. Every time I've used it for marinating, I've had the runs for four days.

"I was at home Sunday, all snuggled up in my jammies, ready for bed, when André bangs at the door. I said, 'What are you doing here?' With a mournful look he pouted, 'You said I could come over sometime.' I said, 'I didn't mean now!' He came over the next day with Hippo and brought the rest of the ribs, so I cooked supper again.

"I explained to him, 'There's never going to be anything between us. Stop pushing me!' If he had teeth it might be different, but he's got that gaping space in front, and the few teeth he has in back are rotten. I can't even sit close to him because of his foul breath. Shakes is the same.

"He said, 'I'm saving my condom supply for you.' I said, 'Don't bother.' I believe in safe sex, but I can just imagine what kind of diseases he's carrying.

"You should see some of the skanks he goes out with. There's one fat bitch who is huge. I can smell her from fifteen feet away. He said he only gets blow jobs from her, but she sleeps in his bed. I don't know how he can put up with the stink.

"He came down here this morning at 8:00. He asked, 'What are you doing?' I said, 'What the fuck do you think I'm doing! I'm working!' Even Big Jake had the sense not to come down for me until 9:00.

"Well, that's my venting for the day."

I asked, "Have you heard from your workers about taking you to the furniture warehouse?"

"I'm going to phone them this afternoon. I'll borrow Chester's phone. One worker was over yesterday. She asked to use the bathroom. It was just an excuse to scope out the place. When she came out she asked, 'Why do you have two tooth brushes and men's hair gel in the bathroom?' I said, 'Hippo brought the Axe, 'cause his hair's getting so long he can't manage it. The two tooth brushes are mine. I use the blue one in the morning, it's newer, but I like to use the green one at night, because it has a tongue cleaner on it.'

I said, "You mentioned that Big Jake was getting out of prison soon."

"Yeah, May 17th. One of his friends was going to sponsor him, but he's been sick, so I guess he'll be going to a halfway house. He's got family here, so this is where he'll be coming. People ask me if I'll be getting back with him. I tell them, 'I don't want to be with anyone, but if he's changed I might consider it.' I'd rather just have him as a fuck buddy.

"Here comes Chester. I wonder what he wants."

I said, "I'll leave you to it."

"That's it, leave me alone with him."

You People

25 April 2013

This morning was sunny but cold, 39 degrees. I usually walk straight to Joy's spot, but I had run out of bus tickets and coffee shop cards, so I had to make two stops, stand in two lineups. When I got to Joy's spot, she was sobbing.

"Thank God you're here. I saw you cross the street and I thought I wouldn't see you. I left my purse at Outcast's place last night. I took a cab, and only after I tried to pay the fare did I realize I didn't have my purse with me. In it I had my cash, my pot, all my phone numbers. I told the guy, 'I'm just going to go up to my friend's place to get some money.' He grabbed my bag and said, 'I'll hold onto this until you get back.' I went to Mariah's place. She wasn't home. Even if she didn't have any money I could have used her phone to call André or Outcast. I went down to the cab and said to the guy, 'Fuck man, I got no money. I can't call my friends. Can I pay you tomorrow? He said, 'I'll give you twenty-four hours, then I call the police. What is it with you people? You think you can get away without paying. I got bills to pay.'

I said to him, 'First of all, what's this **you people**. Do you think I'm a hoe? I wouldn't be wearing nearly this many clothes if I was hooking. Do you think I'm a crack addict? Do I act like a crack addict? Is it because I'm part native?' This guy was a fuckin' immigrant! I was born here.

"This morning I had to beg the bus driver to let me on. I said to him, 'I got no tickets, can I give you four (*each fare is two tickets*) tomorrow. He said, 'Okay, I see you going in to the hotel through the back way. Why don't you go through the front?' The only reason I go in there is to take a piss, but I said to him, 'I work as a cleaner there. Only paying guests are allowed to use the front door.'

"Most of the regulars on the bus think I work in construction. I overheard this woman say that one of her pipes was leaking. I said to her, 'It sounds to me like you just need a plastic elbow. It'll fit inside your pipe and stop the leak.' This other guy says, 'If you're a tradesman, how do you cut marble?' I said, 'I'd use a Jig saw and plenty of water to keep the blade cool.' I just pick this stuff up on programs like How's this Made.

"It's just like when I was in prostitution. For a while I worked in a phone sex chat room. People say I have a sexy phone voice. I've heard myself on tape recorder. I just think it sounds nasal, like I have a sore throat. I went by the name Lincoln. But I'd say 'I'm not that big, but I do purrrr.' It was crazy working in that place. There were about sixty of us in this room, we each had a cubicle. Most of the time we'd have our feet up munching on something. When we'd get a call, we weren't allowed to initiate the conversation. Just like when we were on the street, the guy would have to tell us what he wanted and we'd give him a price. We'd wait until the guy said something like, 'What are you wearing?' I'd say, 'I'm just curled up in my pink baby dolls, waiting for you handsome.' Otherwise we could have been charged with soliciting.

"Big Jake phoned me one time, and, I mean I was living with the guy, right, so he knew how I'd be dressed and what I looked like. We chatted for a while and when I got home he said, 'I had such a hardon all afternoon, I had to leave work, it was such a stiffy' — or woody, or chipmunk, or whatever you want to call it.

"Anyway, I was sure glad you came along this morning. You cheered me up. When I saw you go by, I just put my head down in my lap and started bawling my eyes out. This old lady stopped, not one of my regulars, and asked, 'What's the matter, deary? Is there anything I can do to help?' She reached into her purse and dropped me one blue bus ticket. I don't know if they even take them anymore. That was before the pink ones, the orange ones. And there was only one. I guess I could have told the driver that it was folded and I couldn't get it apart. That might have worked."

We saw Chester coming. "What does that old fart want? It's always something, bus tickets, cigarettes…"

Chester said, "Hi Joy, Dennis. I can't stop. I'm going somewhere."

Joy said, "You're always going somewhere."

"Cheer up," he said, "We get our checks tomorrow. You'll be getting yours too. I'll see you."

"I was hoping that André would be coming down. Last time I saw him was at Mariah's. He was fooling around with this stupid camera. When Mariah saw that he'd taken her picture, she beat the shit out of him, had him in a headlock and was pounding his face. There are a lot of people who don't like to have their picture spread around."

I asked, "What's Mariah worried about?"

"I shouldn't be saying this, but she was with a motorcycle gang in Montreal. They've now joined up with a larger, international gang. Well, she brought the affiliation papers to the larger gang. I'd tell you the names, but then I'd have to kill you."

Next came Toothless Chuck (*not to be confused with his father, Chuck who has teeth*). "Hi Joy! Dennis! Haven't seen you guys for ages. Joy, I got those paints you wanted."

"Cool, man. I've painted some vines on my walls and I wanted to add some color — flowers or something."

"If you see Dan, tell him I have a box of oil pastels that I want to sell. I'm having a barbecue this afternoon. Do you want to come? Shark and Irene will be there."

"I don't know man. Shark and I don't get along so well."

"Just talk to Irene then. There will be lots of other people. I'm on my way to pick up some groceries. I'll pick you up on the way back."

I went to the park at noon. Wolf had mentioned that he didn't have anything to read for the weekend. I brought him

Ian Fleming's, *On Her Majesty's Foreign Service,* a James Bond novel. He was very grateful. He said, "I'll give it back to you once I'm finished."

"No, you keep it, Wolf."

"I really appreciate that. It'll be in my bookshelf if you ever want it back. Books are like gold to me. I can't stand it when people abuse books.

"I'm just coming off a ten day drunk. I was even drinking what these people drink. What is it, Imperial or that Pale Dry. I know why Joy went to hospital. I haven't had a solid shit since I started drinking that stuff. It's back to Blue for me; not even Old Milwaukee. I don't need that extra half percent alcohol.

"If you don't have a solid shit, you're not healthy. That's my advice. Now if you don't mind I'm going to sit down before I fall."

Shakes called me over. He was half sitting half sprawled on the curb. He reached for my hand and pulled me down.

Jake said, "You two are really getting close."

Shakes whispered, "Dennis, can you give me some bus tickets? I'll need six, two for me to get home and four for Danny and I to come down tomorrow. Dan's not like me. I'll say to him, 'Lets jump on at the back door.' He won't, not if he's sober. Did you know that he's living at my place now? He doesn't like the way I live. He's always tidying up. Thanks, Dennis."

I sat between Wolf and Mariah. I asked her, "I guess you heard about Joy leaving her purse at Outcast's place last night?"

"Yeah, she came running up to my apartment, but I didn't have any cash. She should get it back today, unless she dropped it somewhere between Outcast's and the cab. You know how us women depend on our purses."

Wolf leaned over and whispered to me, "I'd be surprised if her money's still there. I don't know if he'd steal from Joy, but he stole from me when he came over to buy some crack. He can't be trusted, but that's just between me and you. Nobody else heard that."

Shakes ambled over, parked himself on a vacant pillow near the curb.

"Yeah, Shakes, you might as well join us. You're already sitting on my toilet seat cushion (*referring to the Montreal Canadians hockey team logo*)."

Shaggy started barking. Wolf reached into Shaggy's buggy and pulled out a tinfoil bag of treats. Shakes was fumbling, trying to open the bag. Wolf said, "If he doesn't get that bag open soon, Shaggy will bite him. She will, she's like that and it doesn't matter what race the person is; black, brown, yellow or white, she'll bite them."

Shakes had the bag opened and put one of the doggy treats in his mouth, then leaned toward Shaggy. Wolf said, "Those treats are pretty small, I don't think he should try that."

Shaggy took the treat without incident. "How old is Shaggy?" asked Shakes.

Wolf said, "She's as old as I've known you. You came here twelve years ago; she's twelve years old."

Jacques said, "Shakes, hand me that bag. I want to see if it has glucosamine in it. I've asked my doctor if glucosamine will help my arthritis. He always changes the subject. He won't give me a straight answer. Yes it has glucosamine, along with pea flour, rice flour, miniblablabla…"

I said, "Ask Shakes how they taste. Maybe you'll like them."

Mariah said, "Glucosamine is good for cartilage. I take it all the time."

It was time for me to go back to work. As I struggled to my feet, Mariah held out her arm. I leaned on it to get my balance.

I said, "Us old people need a helping hand every once in a while."

"You could have leaned harder than that. I'll need a hand up when it's time for me to go."

Same Mother, Different Fathers

26 April 2013

It rained last night, so there were puddles on the sidewalk. I didn't expect Joy to be at her spot, but there she was. I asked, "How was the barbecue yesterday?"

"It was good, except for Shark. I told Chuck that Shark and Irene would bail, and sure enough they did. We were waiting to eat, Chuck had to go to Shark's place to buy some pot. He figured he could talk Shark into coming. When he came back he asked me, 'What is it between you and Shark?' He said to me, 'I'll sit at the same table with Joy, but I'm not going to feed her.' I said, 'It's thirty years of fighting. Don't sweat it. I wouldn't eat any food that Shark's greasy, fuckin' fingers had touched anyway.

"I'm expecting Chester to come by. He'll have his check by now. He wants me to move back with him. He knows how much I hate the place I'm in now, but I don't hate it that much."

"He's still seeing Raven, isn't he?"

"Whenever he thinks he can get a piece of ass. I've had it with her. The last time I had anything to do with her was at his place. I think I told you about it. I was cooking steaks. She

327

came over and leaned her head almost into the frying pan. Her long fuckin' hair was nearly touching our food. I was cool, I just went downstairs to talk to Mariah. What I wanted to do was take the steaks out and push her skinny face into the grease of the pan.

"Since then she's come up to me and said, 'I'm so sorry Joy.' I just said, 'Keep the fuck away from me, and don't ever talk to me again.' I can be a real bitch sometimes."

I asked, "Apart from Shark and Irene not turning up, how was the rest of the party?"

"It was good until Chuck's landlord came over. Chuck laid into him with, 'When are you going to fix my fuckin' window? It's a hazard. A child could fall through there.' I could see this was going bad, so I stepped between them. I took Buddy into the hall. He asked, 'Who are you?' I said, 'I'm Chuck's sister and I may be looking for a place if the price is right.' He said, 'You sure don't look like Chuck.' I said, 'Yeah, well, same mother, different fathers. The only thing we share in common is sperm.' He asked, 'Where are you from and what do you do?' I couldn't decide what to say, but I said, 'I'm from Montreal. I work in housing maintenance. I could fix that window for you, but as far as living here, you're charging way too much. Chuck's paying $890. I know you've done some painting upstairs, but I wouldn't take it for more than $700. It's only one room.

"Chuck came storming out and said, 'Look, you fuckin' nigger. Get out of my place before I put you down right here.' I said, 'Hold on Chuck, I was negotiating a reduction in your rent.' I knew that Buddy had a button on his phone that would have brought a dozen of his black brothers here in minutes. He got in his truck, drove ten feet, then slammed on his brakes. I thought we were in for it then, but he drove off.

"I picked up a butter knife and tightened the screws in the window so it doesn't sag. Chuck said, 'What about the next time it comes loose?' I handed him the butter knife, saluted and left."

In the Realm of Hungry Ghosts

26 April 2013

I've sometimes wondered why I'm drawn to homeless people. I've found some answers in the book, In the Realm of Hungry Ghosts: Close Encounters with Addiction by Gabor Mate, M.D.

Dr. Mate works with drug addicts in the former Portland Hotel, on Hastings Street, in Vancouver's Downtown Eastside, considered Canada's drug capital.

"What keeps me here?" muses Kersten Steuerzbech. "In the beginning I wanted to help. And now ... I still want to help, but it's changed. Now I know my limits. I know what I can and cannot do. What I can do is to be here and advocate for people at various stages of their lives, and allow them to be who they are. We have an obligation as a society to ... support people for who they are, and to give them respect. That's what keeps me here."

"Liz Evans began working in the area at the age of twenty-six. 'I was overwhelmed,' she recalls. 'As a nurse, I thought I had some expertise to share. While that was true, I soon discovered that, in fact, I had very little to give — I could not rescue people from their pain and sadness. All I could offer was to walk beside them as a fellow human being, a kindred spirit.' "

I hope that you've enjoyed reading about my friends. Every person has a story, these are just a few. This is the end of Book 2, but don't worry, Book 3 has been written and is now being edited. Visit my blog, Gotta Find a Home at: http://gottafindahome.com to read about recent adventures, promotions and links to my new book a soon as it has been released.

Thank you for your support in buying and reading my book. If you enjoyed it, I would be very pleased if you posted a review (no matter how short) on Amazon, Goodreads and any of your social networks. All author royalties go directly to people forced onto the streets and to Ottawa Innercity Missions, Street Outreach Program.

More books by the author

Gotta Find a Home: Conversations with Street People

Continue reading similar stories in
Gotta Find a Home 3: Conversations with Street People,
coming soon.

Read about Joy, Shakes, and all the others in real time on
Dennis' blog **_Gotta Find a Home._**

http://gottafindahome.com/

A generous portion of the proceeds from the sale of these
books goes towards helping the homeless.

You can help in this goal by leaving a review on
Amazon.com, Goodreads, wherever you purchased this book,
or on any of your social media networks.

Thank you so much!
Dennis Cardiff, author
Karen Hamilton Silvestri, editor

Connect with the author:

Follow Dennis Cardiff on Twitter:
https://twitter.com/DennisCardiff

Like Gotta Find a Home on Facebook:
https://www.facebook.com/gottafindahome/

Subscribe to Gotta Find a Home blog:
http://gottafindahome.com/

Ottawa Innercity Missions, Street Outreach Program

I can't do much for these people except to show them love, compassion, an ear to listen, perhaps a breakfast sandwich and a coffee. I want to do more. To know them is to love them. What was seen cannot be unseen. I thank my publisher, Karen Silvestri for helping to realize my dream.

All profits from the sale of these books will be used to support the *Ottawa Innercity Missions, Street Outreach Program.*

OIM's *Street Outreach* teams come to walk alongside the poor and homeless in the downtown core. Volunteer teams provide relief provisions, pastoral care, crisis intervention and referrals.

Street Outreach is the main component of OIM's work. Through *Street Outreach* our trained volunteers meet men and women living on the street, create trusting relationships, and can work to filling both physical and personal needs. Last year (2012) OIM connected with 7,672 individuals on the street in downtown Ottawa, 2,735 of whom were youth.

The Red Vests

If you see two or more people walking down the street
wearing a bright red vest with the OIM logo on it then you
have run into one of our mobile outreach teams!

OIM's *Street Outreach* volunteers are out meeting with
people and handing out snacks and toiletries six days a week.

We have teams on the street Monday to Thursday nights
(7pm – 9pm), including late Wednesday (9pm-Midnight).
Additional teams are out during the day on Wednesdays &
Saturdays (10am-1pm) and Thursdays & Fridays (1-3pm).

You may donate directly to *Ottawa Innercity Ministries* by
contacting Canada Helps.org at: http://buff.ly/1pHYBPy

www.ingramcontent.com/pod-product-compliance
Lightning Source LLC
Chambersburg PA
CBHW022329280326
41934CB00006B/579